The DIRECTORY of WOODEN BOAT BUILDERS

by
WoodenBoat Magazine

A Guide to the
Building and Repair Shops
in North America

Compiled by
Anne Bray and Cynthia Curtis

Cover drawings by William Gilkerson

Copyright © 1986
by WoodenBoat Publications, Inc.
ISBN 0-937822-06-X

All rights reserved. Except for use in a review, no
part of this work may be reproduced or utilized in
any form or by any means, electronic or mechanical,
including photocopying, recording, or by any
information storage and retrieval system, without
written permission from the publisher.

Library of Congress Catalog Number: 86-50329

Published by WoodenBoat Publications
Naskeag Road
Brooklin, Maine 04616

INTRODUCTION

The business of wooden boat building and repair in North America has enjoyed a resurgence in recent years. As individuals have sought products that embody craftsmanship and excellence in their construction, wooden boats of all sizes and types have been designed, built, or restored to their former glory. Indeed, a small industry has come of age once again—one that deserves to flourish. It is to this end that we have compiled the *Directory*.

The individual builders and shops listed in the following pages represent our best efforts to uncover the artisans who make up this industry. We extend our thanks to everyone who sent us names of boatbuilders unknown to us. We know there are some who have been missed. But our intent is to update the *Directory* every two years or so, and we will continue to be on the lookout for new and additional information. If you, the reader, have any suggestions or additions (or corrections), we would be most grateful to hear from you.

The Directory of Wooden Boat Builders is an information resource of which we are very proud. The listings are grouped by states, and the whole is indexed by builder's name and company name to make the information accessible to the widest possible range of users. It has been an exciting project, and we hope that this *Directory* serves its users well.

—Jon Wilson, Editor
WoodenBoat Magazine

CONTENTS PAGE

UNITED STATES

ALABAMA...................2	OHIO....................187
ALASKA....................3	OREGON...................191
ARIZONA....................4	PENNSYLVANIA...........197
ARKANSAS..................5	RHODE ISLAND...........199
CALIFORNIA...............6	SOUTH CAROLINA.........204
COLORADO.................20	TENNESSEE...............205
CONNECTICUT.............21	TEXAS....................206
FLORIDA.................34	U.S. VIRGIN ISLANDS.......209
GEORGIA..................46	UTAH......................211
HAWAII...................48	VERMONT.................212
IDAHO....................49	VIRGINIA.................217
ILLINOIS.................50	WASHINGTON..............223
INDIANA..................53	WISCONSIN..............246
IOWA.....................54	
MAINE....................56	
MARYLAND................106	**CANADA**
MASSACHUSETTS.........113	BRITISH COLUMBIA.......256
MICHIGAN...............132	MANITOBA...............263
MINNESOTA..............143	NEW BRUNSWICK..........264
MISSISSIPPI..............147	NOVA SCOTIA............265
MISSOURI.................148	ONTARIO.................274
MONTANA.................149	QUÉBEC..................291
NEVADA..................150	
NEW HAMPSHIRE..........151	
NEW JERSEY.............158	**INDEX** 293
NEW YORK................164	
NORTH CAROLINA........182	

ALABAMA

ALRED MARINA—David Barrow
Rte. 6, Box 418
Guntersville, AL 35976
205-582-4400

Builder Information
Years in business: 27
Carpenters employed: 2
Shop capacity: Boats to 50'
Willing to travel for on-the-site building projects.

Recent Repair Projects
40' Pacemaker cruiser (1967). Rebuilt cabin windshield and foredeck bench. Replaced sections of deck as needed. Refinished hull's exterior. 1985.
18' Chris-Craft Riviera (1953). Rebuilt boat from sheer plank up. Completely refinished hull. 1984.
42' Trojan cruiser (1972). Replaced teak decks and deck framing. Renewed portion of bottom and refinished hull's exterior. 1982.
50' Chris-Craft (1960). Completed major hull repairs to bottom and transom. 1985.

Yard Information
Services:
    Marina facilities
    Launching facilities
    Overland transport
    Moorage
    Gas engine repair
Maintenance:
    Number of boats maintained per year: 100
    Percentage of wooden boats: 50
Retail supplies:
    Supplies for refinishing. Ignition parts, props, impellers.

STAUTER BOATS
6004 Clearview Rd.   *355 Grecno Rd.*
Mobile, AL 36619   or: *Fairhope, AL 36532*
205-666-1152   *205-928-7590*

Builder Information
Years in business: 38
Carpenters employed: 4
Shop capacity: Boats to 20'

Recent New Construction
Boats designed by Stauter Boats:
    12-17' outboard fishing boats. Plywood V-bottom or semi-V-bottom construction.
    12-15' outboard Butt Nose/Jon boats. Plywood V-bottom or semi-V-bottom construction.

Recent Repair Projects
Stauter-built fishing boats, Jon boats, and other small craft. Work has included replacing hull planking and repairing other structural damages.

Yard Information
Retail supplies:
    Glue. Trailer parts for small trailers.

ALASKA

DAVID McFADDEN, BOATBUILDER
P.O. Box 668
Petersburg, AK 99833

Builder Information
Years in business: 15
Carpenters employed: 1
Shop capacity: Boats to 35'
Willing to travel for on-the-site building projects.

Recent New Construction
14'3" Boston Whitehall. Lapstrake construction, traditional design. Built 1971.

Recent Repair Projects
27' Monterey fishing boat. Renewed stem, sternpost, and deadwood. Replaced frames, butt blocks, deckbeams, and deck. Renewed cabin, pilothouse, and fish hold. Refastened hull and installed new engine. 1985.
15' Poulsbo boat. Replaced keel, stem, decks, and cabin. Refastened hull and installed 1-cyl diesel. Rigged boat for hand trolling. 1981.
27' Gillnet skiff. Renewed foredeck, side decks, and coaming. Strengthened stern for outboard engine. 1980.

Yard Information
Maintenance:
    Number of boats maintained per year: 3
    Percentage of wooden boats: 100

TOLMAN SKIFFS—Renn Tolman
Box 1343
Homer, AK 99603

Builder Information
Years in business: 7
Carpenters employed: 1
Shop capacity: Boats to 34'
Willing to travel for on-the-site building projects.

Recent New Construction
Boats of plywood and epoxy construction:
    34' cutter. Benford design. Built 1980.
    24' seiner. Tolman design. Built 1978.
    18–22' V- and flat-bottomed power skiffs. Tolman designs. 37 built 1982–'85.
    12' Yankee Tender skiff. WoodenBoat design. Built 1981.
    8' pram. 4 built 1983–'85.

Recent Repair Projects
36' salmon seiner. Replaced hatch and flying-bridge windshield. 1983.
24' Bayliner cabin cruiser. Renewed deck. 1985.
19' dory. Replaced keel. 1983.

ARIZONA

Z-CRAFT CUSTOM RACE BOATS—Frank Zorkan
1501 E. Cambridge
Phoenix, AZ 85006
602-277-9028

Builder Information
Years in business: 35
Carpenters employed: 1
Shop capacity: Boats to 30'
Willing to travel for on-the-site building projects.

Recent New Construction
Hydroplanes, runabouts, tunnels, V-bottomed racing boats.
  Plywood construction, Z-Craft designs. 10 built per year for last 35 years.

Recent Repair Projects
Hydroplanes, runabouts, tunnels, V-bottomed racing boats.
  Racing damage repairs from minor holes to major reconstructions.
  Approximately 10 boats repaired per year.

Yard Information
Services:
  Overland transport
  Gas engine repair
  Rigging
Storage:
  Number of boats stored per year: 6
  Percentage of wooden boats: 100
  Maximum size for hauling and storing:
    Length: 30'
Maintenance:
  Number of boats maintained per year: 6
  Percentage of wooden boats: 100
  Owner maintenance allowed.

BUFFALO BATEAUS—Jim Boone
Rte. 1, Box 169
St. Joe, AR 72675
501-439-2377

Builder Information
Years in business: 10
Carpenters employed: 1
Shop capacity: Boats to 24'
Willing to travel for on-the-site building projects.

Recent New Construction
7'9" sailing punts and prams. Plywood construction. Phil Bolger design. 2 built 1985.
20' plywood bateau. Neison/Gardner design. Built 1983.
18' plywood punt. Neison design. Built 1984.
18' lapstrake bateau. Neison design. Built 1981.
16' Quincy skiff. Lapstrake construction. Gardner design. Built 1983.
15'6" plywood dory. Phil Bolger design. Built 1982.
12' lapstrake skiff. Arno Day design. Built 1983.

Recent Repair Projects
18-20' bateaux. Repairwork has involved structural repairs and hull finishing.

REVERENCE FOR WOOD BOATSHOP—Roy Hebert
15 Douglas
Eureka Springs, AR 72632
501-253-8359

Builder Information
Years in business: 3
Carpenters employed: 1
Shop capacity: Boats to 17'
Willing to travel for on-the-site building projects.

Recent New Construction
16'5" lapstrake wherry. Pete Culler design.
15' St. Lawrence river skiff. Lapstrake construction. Zavier Colon design.

CALIFORNIA

BRIGHT CRAFT BOATWORKS—Erik Wahlman
6525 Barbara Dr.
Sebastopol, CA 95472
707-823-0314

Builder Information
Years in business: 2
Carpenters employed: 1
Shop capacity: Boats to 25'
Willing to travel for on-the-site building projects.

Recent New Construction
16'8" sea kayak. Plywood and strip-plank construction. E. Wahlman design. Built 1985.
15'6" wood-and-fabric touring kayak. Blandford design. 2 built 1984.

Recent Repair Projects
15' outboard runabout. Repaired bow damage and decks. Rebuilt windshield and refinished boat. 1985.
17' Chris-Craft runabout. Renewed frames, keel, chine logs, and hull bottom. Refinished boat. 1983–'84.
16' Old Town wood-and-canvas canoe. Repaired planking and stems. Replaced deck and outwales. Recanvased and refinished hull. 1985.
16' wood-and-canvas canoe (ca. 1925). Replaced 3 ribs and planking as needed. Renewed decks and closed gunwales. Recanvased and refinished hull. 1985.

CALIFORNIA CUSTOM YACHTS AND MARINE HARDWARE, INC.
Robert Perkins
P.O. Box 3149
Redondo Beach, CA 90277
213-376-0469

Builder Information
Years in business: 15
Carpenters employed: 3+
Shop capacity: Boats to 75'
Willing to travel for on-the-site building projects.

Recent New Construction
46' cold-molded high-performance trimaran. Kantola design. Built 1985.
38' cold-molded high-performance trimaran. Kantola design. Current project.
25' cold-molded fantail steam launch. Weston Farmer design. Built 1983.
25' 4-man ocean-racing pulling boat. Plywood construction. Joseph Dobler design. Built 1983.
20' single ocean-racing pulling boat. Plywood construction. Joseph Dobler design. Built 1984.

Recent Repair Projects
34' Herreshoff sloop. Renewed hull with cold-molded overlay, laid new teak deck, renewed interior. 1978.
18' Chris-Craft. Rebuilt entire hull. 1979.

Yard Information
Services:
   Rigging
Wholesale supplies:
   Distributor for WEST System epoxy, paint, and accessories.

C AND B MARINE— Bob Thomsen
410 Escalona Dr.
Capitola, CA 95010
408-722-6276

Builder Information
Years in business: 13
Carpenters employed: 6-12
Shop capacity: Boats to 95'

Recent New Construction
73' strip and cold-molded schooner. John Alden design. Current project.
49' cold-molded schooner. Chuck Burns design. Built 1984.
73' strip and cold-molded schooner. John Alden design. Built 1983.

Recent Repair Projects
50' 8-meter sloop ANGELITA (Owen Churchill's 1932 Olympic Gold medal winner). Totally restored boat. Cold-molded overlay to existing hull, renewed deck, interior, rigging, spars, rudder, and hardware. 1984.

Yard Information
Services:
 Rigging

CAMBER CRAFT—Louie Brochetti
4150 Hillside Dr.
Carlsbad, CA 92008
619-729-6792

Builder Information
Years in business: 6
Carpenters employed: 1-2
Shop capacity: Boats to 30'
Willing to travel for on-the-site building projects

Recent New Construction
32' trimaran. Constant Camber construction. Jim Brown and John Marples design. Built 1984.
15' plywood daysailer NANCY'S CHINA. Sam Devlin design. Built 1984.
8' plywood tender for oar and sail. 5 built 1984-'85.
17' plywood dory. 4 built 1984-'85.

Recent Repair Projects
25' powerboat. Renewed deck, cabin sole, console, and interior. 1985.

Yard Information
Services:
 Rigging
Retail supplies:
 Marine hardware, System Three Epoxy, line, chain, oars, spars.

CALIFORNIA

CLARK CUSTOM BOATS—Bill Clark
3665 Hancock St.
San Diego, CA 92110
619-297-8121

Builder Information
Years in business: 25
Carpenters employed: 2
Shop capacity: Boats to 60′

Recent New Construction
30′ cold-molded cutter. Jacobs design. Built 1983-'85.
22′ cold-molded cat. Phil Bolger design. Built 1984-'85.

Repair Projects
44′ yawl. Completely restored boat. 1980-'85.
30′ Angleman ketch. Renewed deck, cockpit, bulwarks, main bulkhead. Installed new tanks and ice box.
61′ Alden schooner. Rebuilt mast and rig. 1985.
28′ H-28 ketch. Rebuilt rig. 1985.
57′ Alden yawl. Prepared for race to Hawaii. 1985.

Yard Information
Services:
  Rigging

DAWE CRAFT BOATS—Ernie Dawe
82-138 Tahquitz
Indio, CA 92201
619-347-3287

Builder Information
Years in business: 15
Carpenters employed: 1
Shop capacity: Boats to 15′
Willing to travel for on-the-site building projects.

Recent New Construction
12′ outboard runabouts, plywood construction. Ernie Dawe design. 3 built 1985.

Yard Information
Services:
  Gas engine repair

STEVAN DERWINSKI
Box 343
Philo, CA 95466
707-895-3053

Builder Information
Years in business: 4
Carpenters employed: 1
Shop capacity: Boats to 20′

CALIFORNIA

Recent New Construction
13'6" sailing skiff. R.D. Culler design. Built 1985.
17' decked sailing canoe. Glued lapstrake construction. Derwinski design. Built 1984.
14' double-paddle solo canoe. Glued lapstrake construction. Derwinski design. 2 built 1984.
17' Swampscott dory. Lapstrake construction. Lines from Mystic Seaport. Built 1983.
17'6" lapstrake beach boat JAVA. Modified R.D. Culler design. Current project.

DRISCOLL CUSTOM BOATS, INC.—Gerald Driscoll
2438 Shelter Island Drive
San Diego, CA 92106
619-224-3575

Builder Information
Years in business: 40
Carpenters employed: 6
Shop capacity: Boats to 65'

Recent New Construction
48' cold-molded racing sloop. Driscoll design. Built 1984.

Yard Information
Services:
    Launching facilities
    Diesel and gas engine repair
    Rigging
Maintenance:
    Number of boats maintained per year: 500
    Owner maintenance allowed.

ART HOBAN, BOATBUILDER—Art Hoban
512 W. California Ave. #205
Vista, CA 92083
619-941-5584

Builder Information
Years in business: 7
Carpenters employed: 1
Shop capacity: Boats to 50'
Willing to travel for on-the-site building projects.

Recent New Construction
18' cold-molded Itchen Ferry cutter. Lyle Hess design. 2 built 1985.
19' cold-molded Newfoundland sloop. Design by Walt Simmons and Art Hoban. Built 1984.
14' Whitehall. John Gardner design. Built 1979-'80.
16'10" cold-molded pocket cruiser. Bill Allen design. Built 1985.
16' cold-molded wherry. Art Hoban design. 20 built 1980-'85.
20' cold-molded wherry. Art Hoban design. 4 built 1983-'85.
20' cold-molded Whitehall. Design by John Gardner and Art Hoban. Built 1984.

Recent Repair Projects
25' sloop. Repaired tiller, dropboards, worked on galley. 1985.
36' sloop. Repaired lazarette covers and hatches. 1983.
24' Alden sloop. Restored deck. 1984.
32' Gillmer ketch. Restored boat. 1985-'86.
(continues)

CALIFORNIA

(Art Hoban, Boatbuilder, continued)
Yard Information
Services:
    Overland transport
    Rigging
Storage:
    Number of boats stored per year: 4
    Percentage of wooden boats: 100
Retail supplies:
    Wheel-a-weighs, oars, rowing parts, marine supplies.

WILLIAM KRASE, BOATWRIGHT
P.O. Box 1454
Mendocino, CA 95460
707-937-0830

Builder Information
Years in business: 10
Carpenters employed: 1
Shop capacity: Boats to 18'

Recent New Construction
Boats designed by W.H. Krase for plywood lapstrake construction:
    14' cat yawl. Built 1980.
    10' sprit-rigged catboat. 2 built 1981.
    8' pram dinghy. 4 built 1982.
    16' and 18' modified Whitehalls. 3 built 1981-'82.

RON LINK
P.O. Box 2441
Fort Bragg, CA 95437

Builder Information
Years in business: 22
Carpenters employed: 1
Shop capacity: Boats to 20'

Recent New Construction
17' Rangeley Lake boat. Lapstrake construction. Ellis design. Built 1982.

Recent Repair Projects
14' International 14-class sloop. Completely restored boat. 1983.

DON L. MACEY
P.O. Box 581,
Carnelian Bay, CA 95711
916-583-2263

Builder Information
Years in business: 5
Carpenters employed: 1
Shop capacity: New construction to 36'
Willing to travel for on-the-site building projects.

CALIFORNIA

Recent New Construction
22′ cold-molded MORC racing sloop. Gary Mull design. Built 1981-'82.
8′ cold-molded sailing dinghy. Jay R. Benford design. 2 built 1982-'83.
35′ cold-molded ULDB cruiser. Gary Mull design. Current project.
16′ batten-seam single-cockpit runabout. John Hacker design. Current project.

Recent Repair Projects
55′ Hacker day cruiser THUNDERBIRD. Repaired topside planking and some interior cabinets. 1985.
19′ Chris-Craft racing runabout. Replaced deck and half of topside planking. 1985.

Yard Information
Services:
  Rigging
  Engine repair

THE MARINE EXCHANGE—John D. Skoriak
Schoonmaker Point
Sausalito, CA 94965
415-332-9231

Builder Information
Years in business: 6
Carpenters employed: 1-2, as needed

Recent Repair Projects
Specialize in the repair and restoration of classic and antique runabouts (Gar Wood, Chris-Craft, Century, and others). Have also worked on cabin cruisers and sailboats, 8-78′. Offer surveying, appraisal, and consulting services for antique runabouts.

Yard Information
Services:
  Overland transport
  Moorage
  Diesel and gas engine repair
  Sailmaking
Storage:
  Number of boats stored per year: 6-20, trailerable boats only
  Percentage of wooden boats: 50
Maintenance:
  Number of boats maintained per year: 20-30
  Percentage of wooden boats: 50-60
  Owner maintenance allowed.
Retail supplies:
  Electronics—will order on request.

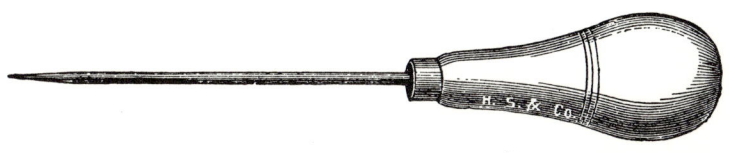

CALIFORNIA

ARTHUR F. MULVEY FINE WOODWORKING—Arthur F. Mulvey
1620 Alvarado St.
Oceanside, CA 92054
619-757-3209

Builder Information
Years in business: 14
Carpenters employed: 1
Shop capacity: New construction to 28'
Willing to travel for on-the-site building projects.

Recent New Construction
8' plywood sailing pram. Arthur F. Mulvey, Sr. design. Built 1985.
12' plywood sailing skiff. Asa Thomson design. 3 built 1983–'85.
18' gunning dory of lapstrake plywood. Chamberlain design. Built 1984.
21' semi-dory of lapstrake plywood. John Gardner design. 3 built 1984–'85.
8' plywood pram. A.F. Mulvey, Sr. design. 75 built 1980–'85.
10' plywood skiff. A.F. Mulvey, Sr. design. 12 built to date.
12' plywood skiff. Asa Thomson design. 4 built to date.
12' lapstrake skiff. Asa Thomson design. 6 built to date.
21' Swampscott dory of lapstrake plywood. Chamberlain design.
10' dory tender of lapstrake plywood. Chaisson design. Built 1985.

Recent Repair Projects
36' sportfisherman. Replaced aft deck with plywood and fiberglass, installed new engine hatch. 1985.
100' minesweeper. Replaced sheer planks, rubrail, stanchions, and caprail. Renewed bridge deck and transom. 1983–'84.

NATIONAL MARITIME MUSEUM at San Francisco—Gus Block
2905 Hyde St.
San Francisco, CA 94109
415-556-6435

Builder Information
Years in business: 3
Carpenters employed: 1
Shop capacity: Boats to 40'

Recent Repair Projects
26' Monterey gillnetter. Restored and refinished. Replaced frames, planking, and renewed joinerwork.
12'3" lapstrake wherry. Restored and refinished. Installed new frames, replaced planking, quarterknees, thwart knees.

Yard Information (for National Maritime Museum boats only)
Services:
    Marina facilities
    Launching facilities
    Overland transport
    Moorage
    Diesel and gas engine repair
    Rigging
Storage:
    Number of boats stored per year: 68
    Percentage of wooden boats: 95
    Inside storage facilities

CALIFORNIA

Maintenance:
　　Number of boats maintained per year: 6
　　Percentage of wooden boats: 100

CHUCK PETTY CUSTOM BOATS—Chuck Petty
633 Escondido Circle
Livermore, CA 94550
415-447-4704

Builder Information
Years in business: 3
Carpenters employed: 1 (part-time)

Recent New Construction
8-17' plywood racing-tunnel catamarans. C. Petty design. Current projects.

Yard Information
Services:
　　Gas engine repair
　　Rigging
Maintenance:
　　Number of boats maintained per year: 2
　　Percentage of wooden boats: 100
Retail supplies:
　　Racing hardware, fiberglass parts.

PT. LA JOLLA CUSTOM BOATS—Jake Russell
4342 Bayard St.
San Diego, CA 92109
619-459-5261

Builder Information
Years in business: 5
Carpenters employed: 2
Shop capacity: Boats to 100'
Willing to travel for on-the-site building projects.

Recent New Construction
100' topsail schooner. Melbourne Smith design. Built 1983-'84.

RUTHERFORD'S BOAT SHOP—Jeffrey Rutherford
320 West Cutting Blvd.
Richmond, CA 94804
415-233-5441

Builder Information
Years in business: 10
Carpenters employed: 3
Shop capacity: Boats to 50'
(continues)

CALIFORNIA

(Rutherford's Boat Shop, continued)
Recent New Construction
28′ sharpie. Lines by H.I. Chapelle. Built 1980.
21′ plywood Long Island skipjack. Lines by H.I. Chapelle. Built 1984.
8′ cold-molded pram. Davis design. Built 1985.
14′ flat-iron skiff. 5 built 1981.
18′ lifeboat. Built 1983.

Recent Repair Projects
52′ Alden schooner BARBARA. Replaced trunk cabin and cabintop. Renewed cockpit, rig, and masts. Repaired framing and planking where necessary. 1983.

Yard Information
Services:
  Rigging

SALT CREEK BOAT WORKS AND TRADING COMPANY—Jim Hetrick
P.O. Box J-B
Dana Point, CA 92629

Builder Information
Years in business: 5
Carpenters employed: 1-2
Shop capacity: New construction to 30′
Willing to travel for on-the-site building projects.

Recent New Construction
Boats of lapstrake construction:
  8′ sailing dinghy SALTY TENDER. Barnes and Hetrick design. 10 built 1984-'85.
  7′2″ sailing pram SALTY II. Barnes and Hetrick design. 4 built 1984-'85.
  8′ Acorn pram for oar and sail. Iain Oughtred design. 5 built 1984.
  12′ Acorn skiff. Iain Oughtred design. 2 built 1984-'85.
  17′ canoe. Walt Simmons design. Built 1984.

Recent Repair Projects
28′ Rhodes cutter (1932). Cold-molded overlay. Current project.
70′ Baltic ketch ARGUS. Worked with others on restoration project. Replaced stem, frames, keel, and bow planking. 1985.
22′ Swampscott dory. Restored boat. 1985.
36′ Mariner. Repaired dry rot. 1985.
8-12′ prams and dinghies. General repairs and restoration. 1985.

SANFORD BOAT CO.—Alfred Sanford
530 W. Cutting
Richmond, CA 94804
415-236-6633

Builder Information
Years in business: 8
Carpenters employed: 6
Shop capacity: Boats to 70′

Recent New Construction
26′ Alerion-class sloop. Cold-molded construction. N.G. Herreshoff design. 22 built since 1978.
51′ ocean-sailing racer/cruiser. Cold-molded, composite-keel construction. In-house design. Built 1985.

Recent Repair Projects
45' Fife yawl. Renewed transom. 1985.
55' Alden ketch. Renewed framing and planking. 1985.
40' trawler. Restored one side of hull. 1984.
40' Abeking & Rasmussen sailboat. Replaced keelbolts. 1984.
35' motorcruiser. Renewed deck canvas. 1985.

Yard Information
Services:
  Marina facilities
  Launching facilities
  Rigging
Storage:
  Number of boats stored per year: 40
  Percentage of wooden boats: 20
  Maximum size for hauling and storing:
    Length: 90'
    Tonnage: 60
Maintenance:
  Owner maintenance allowed above and below rail.
Retail supplies:
  Well stocked ship's chandlery. Will do pattern work for bronze castings.

SAUSALITO SHIPWRIGHT'S CO-OP—Jon Bielinski
Waldo Point #738
Sausalito, CA 94965
415-332-9832

Builder Information
Years in business: 12
Carpenters employed: 21 co-op members
Shop capacity: Boats to 60'
Willing to travel for on-the-site building projects.

Recent New Construction
39' SPRAY replicas. 1 of lapstrake construction. 2 built 1981 and 1985.
35' Block Island boat. Built 1983.
51' French pilot cutter. Current project.
8' pram. John Gardner design. 2 built 1985.
16' double-paddle canoe. Lapstrake construction, design by L.F. Herreshoff. 2 built 1982.
10' pram. Plywood lapstrake constructon. L.F. Herreshoff design. Built 1980.

Recent Repair Projects
40' Spitzgatter double-ender. Renewed planking, bulwarks, and interior. 1985.
31' sailboat. Replaced garboard, repaired backbone. 1985.
30' Knarr-class sloop. Replaced toerail, planking, and deck framing. Refinished hull and deck. 1984.
39' Navy buoy boat. Converted for fishing. 1982.
50' William Hand yacht BALI. Repaired plank damage, converted for fishing. 1985.

Yard Information
Services:
  Diesel and gas engine repair
  Rigging
(continues)

CALIFORNIA

(Sausalito Shipwright's Co-op, continued)
Storage:
    Number of boats stored per year: 12
    Percentage of wooden boats: 80
    Maximum size for hauling and storing: Boats that can be trailered from nearby Travelift. Approx. 20-30 tons.
Maintenance:
    Number of boats maintained per year: 21
    Percentage of wooden boats: 90
    Owner maintenance allowed above and below rail.

SIERRA BOAT COMPANY—Dick Clarke
P.O. Box 69
Carnelian Bay, CA 95711
916-546-2552

Builder Information
Years in business: 33
Carpenters employed: 19-41
Shop capacity: Boats to 40'

Recent Repair Projects
28' Gar Wood (1932). Renewed hull bottom, replaced deck, did major restoration work. 1985.
30' offshore speedboat. Totally restored boat.
Canoes, dinghies, and antique classic powerboats. Minor repairs to complete restorations.
8-10 major projects in progress.

Yard Information
Services:
    Marina facilities
    Launching facilities
    Gas engine repair
Storage:
    Number of boats stored per year: 533
    Percentage of wooden boats: 48
    Inside storage facilities
    Maximum size for hauling and storing:
        Length: 40'
        Draft: 4'
        Tonnage: 10
Maintenance:
    Number of boats maintained per year: 450
    Percentage of wooden boats: 60
Retail supplies:
    Engine parts, fastenings, mahogany. Skis, jackets, radios.

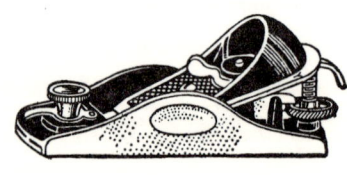

CALIFORNIA

SORENSEN WOODCRAFT—Darrell Sorensen
13307 Avenue 22 1/2
Chowchilla, CA 93610
209-665-5236

Builder Information
Years in business: 16
Carpenters employed: 1
Shop capacity: Boats to 18'

Recent New Construction
Boats designed by D. Sorensen for plywood construction:
- 16' hydroplane. 4 built 1985.
- 14' hydroplane. 3 built 1985.
- 13' runabout. Built 1985.
- 12' runabout. 5 built 1985.
- 11'6" runabout. 8 built 1985.
- 10' hydroplane. 6 built 1985.

Repair Projects
11' runabout. Repaired deck and side. 1985.

Yard Information
Services:
  Rigging

Retail supplies:
  Hardware required for above construction projects.

VOYAGER MARINE—Gene O'Riley
P.O. Box 123, 1296 State St.
Alviso, CA 95002
408-263-7633

Builder Information
Years in business: 12
Carpenters employed: 2-6
Shop capacity: Boats to 50'
Willing to travel for on-the-site building projects.

Recent New Construction
- 31' plywood Searunner trimaran. Jim Brown design. 8 built.
- 37' plywood Searunner trimarans. Jim Brown design. 6 built
- 40' plywood Searunner trimarans. Jim Brown design. 2 built.
- 53' cold-molded cutter. Roberts design. 1 built.
- 40' cold-molded trawler. Tippett design. 1 built.
- 8' cold-molded prams. Gougeon Brothers design. 2 built.
- 10' cold-molded prams. Gougeon Brothers design. 2 built.

Recent Repair Projects
8-50' powerboats and sailboats. Repair projects have involved rigging work, interior carpentry, engine installations and overhauls, electrical system work. Also, hull, deck, and cabin reconstructions.

(continues)

CALIFORNIA

(Voyager Marine, continued)
Yard Information
Services:
    Launching facilities
    Overland transport
    Diesel and gas engine repair
    Sailmaking and repair
    Rigging
Storage:
    Number of boats stored per year: 10
    Maximum size for hauling and storing:
        Length: 40'
        Tonnage: 20
Maintenance:
    Number of boats maintained per year: 30-40
    Percentage of wooden boats: 20
    Owner maintenance allowed above and below rail.
Retail supplies:
    Complete chandlery for sail and power boats.

WOODEN BOAT CENTER—Ronald Blair
13000 Culver Blvd.
Marina Del Rey, CA 90292
213-306-2770

Builder Information
Years in business: 4
Carpenters employed: 4-6
Shop capacity: Boats any size
May be willing to travel for on-the-site building projects.

Recent New Construction
8' multi-chined rowing boat. Plywood construction. Dave Webb design.
    3 built 1981-'84.
Lapstrake tender for oar and sail. Dave Webb design. 4 built 1981-'84.

Recent Repair Projects
16' lugger. Renewed interior and thwarts. 1985.
16-22' Chris-Crafts. Planking repairs to total restorations. 1982-'85.

Yard Information
Storage:
    Number of boats stored per year: 6
    Percentage of wooden boats: 80
    Maximum size for hauling and storing:
        Length: no limit
Maintenance:
    Number of boats maintained per year: 100
    Percentage of wooden boats: 70
    Owner maintenance allowed above and below rail.
Retail supplies:
    Wood, plywood, fastenings, paints, varnishes, epoxies, fiberglass, and other building and maintenance products. Pre-made cabinets, moldings and fittings, books, plans, videos.

WOODEN SHIP BOATWORKS—Gary Minnis
2421 Front St.
West Sacramento, CA 95691
916-371-7447

Builder Information
Years in business: 19
Carpenters employed: 3
Shop capacity: Boats to 36'

Recent New Construction
19' plywood pirogue. Gary Minnis design. Built 1985.
16' plywood pirogue. Gary Minnis design. 2 built 1985.
14' plywood drift boat. Glen-L Marine design. Current project.

Recent Repair Projects
19' Chris-Craft Capri. Completely restored 2 boats.
17' Chris-Craft Sportsman (1956). Completely restored boat.
17' Chris-Craft ski boat (1959). Completely restored boat.
21' Chris-Craft Continental (1957). Rebuilt and restored boat.
18' Chris-Craft Continental (1957). Completely restored boat.
21' Coronado Century (1958). Cold-molded bottom.
18' Coronado Resorter (1956). Refastened and recaulked bottom.
19' Chris-Craft racing runabout (1952). Rebuilt and restored boat.
16' Mercury Sabre (1956). Completely restored boat.
19' Mercury runabout (1949). Rebuilt and restored boat.

Yard Information
Services:
    Overland transport
    Engine repair

WOODWINDS—Gary Young
4901 E. 12th St.
Oakland, CA 94601
415-436-8616

Builder Information
Years in business: 20
Carpenters employed: 5+
Shop capacity: Boats to 16'

Recent New Construction
8'3"-12'6" cold-molded sailboards. Designs by Gary Young
    and others. Approximately 300 built 1979-'85.

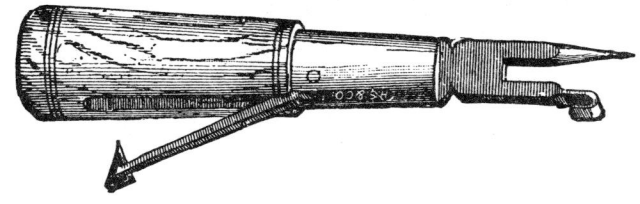

COLORADO

DAN BRECHTEL
635 Graefe Ave.
Ault, CO 80610
303-834-1465

Builder Information
Years in business: 2
Carpenters employed: 1
Shop capacity: Boats to 20'
Willing to travel for on-the-site building projects.

Recent New Construction
8' plywood dinghy/pram. Built 1985.
6' plywood dinghy. Built 1984.

Recent Repair Projects
90' ketch. Interior joinerwork: bunks, shelving, head, and pilothouse paneling. 1984.

CONNECTICUT

AQUATEC BOAT CO.—Ken Bauser
Rte. 61, P.O. Box 53
Morris, CT 06763
203-567-4190

Builder Information
Years in business: 6
Carpenters employed: 1
Shop capacity: Boats to 20'

Recent New Construction
13'6" Blue Jay-class sloop. Plywood construction. Sparkman & Stephens design.
    8 built 1981-'85.
12' DN-class ice yacht. Aircraft type construction. Archie Aarel design.
    14 built 1980-'85.
7'9" Aero-B pram for power, sail, or oar. Composite construction. Ken Bauser design.
    120 built 1980-'85.
9'8" power pram, compact runabout. Composite construction. Ken Bauser design.
    Built 1985.
13' utility rowboat, Berkshire Skiff. Plywood construction. Wescon Design Team design.
    5 built 1983-'85.

Recent Repair Projects
13'6" Blue Jay-class sloops. Replaced bottom frames and planking.
    Renewed coaming, rails, rudder, and spars. Stripped and refinished boat. 1985.
17' Chris-Craft Deluxe runabout (1947). Stripped and refinished hull. 1985.
16' Ventnor Special runabout (1948). Replaced part of keel and bottom planking.
    Built new deck structure and cockpit. Refinished hull. 1985.

Yard Information
Retail supplies:
    Paint. Rigging and hardware for boats built. Custom racing centerboards and rudders for many class sailboats.

CARL'S CANVAS CANOE CARE CO.—Carl H. Williams
Salisbury School
Salisbury, CT 06068
203-435-2160

Builder Information
Years in business: 35
Carpenters employed: 2
Shop capacity: Boats to 20'
Willing to travel for on-the-site building projects.

Recent Repair Projects
16' Morris canoe. Completely rebuilt hull. 1985.
17' Old Town Otca canoe. Repaired and recanvased hull. 2 boats completed in 1985.
16' Old Town rowing canoe. Repaired and recanvased hull. 2 boats completed 1985.
18' Chestnut Ogilvy canoe. Completely rebuilt hull, converted to square-stern. 1985.
11' Old Town canoe. Repaired and recanvased hull. 1985.
16' motorboat. Repaired and recanvased hull. 1985.
18' E.M. White guide-model canoe. Repaired and recanvased hull. 1985.

CONNECTICUT

DEXTER BOATS—Dexter C. Avery
Mashapaug Lake Rd.
Union, CT 06076
203-684-2229

Builder Information
Years in business: 5
Carpenters employed: 1
Shop capacity: Boats to 24'
Willing to travel for on-the-site building projects.

Recent New Construction
9'3" Class X sailing tender, ¾ scale. Modified Lawley design. Built 1985.
11'6" Class X sailing tender. Lapstrake construction. Designed in-house. Built 1985.
14'10" and 17'9" power skiffs. Plywood lapstrake construction. Designed in-house. 2 built 1985.
9'3" lapstrake tender. Lawley design. 2 built 1984-'85.
15' single rowing scull. Lapstrake construction, reproduction of 1890s Norwegian boat. Built 1985.
9'3" tender. Plywood lapstrake construction. Modified Lawley design. Current project.

Recent Repair Projects
14' Old Town runabout (1955). Replaced deck and refinished boat. 1985.
14' Thompson runabout (ca. 1950). Complete rebuild. Replaced deck and seats, reshaped keel and refinished boat. 1985.
10'6" plywood hydroplane (1955). Refastened and refinished hull. 1985.
16' Lyman runabout (1958). Replaced 2 frames, refinished boat. 1985.
12' Old Town rowboat (ca. 1950). Complete restoration. Renewing transom, thwarts, and canvas. Refinishing hull. Current project.
16' Century (1956). Replaced engine with modern power plant. 1985.

Yard Information
Services:
    Launching facilities
    Overland transport for boats under 24' (by special arrangement)
    Moorage
    Gas engine repair
Maintenance:
    Number of boats maintained per year: 10
    Percentage of wooden boats: 80
Retail supplies:
    Used outboard motors. Some materials by order.

GRAHAM ERO WOODEN BOAT SHOP—Graham Ero
875 Quinnipiac Ave.   *NEW* | *Church Street*
New Haven, CT 06513   *ADDRESS* | *Still Pond, MD 21667*
203-468-6665

Builder Information
Years in business: 8
Carpenters employed: 1
Shop capacity: Boats to 30'

CONNECTICUT

Recent New Construction
28'2" sharpie EGRET. R.M. Munroe design. Built 1985.
16' New Haven oyster sharpie. Traditional design and construction. Current project.
15' yawlboat for bugeye J.N. CARTER. Plywood construction. Graham Ero design. Built 1983.
15'9" pulling boat WHISP. Steve Redmond design. Current project.

Recent Repair Projects
48' motorsailer research vessel R.V. ESTRELLITA. Replaced transom, rubrails, bowsprit, and boomkin. Renewed rudders and rudder blocks, refastened butt blocks, and repaired stem and forefoot damage. Extensively rebuilt pilothouse. 1984.
26' New Haven lobsterboat. Replaced cockpit sole, ceiling, and flush hatches. 1983.
25' Wianno Senior-class sloop. Total restoration.
12' Beetle Cat. Total restoration.
16' Bahamian skiff. Completed major repairs and partially restored.
16' Herreshoff 12½-class sloop. Completed extensive repairs.

Yard Information
Services:
　Overland transport
　Rigging
　Maintenance

ESSEX BOAT WORKS—J. Ridgway
Ferry St.
Essex, CT 06426
203-767-8276

Builder Information
Years in business: 53
Carpenters employed: 6-8
Shop capacity: Boats to 72'

Recent Repair Projects
62' New Haven oyster boat FLORA (1906). Renewed frames, planking, deckbeams, deck, and bulwarks. 1983-'85. Boat has been maintained by Essex for last 27 years.
43' Sparkman & Stephens sloop (1965). Repowered boat, renewed planking. 1982-'83.
26' Laker launch (1906). Sistered frames and renewed planking. Replaced fuel tank and refurbished hull. 1984-'85.
39' Concordia yawl (1951). Renewed planks, rebuilt icebox. 1982.
28' Herreshoff sloop-rigged H-28 (1946). Replaced or sistered frames, refastened hull. 1984-'85.
42' Kinney sloop (1967). Renewed forward end of cabin trunk, tightened backbone fastenings, replaced engine, and refinished hull. 1983-'84.
　Boat has been maintained by Essex for last 17 years.
51' West Haven Shipyard trawler (1951). Sistered frames, replaced decks and cabinhouse. 1979 and 1983.
62' Chris-Craft bullnose-type power cruiser (1952). Sistered frames, replaced bottom planks and cabinsides. Repaired underwater gear. 1983-'84.
45' German Frers, Sr., yawl (1960). Replaced keel, transom, and some planking. Renewed toerails and caprails. Refastened and refinished hull. 1980-'81.
60' Walstead-built sloop (1963). Altered interior and fabricated aft cabin hatch. Completed minor hull repairs. 1981.
63' Sparkman & Stephens schooner BRILLIANT. Repaired rudder and small amount of rot. 1983-'84. Ongoing maintenance work done each year.
(continues)

CONNECTICUT

(Essex Boat Works, continued)
Yard Information
Services:
    Launching facilities
    Limited overland transport
    Moorage
    Diesel and gas engine repair
    Rigging
Storage:
    Number of boats stored per year: 65
    Percentage of wooden boats: 20-30
    Inside storage facilities for 65 boats
    Maximum size for hauling and storing:
        Length: 70'
        Draft: 10'
        Tonnage: 60
Maintenance:
    Number of boats maintained per year: 125
    Percentage of wooden boats: 20
    Owner maintenance allowed above rail.
Retail supplies:
    Materials for repair.

RICHARD A. FEWTRELL
25 Billow Rd.
Old Saybrook, CT 06475
203-388-1765

Builder Information
Years in business: 20
Carpenters employed: 1

Recent Repair Projects
27' Chapelle sloop (1953). Renewed transom, garboards,
    deck, centerboard, bunks, and rigging.
47' Hilliard ketch (1928). Renewed transom, deck, spars, rigging, sails,
    and interior accommodations.
120' Camper and Nicholson schooner (1928). Replaced all standing rigging.
50' Herreshoff ketch (1925). Renewed transom, horn timber, sternpost,
    and rudder.
46' English yawl (1924). Replaced topside and bottom planking, refastened and
    recaulked hull. Renewed engine bed.
46' Jersey oyster sloop (1947). Replaced mainsail and steering gear.
    Repaired hull as needed.
25' Honduran sloop (1953). Renewed transom, garboards, and mast.

CONNECTICUT

MORTIMER LAPOINTE WOODEN BOAT RESTORATION & REPAIR
Mortimer LaPointe II
P.O. Box 503
Old Mystic, CT 06372
203-536-7438

Builder Information
Years in business: 7
Carpenters employed: 2
Willing to travel for on-the-site building projects.

Recent Repair Projects
27'5" Herreshoff S-class sloop. Complete restoration. Renewed floors, frames,
   decks and deckbeams, cabin, and mast. Replaced deck canvas.
17' Whitehall. Renewed frames.
25' Herreshoff E-class sloop. Renewed frames, coaming, and boom. Replaced garboard planks.
37' Egg Harbor (1952). Replaced stem.

Yard Information
Retail supplies:
   8-10' solid spruce spoon oars.

MARINE EXHIBITS RESTORATION CO.—Paul T. Stubing
Box 254
Noank, CT 06340
203-572-0066

Builder Information
Years in business: 40
Carpenters employed: 1+
Shop capacity: Boats to 48'

Recent Repair Projects
29'7" Mt. Desert Island lobsterboat. Renewed frames and floor timbers.
   Replaced horn timber, transom, deck, ceiling, trunk cabin, and standing shelter. 1984-'85.
39' Concordia yawl. Replaced forward sister frames and keelbolts. 1983-'85.
37'8" Swedish sloop. Renewed keel, deadwood, stern post, and knee. Replaced
   wooden floors with Stubing-designed cast-bronze floors. Renewed maststep.
43'6" New York 30-class sloops. Completely restored 2 boats.
26' Hackercraft. Completely restored.

Yard Information
Maintenance:
   Number of boats maintained per year: 7
   Percentage of wooden boats: 100

MILFORD BOAT WORKS—Barry Peale
1 High St.
Milford, CT 06460
203-877-1475

Builder Information
Years in business: 40
Carpenters employed: 1+
Shop capacity: Boats 40'+
(continues)

CONNECTICUT

(Milford Boat Works, continued)

Recent New Construction
24' cold-molded ¼-tonner. Kirby design. 2 built 1976.

Recent Repair Projects
45' Eldredge-McInnis motorsailer. Renewed transom and planking. 1982.
33' Knutson Pilot-class sloop. Repaired maststep and framing. 1980.
39' Concordia yawl. Replaced rudder. 1980.
39' Concordia yawl. Renewed rudder and planking. 1982.
50' Eldredge-McInnis trawler. Renewed stem and planking. 1985.

Yard Information
Services:
    Marina facilities
    Launching facilities
    Overland transport
    Diesel and gas engine repair
    Sail repair
    Rigging
Storage:
    Number of boats stored per year: 250
    Percentage of wooden boats: 10
    Inside storage facilities
    Maximum size for hauling and storing:
        Length: 45'
        Draft: 8'
        Tonnage: 25
Maintenance:
    Number of boats maintained per year: 125+
    Percentage of wooden boats: 5+
    Owner maintenance allowed above and below rail.
Retail supplies:
    Extensive inventory, complete marine store.

MYSTIC SEAPORT SMALL BOAT SHOP
Mystic Seaport Museum
Mystic, CT 06355

Builder Information
Years in business: 12
Carpenters employed: 3
Shop capacity: Boats to 20'

Recent New Construction
20' catboat. Crosby design. Current project.
14' lapstrake double-ender. Original built by J.H. Rushton. 15 built 1984-'85.

CONNECTICUT

SETH PERSSON BOATBUILDERS—Jon Persson
18 Riverside Ave.
Old Saybrook, CT 06475
203-388-2343

Builder Information
Years in business: 58
Carpenters employed: 1
Shop capacity: Boats to 50'

Recent New Construction
Boats designed by Jon Persson:
    27' motorsailer. Built 1981-'83.
    21' bassboat/power launch. Plywood construction. Built 1984.
    18' pulling boat. Plywood lapstrake construction. Built 1983.
    15', 17', and 18' kayak-type pulling boats. Wood-and-canvas construction.
      7 built 1984-'85.
Other new construction:
    17' Buzzards Bay 14-class sloop. L.F. Herreshoff design. Built 1980.

Recent Repair Projects
45' Rhodes sloop. Replaced transom, bowrail, handrails,
    3' section of stem, and 700-lb fairing piece forward of ballast.
    Renewed aft end of cabin, butt block bolts, stem and masthead fittings,
    and rudder. Built raised-panel icebox, replaced cabin moldings,
    and renewed plumbing and hot water systems. Refastened all hardware
    and refinished boat. 1979-'80.
38' Crocker cutter. Replaced main and mizzenmasts. 1981.
35' Herreshoff Newport 29-class sloop. Refastened bottom and
    recaulked deck. Renewed stern rail and keelbolts. 1981.
42' Alden Off Soundings yawl. Renewed keelbolts, recaulked deck, and
    installed stainless steel maststep. 1981-'82.
36' Bunker & Ellis power launch. Replaced carlings and deck planking.
    Renewed deck canvas, coamings, and toerails. 1981-'82.
36' Ohlson yawl. Sistered 50 frames, replaced 9 planks. 1982-'83.
36' Hinckley yawl. Installed stainless steel maststep. Renewed 13 frames
    and cabintop canvas. 1982-'83.
30' Yankee One-Design sloop. Replaced forefoot, garboards, broadstrakes,
    deckbeams, deck planking and canvas, toerails, and engine. 1984.

Yard Information
Services:
    Launching facilities
    Rigging
Storage:
    Number of boats stored per year: 20
    Percentage of wooden boats: 100
    Maximum size for hauling and storing:
      Length: 50'
      Draft: 7'
      Tonnage: 25
Maintenance:
    Number of boats maintained per year: 5
    Percentage of wooden boats: 100
    Owner maintenance allowed above and below rail.
Retail supplies:
    Used hardware, paint, fastenings, and other supplies.

CONNECTICUT

PILOTS POINT MARINE—Rives Potts
63 Pilots Point Dr.
Westbrook, CT 06498
203-399-7906

Builder Information
Years in business: 10
Carpenters employed: 9

Recent Repair Projects
"Over the past 5 years, we have rebuilt, repaired, replanked, cast new keels, etc., on approximately 36 sail and powerboats, ranging from 40' to 80'. The latest is repairs to the schooner NINA."

Yard Information
Services:
  Marina facilities
  Launching facilities
  Diesel and gas engine repair
  Rigging
Storage:
  Number of boats stored per year: 700
  Percentage of wooden boats: 10
  Inside storage facilities
  Maximum size for hauling and storing:
    Length: 85'
    Draft: 14'
    Tonnage: 65
Maintenance:
  Number of boats maintained per year: 1,500
  Percentage of wooden boats: 10
  Owner maintenance allowed above and below rail.
Retail supplies:
  Everything!

CURTIS RINDLAUB, AMATEUR BOATBUILDER
8 Hill Lane
Riverside, CT 06878
203-637-4441

Builder Information
Years in business: 4
Carpenters employed: 1
Willing to travel for on-the-site building projects.

Recent New Construction
14'6" solo ocean kayak. Strip-plank construction. Curtis Rindlaub design. Built 1982.
28' single rowing shell. Cold-molded construction. M. Bryan-Brown design. Built 1980.

CONNECTICUT

Recent Repair Projects
Assisted in following projects while employed at Day Boats,
   Inc., Norwalk, Ct.:
   72′ Herreshoff ketch TICONDEROGA. Renewed cabintop canvas and
   restitched mast boots. Rebedded hatches and replaced keel to deck
   tie-rod. 1982.
   40′ Hinckley yawl. Renewed deck canvas, replaced toe and taff rails.
   Replaced all through-hull fittings. 1982.
   40′ Sparkman & Stephens sloop. Replaced keelbolts, garboards, and planking
   as needed. 1982.
   16′, 18′, and 22′ Chris-Craft and Century runabouts. Replaced frames,
   planking, and decks. Stripped and refinished hulls. 1982.
Other repairwork:
   42′ Hubbard cold-molded ketch. Reinforced keel chamber bulkhead.
   Fabricated and installed cantilever mechanism parts for
   pendulum keel. 1982.

RYDER & SON WOODWORKING—Richard G. Ryder
14 Marion Dr.
East Lyme, CT 06333
203-739-0561

Builder Information
Years in business: 5
Carpenters employed: 1
Shop capacity: Inside to 18′
Willing to travel for on-the-site building projects.

Recent New Construction
16′ lapstrake dory-skiff. J. Gardner design. Built 1984.
7′6″ lapstrake skiff. Atkin design. Built 1983.
12′6″ Yankee Tender for oar and sail. Lapstrake construction, WoodenBoat design. Built 1978.
14′ lapstrake Whitehall. Baxter design. Built 1985.

Recent Repair Projects
42′ Herreshoff yawl TRADITION. Renewed rails and double-planked hull. 1984.
16′ Herreshoff 12½-class sloop (1939). Replaced lower section of transom,
   garboards, and first broad planks. 1985.
16′ Herreshoff 12½-class sloop (1915). Replaced four frames, other
   selective repairs. Refinished brightwork. 1985.

Yard Information
Maintenance:
   Number of boats maintained per year: 1
   Percentage of wooden boats: 100
Retail supplies:
   On order basis only.

CONNECTICUT

SKIP SNAITH CANOES & KAYAKS—Skip Snaith
40 Lonetown Rd., P.O. Box 141
Redding, CT 06875
203-938-9158

Builder Information
Years in business: 8
Carpenters employed: 1-2
Shop capacity: Boats 30' +
Willing to travel occasionally for on-the-site building projects.

Recent New Construction
18'6" flat-bottomed power work launch. Lapstrake construction. Skip Snaith design. Built 1983.
20' Carolina power dory-skiff. Plywood construction. Gardner/Texas Dory design. Built 1983.
10'6" double-paddle canoe Dragonfly. Glued lapstrake construction. Rushton Wee Lassie design. 6 built 1984-'85.
13'8" sea kayak Alaskin. Glued lapstrake construction. Skip Snaith design. Built 1985.
16' sea kayak Aleutka. Glued lapstrake construction. Skip Snaith design. Built 1985.
18' + double sea kayak. Glued lapstrake construction. Skip Snaith design. Current project.

Recent Repair Projects
16' lapstrake sailing dinghy. Repaired planking and transom. Replaced rails. 1983.

THOMSON CANOE WORKS—Schuyler Thomson
343 Weekeepeemee Rd.
Woodbury, CT 06798
203-263-3404

Builder Information
Years in business: 18
Carpenters employed: 1
Shop capacity: Boats to 25'
Willing to travel for on-the-site building projects.

Recent Repair Projects
Canoes, Folbots, kayaks, lapstrake boats, and other small craft.
Minor repairs to complete restorations. Recanvasing, refinishing, plank, keel, and thwart renewals. 1967-'85.

Yard Information
Retail supplies:
Wood, fastenings, and other materials necessary for the repair or construction of canoes.

RICK WATERS, BOATBUILDER
13 Main St.
Noank, CT 06340
203-572-9044

Builder Information
Years in business: 10
Carpenters employed: 1
Shop capacity: Boats to 30'
Willing to travel for on-the-site building projects.

CONNECTICUT

Recent New Construction
28' whaleboat. Lapstrake and batten-seam construction. Built 1983.
29' strip-planked sailing cruiser. T. MacNaughton design. Built 1978.
32' strip-planked lobsterboat. S. Lincoln design. Built 1977.
13' peapod. Design by Eric Dow, et al. Built 1976.

Recent Repair Projects
295' USCGC EAGLE barque. Replaced deck seam caulking. 1985.
58' sloop NEITH (1907). Herreshoff design. Worked with other people to restore interior and deck structures. 1984-'85.
200' barque ELISSA. Replaced pin rails, deckhouse, and crosstrees. 1982.
16' Old Town canoe. Repaired planks and ribs. Replaced hull canvas and revarnished interior. 1985.

GARY WEISENBURGER, BOATBUILDER
63-A Lake Dr.
Oakdale, CT 06370
203-859-1613

Builder Information
Years in business: 12
Carpenters employed: 1-2
Willing to travel for on-the-site building projects.

Recent New Construction
17' sailing Whitehall. John Gardner design. 4 in progress.

Recent Repair Projects
9'9" yacht tender. Replaced frames and rubrail. Stripped and refinished hull, inside and out. 1985.
30' steam launch. Replaced stem, keel, frames, planking, deck framing, and deck. Completely restored hull. 1984.
18' Chris-Craft (1940). Rebuilt transom. Replaced frames and some planking. Revarnished hull. 1983.
17' Old Town canoe (1947). Replaced stems, gunwales, and some frames. Recanvased and refinished hull. 1983.

Yard Information
Services:
    Launching facilities
Maintenance:
    Number of boats maintained per year: 3-4
    Percentage of wooden boats: 100
    Owner maintenance allowed above and below rail.
Retail supplies:
    Wood, paint, fastenings, and other traditional marine supplies.

CONNECTICUT

R.K. WILMES, BOATBUILDER
120 Warner Rd.
East Haddam, CT 06423
203-873-1051

Builder Information
Years in business: 40
Carpenters employed: 1
Shop capacity: Boats to 40'

Recent New Construction
21'6" strip-planked yawl. Laurent Giles design. Built 1984-'85.
24' sloop. Fred Bingham design. Built 1985.
18' power launch. Lapstrake construction. William Deed design. Built 1984.
19' plywood outboard dory. John Gardner design. Built 1985.
16' Cape Split peapod. Lapstrake construction. Plans from Mystic Seaport Museum. Built 1985.
7'6" lapstrake skiff. John Atkin design. Built 1985.

Recent Repair Projects
32' Quoddy Pilot sloop. Redesigned and refitted interior. 2 boats completed in 1984.
30' Owens power cruiser. Replaced bottom and windshield. 1985.
24' Groton Long Point-class sloop. Repaired and refastened hull, replaced deck canvas. 1985.
34' Crowninshield sloop (1902). Completely rebuilt boat. Renewed frames, spars, etc. 1985.
16' Zip-class sloop. Completely rebuilt boat. 1985.
32' Sumner Craft powerboat. Completed boat. 1984.
34' Columbia power cruiser. Repaired hull and cabin, sheathed deck with fiberglass. 1985.
30' Pembroke power cruiser. Replaced transom. 1985.

Yard Information
Retail supplies:
  Small supply of paint. Will order parts and other materials by request.

WISNER BROS.—J.D. Wisner
10 N. Water St.
South Norwalk, CT 06854
203-866-2252

Builder Information
Years in business: 10
Carpenters employed: 2
Shop capacity: Boats to 60'
Willing to travel for on-the-site building projects.

Recent New Construction
38' sloop. Composite construction. Marshall design. Built 1984-'85.

Recent Repair Projects
22' catboat. Renewed frames, planking, transom, cockpit, cabin sides, and top. Installed new diesel and tankage. 1985.

Yard Information
Services:
  Marina facilities
  Launching facilities
  Overland transport
  Moorage
  Diesel and gas engine repair

CONNECTICUT

Storage:
    Number of boats stored per year: 20-30
    Percentage of wooden boats: 50
    Inside storage facilities
    Maximum size for hauling and storing:
        Length: 50'
        Draft: 12'
        Tonnage: 20
Maintenance:
    Number of boats maintained per year: 15
    Percentage of wooden boats: 50
    Owner maintenance allowed above and below rail.

FLORIDA

ADAMS BOATBUILDING CO.—Albert E. (Bud) Adams
5420 Maule Way
West Palm Beach, FL 33407
305-844-9818

Builder Information
Years in business: 60
Carpenters employed: 4
Shop capacity: Boats to 50′

Recent New Construction
36′ custom sedan cruiser. Epoxy and fiberglass sheathing over carvel planking. A.E. Adams design. Built 1984.
32′ commercial fishing boat. Epoxy and fiberglass sheathing over carvel planking. A.E. Adams design. Built 1980.

Recent Repair Projects
All types of repair and remodeling.

Yard Information
Services:
    Diesel engine repair
    Rigging

ADAMS CUSTOM BOATS INC.—Kim Adams
950 Mullet Rd.
Port Canaveral, FL 32920
305-784-2013 or 784-2028

Builder Information
Years in business: 10
Carpenters employed: 6
Shop capacity: Boats to 65′ on site
Willing to travel for on-the-site building projects.

Recent New Construction
65′ composite sloop. James Krogen design. 3 built 1978–'85.
28′ cat-ketch. Composite construction. Phil Bolger design. Built 1985.
8′ plywood pram. 6 built 1982–'83.
16′ plywood dory. Phil Bolger design. 4 built 1982–'83.

Recent Repair Projects
41′ Formosa ketch. Total restoration. Renewed interior, cockpit, cabin trunk, and spars. Replaced hardware, generator, wiring, and electronics. Refinished boat. 1982–'85.
Correct-Craft Commuter (1954). Replaced stem, chines, and bottom frames. Renewed double-diagonal bottom planking. 1984.
30′ Egg Harbor. Sistered 38 frames, refastened bottom, and replaced teak covering boards. 1983.

Yard Information
Services:
    Launching facilities
    Sailmaking
    Rigging
    Canvas and upholstering

Maintenance:
    Number of boats maintained per year: 6
    Percentage of wooden boats: 50
    Owner maintenance sometimes allowed above and below rail.
Retail supplies:
    Paints, varnishes, lumber, fastenings, plywood, adhesives, abrasives, and teak accessories.

BITTERROOT BOAT WORKS—Lawrence Bausman
P.O. Box 732
San Antonio, FL 34266

Builder Information
Years in business: 14
Carpenters employed: 1
Shop capacity: New construction to 30'

Recent New Construction
12-20' plywood johnboats. Traditional Ozark design. 4 built 1984-'85.
14' plywood wherry. Lines by H.I. Chapelle. Built 1984.
28' sharpie. Carvel-and-plywood construction. L. Bausman design. Built 1984-'85.
16' strip-planked canoe. L. Bausman design. Built 1984-'85.
12' strip-planked sneakbox. Lines by H.I. Chapelle. 2 built 1982 and 1984.

Recent Repair Projects
32' Nicholson sloop. Renewed frames and floors. 1985.
36' Spanish-built sloop. Repaired strip-planked hull. 1984-'85.
17' Thistle-class sloop. Repaired hull damage. 1982.
25' Folkboat-class sloop. Replaced rotten planking, renewed rig. 1983.

Yard Information
Services:
    Marina facilities by arrangement
    Launching facilities by arrangement
    Overland transport
    Diesel and gas engine repair
    Sailmaking
    Rigging
Storage:
    Number of boats stored per year: 20
    Percentage of wooden boats: 30
    Maximum size for hauling and storing:
        Length: 40'
        Tonnage: 20
Maintenance:
    Number of boats maintained per year: 10
    Percentage of wooden boats: 100
    Owner maintenance allowed above rail.

FLORIDA

BRUNO'S MARINE SERVICE—Peter and Steven Bruno
2868 S.E. Iris St.
Stuart, FL 33494
305-283-0790

Builder Information
Years in business: 20
Carpenters employed: 2
Shop capacity: New construction to 40′
Willing to travel up to 5 miles for on-the-site building projects.

Recent New Construction
12′ plywood catamaran. Lines published in *Popular Mechanics*. Built 1968.
13′ plywood outboard runabout. Pete Bruno design. Built 1975.
27′ cruising tugboat. Strip-planked with cypress. Pete Bruno design. Current project.
14′ lapstrake peapod. John Gardner design. Current project.

Recent Repair Projects
43′ Rybovich sportfisherman (1963). Remodeled saloon using Honduras mahogany. Installed cockpit cabinets, tackle lockers. 1983.
34′ Hatteras sportfisherman. Replaced aft cabin bulkhead and sliding doors. Installed cockpit cabinets, freezer, and tackle locker, using teak and teak veneers. Remodeled saloon and galley. 1984.

Yard Information
Retail supplies:
  Teak, mahogany, cypress, Bruynzeel and other marine plywood. Epoxy glue, stainless steel fastenings, paints. Large selection of marine equipment and hardware. Custom-made tackle lockers, deck boxes, and exterior/interior cabinets.

DERECKTOR-GUNNELL, INC.—Skip Gunnell
775 Taylor Lane
Dania, FL 33004
305-920-5756

Builder Information
Years in business: 16
Carpenters employed: 20
Shop capacity: Boats to 100′

Recent Repair Projects
Planking and worm shoe replacement on following boats, 1984–'85:
  65–105′ Trumpys.
  54–75′ Grebes.
  Minesweepers to 110′.
  106′ Feadship power cruiser.

Yard Information
Services:
  Marina facilities
  Launching facilities
  Overland transport
  Moorage
  Diesel engine repair
  Rigging

Storage:
    Number of boats stored per year: 20-25
    Maximum size for hauling and storing:
        Length: 100'
        Draft: 12'
        Tonnage: 150
Maintenance:
    Number of boats maintained per year: 100
    Percentage of wooden boats: 10-20
Retail supplies:
    Materials for maintenance.

DESCO MARINE, INC.—Thomas J. Collins, Jr.
P.O. Box 1480
St. Augustine, FL 32085
904-824-4461

Builder Information
Years in business: 43
Carpenters employed: 4-5
Shop capacity: Boats to 73'

Recent Repair Projects
85' Trumpy motoryacht. Major reconstruction. Current project.
Fishing trawlers. Repairwork has included renewing planking and worm shoes, recaulking and refinishing hulls. 20-30 boats repaired per year.

Yard Information
Services:
    Launching facilities
    Moorage
    Engine repair
Maintenance:
    Number of boats maintained per year: 150
    Percentage of wooden boats: 40
    Maximum size for hauling and storing:
        Length: 105'
        Draft: 10'
        Tonnage: 150

ERA-PAST BOAT CO.—Dale Tassell
Rte. #1, Box 25H
Mount Dora, FL 32757
904-383-6203

Builder Information
Years in business: 2
Carpenters employed: 1
Shop capacity: Boats to 22'
Willing to travel for on-the-site building projects.

(continues)

FLORIDA

(Era-Past Boat Co., continued)
Recent Repair Projects
19' Chris-Craft Rocket runabout (1953). Replaced 2 planks and refinished boat.
27' Chris-Craft Constellation power cruiser (1957). Refinished hull.

Yard Information
Services:
  Launching facilities
  Gas engine repair
  Consultant for Chris-Craft restoration
Maintenance:
  Number of boats maintained per year: 5
  Percentage of wooden boats: 100
  Owner maintenance allowed.
Retail supplies:
  Engine parts and hardware for older Chris-Crafts. Paint.

FEATHER CANOES, INC.—Henry McCarthy
1705 Andrea Place
Sarasota, FL 33580
813-953-7660

Builder Information
Years in business: 7
Carpenters employed: 1
Shop capacity: Boats to 20'

Recent New Construction
Boats of strip-plank construction:
  14' Melon Seed gunning skiff. Lines by H.I. Chapelle, modified by McCarthy. 2 built 1985.
  20' square-sterned canoe. Original design. Built 1985.
  14' and 16' solo canoes. Rushton Arkansas Traveler models. 2 built 1985.
  12' rowboat. Henry McCarthy design. Built 1985.
  17' square-sterned canoe. Henry McCarthy design. Built 1985

Yard Information
Services:
  Overland transport
Storage (canoes only):
  Number of boats stored per year: 2
  Percentage of wooden boats: 100
  Inside storage facilities
  Maximum size for hauling and storing:
    Length: 20'

FITZGERALD & HOLLINS—Kim Hollins
1603 S.W. 2nd Ave.
Ft. Lauderdale, FL 33315
305-522-5636

Builder Information
Years in business: 12
Carpenters employed: 3
Shop capacity: Boats to 30'

FLORIDA

Recent New Construction
24' cold-molded centerboard sloop. C.W. Paine design. Built 1985.
12' cold-molded dinghy for sail and oar. Fitzgerald & Hollins design. Built 1982.
8' cold-molded dinghy for sail and oar. Frank Davis design. 2 built in 1983.

FLAHERTY MARINE, INC.
Rte. 1, Box 300, Anclote Rd.
Tarpon Springs, FL 33589
813-934-9394

Builder Information
Years in business: 23
Carpenters employed: 2
Shop capacity: Boats to 50'

Recent New Construction
32' sportfisherman. Cold-molded plywood construction. Wherbeck design. Built 1985.
16' skiff. Cold-molded plywood construction. Built 1984.

Recent Repair Projects
25' Friendship sloop. Replaced 36 frames and 8 planks.
    Refastened as needed. 1983.
42' Grand Banks trawler. Replanked, refastened, and recaulked bottom. 1983.
42' Colonial Cruiser. Renewed floor timbers, shaftlogs, and planking.
    Refastened and recaulked hull. 1984.
43' shrimper. Replaced $2/3$ of bottom planking. 1985.
36' Pacemaker. Refastened and recaulked bottom. 1984.
23' fishing boat (1958). Renewed frames, keel, and deck engine box. 1984.
30' houseboat. Rebuilt house, decks, and interior. 1984.
25' Folkboat-class sloop. Renewed frames and bottom planking. 1985.

Yard Information
Services:
    Marina facilities
    Launching facilities
    Moorage
    Diesel and gas engine repair
    Rigging
Maintenance:
    Number of boats maintained per year: 150
    Percentage of wooden boats: 20
    Owner maintenance allowed above and below rail.
    Maximum size for hauling:
        Length: 60'
        Draft: 6'6"
        Tonnage: 30
Retail supplies:
    Teak, mahogany, cypress, marine plywood. Paints, fastenings, rope, and some hardware.

FLORIDA

HUCKINS YACHT CORP.
3482 Lake Shore Blvd.
Jacksonville, FL 32210
904-389-1125

Builder Information
Years in business: 57
Carpenters employed: 30
Shop capacity: Boats to 90'

Repair Projects
30-90' Huckins, Trumpys, Matthews, and Chris-Crafts. Restoration work has included plank replacement and repair, superstructure repair, refurbishing of electrical and mechanical systems, and hull refinishing. Specialize in the repair and restoration of Huckins craft.

Yard Information
Services:
  Marina facilities
  Launching facilities
  Diesel and gas engine repair
  Maximum size for hauling:
    Length: 90'
    Draft: 6'
    Tonnage: 60

GEORGE LUZIER BOATBUILDER, INC.—George Luzier
2135 Princeton St.
Sarasota, FL 33577
813-953-4989

Builder Information
Years in business: 25
Carpenters employed: 4
Shop capacity: Boats to 51'

Recent New Construction
49' strip-planked cutter. Current project.
26' sportfisherman. Batten-seam construction. Luzier design. 5 built 1985.

Recent Repair Projects
26' Luders 16. Completely rebuilding boat. Current project.
22' Luzier sloop. Replaced trim and toerails. Rebuilt galley and refinished boat. 1985.
20' Lotus sloop. Installed seats. Refinished boat. 1985.
Sportfisherman. Repowered and refinished boat. 1985.

FLORIDA

OLD TIME BOAT CO.
1654 Baywinds Lane (mail)
4945 Samuel St. (shop)
Sarasota, FL 33581
813-921-7286

Builder Information
Years in business: 5
Carpenters employed: 1
Shop capacity: Boats to 30'
Willing to travel for on-the-site building projects.

Recent Repair Projects
19' Chris-Craft Race runabout. Renewed bottom, interior, and engine. 1983.
17' Chris-Craft Sportsman. Completely rebuilt and refinished boat. 1984.
18' Chris-Craft Super Sport. Completely rebuilt and refinished boat. 1983.
17' Chris-Craft Special. Rebuilt boat and replaced deck. 1985.
17' Chris-Craft Barrelback. Completely rebuilt boat. 1980.
22' Chris-Craft Sportsman. Completely rebuilt boat. 1979.
17' Chris-Craft Sportsman. Rebuilt boat and converted to rear-cockpit racer. 1985.

Yard Information
Services:
    Overland transport
    Gas engine repair
    Rigging
    Maintenance
Retail supplies:
    Complete inventory of supplies.

OLD WOODEN BOATWORKS—W. Jack Fesenmeyer
106 8 St. E.
Bradenton, FL 33508
813-747-8898

Builder Information
Years in business: 23
Carpenters employed: 1
Shop capacity: Boats to 30'

Recent New Construction
Boats designed by W. Jack Fesenmeyer:
    7'6" lapstrake dinghy for oar and sail. 72 built, 1983 to present.
    9'6" lapstrake dinghy for oar and sail. 21 built, 1984 to present.
    20' plywood dinghy for oar and sail. Built 1985.
    18' deadrise power skiff. Plywood lapstrake construction. 2 built 1985.
Other new construction:
    15'9" lapstrake powerboat. Lyman replica. Built 1985.
    9'6" lapstrake canoe. J.H. Rushton design. 4 built 1983-'84.
    12' lapstrake canoe. J.H. Rushton design. 8 built 1983-'85.
    15' lapstrake canoe. J.H. Rushton design. 7 built 1983-'84.

Yard Information
Services:
    Sailmaking
    Rigging

FLORIDA

SAINT MARINE REPLICRAFT—Col. Hugh M. Saint, USAF (Ret)
838 S.E. 9th St.
Cape Coral, FL 33904

Builder Information
Years in business: 1
Carpenters employed: 1
Shop capacity: Boats to 23'6"

Recent New Construction
23'6" cold-molded runabout. John Hacker design. Built 1985.

SAROUKOS BOAT BUILDING—George Saroukos
1055 N. Pinellas Ave.
Tarpon Springs, FL 33589
813-934-8600

Builder Information
Years in business: 18
Carpenters employed: 6
Shop capacity: Boats to 85'

Recent New Construction
Boats designed by George Saroukos:
   55', 58', and 65' powerboats for pleasure and commercial fishing. Composite and lapstrake construction. 18 built 1972-'85.
   12' dinghies for oar and sail. Cold-molded construction. 48 built 1983-'85.

Yard Information
Services:
   Moorage
   Diesel and gas engine repair
Maintenance:
   Number of boats maintained per year: 150
   Percentage of wooden boats: 80
   Owner maintenance allowed above rail.
   Maximum size for hauling:
    Length: 100'
    Draft: 9'
    Tonnage: 80
Retail supplies:
   Paint, fastenings.

SEAWAY BOAT REPAIRS—Larry Bulman
1118 W. Church St.
Orlando, FL 32805
305-843-3636

Builder Information
Years in business: 2
Carpenters employed: 1
Shop capacity: New construction to 18'
Willing to travel for on-the-site building projects.

FLORIDA

Recent New Construction
7'10" pram dinghy for oar and sail. Plywood construction. Larry Bulman design. 5 built 1983-'85.

Recent Repair Projects
12' Old Town canoe (1959). Replaced 3 planks, renewed bow, stem, and gunwales.

36' Owens launch (1967). Replaced several planks. Renewed stern cockpit and redesigned hatch to accommodate scuppers. Refinished boat.

38' Richardson launch (ca. 1968). Renewed stem and breasthook, refastened and recaulked hull.

38' Alden cruiser (1930s). Refastened and recaulked hull. Redesigned cockpit and refinished boat.

14' outboard WOLVERINE (1936). Repaired rot in stem. Refinished boat.

21' Century Coronado (1967). Renewed frames and planking. Refinished hull.

19' Chris-Craft Capri (ca. 1936). Replaced 2 frames, removed engine, and refinished boat.

18'6" Thompson (1967). Renewed decks and refinished boat.

16' Chris-Craft (1967). Scarfed piece in engine bearer. Renewed deckbeams and forward plywood deck.

16' outboard boat (1958). Renewed transom and outboard well area.

16' Century Resorter (1950s). Renewing transom, deckbeams, foredeck, and hull planking. Current project.

Yard Information
Services:
  Overland transport
  Diesel and gas engine repair
  Rigging
Maintenance:
  Number of boats maintained per year: 50
  Percentage of wooden boats: 20
Retail supplies:
  Epoxy, paint, hardwoods, marine plywood, and fastenings.

SPENCER BOAT CO.—James E. Bronstien
4000 N. Dixie Hwy.
West Palm Beach, FL 33407
305-844-3521

Builder Information
Years in business: 36
Carpenters employed: 18
Shop capacity: Boats to 120'

Recent Repair Projects
56' Abeking & Rasmussen motorsailer ANNIE B. Complete renovation. Repowered main engine and generator. 1984-85.

55' Trumpy CAROUSEL. Complete renovation. 1984-'85.

57' Elco GEMINI. Complete renovation. Renewed hull, cabintop, decks, and superstructure. 1984-'85.

85' Trumpy DREAMBOAT. Complete interior renovation. Renewed aft deck and flying-bridge area. 1984-'85.

(continues)

FLORIDA

(Spencer Boat Co., continued)
Yard Information
Services:
    Marina facilities
    Launching facilities
    Moorage
    Diesel and gas engine repair
    Rigging
Maintenance:
    Number of boats maintained per year: 1,000
    Percentage of wooden boats: 15
    Maximum size for hauling:
        Length: 100'
        Draft: 11'
        Tonnage: 160

VAN MAR BOAT CO.—V.H. Van Bibber
4201 Mariner Dr.
Panama City, FL 32407
904-234-5020

Builder Information
Years in business: 35
Carpenters employed: 1
Shop capacity: Boats to 35'

New Construction
Boats designed by V.H. Van Bibber:
    19' plywood hydrofoil runabout. 2 built 1965 and 1985.
    30' plywood hydrofoil day cruiser. Built 1960.
    16' utility ski-boat. 100 built 1950-'53.
    18'6" double-cockpit runabout. 2 built 1951.
    24' cold-molded utility boat. Built 1952.
    18' cold-molded runabout. Built 1953.

Repair Projects
25' hydrofoil craft. Rebuilt main and cockpit decks, refastened bottom. 1957.
18' Chris-Craft runabout. Renewed bottom, deck, and cockpit. Rebuilt engine. 1970.
16' Chris-Craft runabout. Refastened hull, renewed deck and cockpit. Rebuilt engine. 1975.
21' Century utility. Renewed bottom and decks. Rebuilt engine. 1976.
21' Century utility. Renewed bottom planking and frames, rebuilt deck and engine. 1976.
18' Gar Wood runabout. Renewed bottom, deck, and cockpit. Rebuilt engine. 1978.
25' Gar Wood runabout. Renewed bottom, rebuilt deck, cockpit, and engine. 1979.
20' Hacker runabout. Renewed bottom, rebuilt deck and engine. 1981.
17', 18', and 19' Chris-Craft utilities. Refastened hulls, renewed decks, and rebuilt engines. 1982-'84.

Yard Information
Services (provided for boats undergoing repair):
    Marina facilities
    Overland transport
    Diesel and gas engine repair
    Rigging
Maintenance:
    Number of boats maintained per year: 10
    Percentage of wooden boats: 90

FLORIDA

WHITICAR BOAT WORKS INC.—Jim Dragseth
3636 S.E. Old St. Lucie Blvd.
Stuart, FL 33494
305-287-2883

Builder Information
Years in business: 39
Carpenters employed: 5
Shop capacity: Boats to 62'
Willing to travel for on-the-site building projects.

New Construction
Boats designed by G.C. Whiticar:
    38' sportfisherman. Built 1954.
    61' flush-deck power yacht. Built 1963.
    62' sportfishing power yacht. Built 1970.
    45', 51', and 54' sportfishermans. Cold-molded construction. 4 built 1975,
       1983, 1984, and 1985.

Recent Repair Projects
Work has included planking repairs, interior renovations, and
    running gear and engine installations.

Yard Information
Services:
    Diesel and gas engine repair
Maintenance:
    Number of boats maintained per year: 80
    Percentage of wooden boats: 35
    Owner maintenance allowed above rail.
Retail supplies:
    Lumber, fastenings, paint and painting supplies, hardware, tools, and maintenance
       products. Engine parts, pumps, and parts.

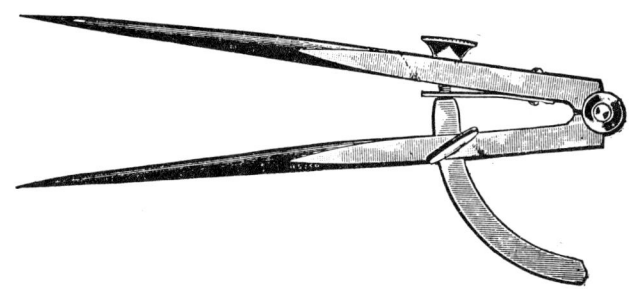

GEORGIA

DE SILVA BOATS
335 E. Foster Ave., P.O. Box 578
Dallas, GA 30132
404-445-1821

Builder Information
Years in business: 40
Carpenters employed: 2
Shop capacity: Boats to 30'

Recent New Construction
9-22' racing powerboats of plywood batten-seam construction. In-house design.

Yard Information
Retail supplies:
  Wood, plywood, fastenings, glue, paint.

HALLS BOAT HOUSE—Jean T. White
Box 36
Lakemont, GA 30552
404-782-4981

Builder Information
Years in business: 60
Carpenters employed: 2
Shop capacity: Boats to 22'

Repair Projects
Have repaired powerboats to 22'.
Offer restoration, refinishing, and mechanical services.
Average about 6 boats each winter.

Yard Information
Services:
  Marina facilities
  Launching facilities
  Gas engine repair
Storage:
  Number of boats stored per year: 50
  Percentage of wooden boats: 10
  Maximum size for hauling and storing:
    Length: 22'
Maintenance:
  Number of boats maintained per year: 200
  Percentage of wooden boats: 30
Retail supplies:
  Some general marine supplies.

JOHN WERMESCHER BOATBUILDER
953 Virginia Circle, N.E.
Atlanta, GA 30306
404-659-2468

Builder Information
Years in business: 32
Carpenters employed: 1

Recent New Construction
10'2" Wiscasset dinghy. Plywood lapstrake construction. M. Roth design. Built 1983.
15'7" skiff Whisp. Steve Redmond design. Current project.
20' cold-molded rowing wherry Bangor Packet. Joel White design. Built 1984.

Recent Repair Projects
15'6" Snipe-class sloop. Reframed, installed new decks, replaced part of keel. 1985.
Rowing shells to 47'. Various repairs to singles, doubles, 4s.

Yard Information
Services:
  Rigging
Storage:
  Number of boats stored per year: 1-2
  Percentage of wooden boats: 100
Retail supplies:
  Dealer for marine supplies.

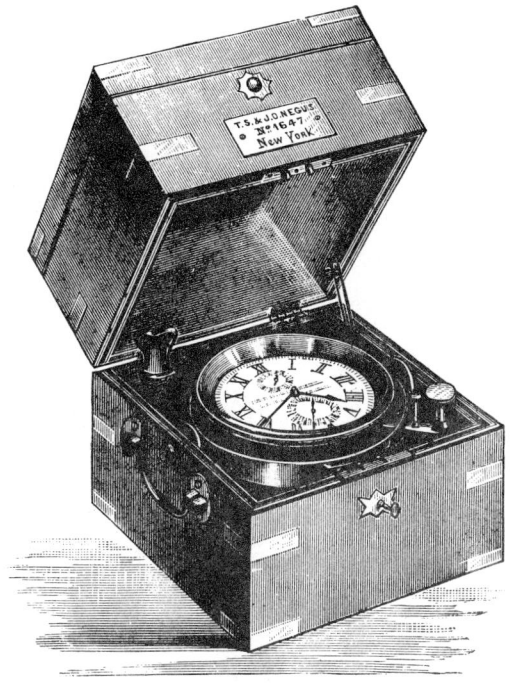

HAWAII

HOGAN BOAT WORKS—Robert Hogan
P.O. Box 2825
Kailua-Kona, HI 96745
808-329-4666

Builder Information
Years in business: 25
Carpenters employed: 1-3
Shop capacity: Boats to 50'
Willing to travel for on-the-site building projects.

Recent Repair Projects
48' Matsumoto Haole sampan. Rebuilt boat. 1982.
42' Merritt BLACK BART. Partially rebuilt boat. 1984-'85.
37' Merritt FINEST KIND. Replaced deck and partially rebuilt boat. 1985.
40' Offshore 40 HAVAIKI. Rebuilt boat, renewed interior woodwork. 1984.
37' Lidgard sloop. Replaced cockpit and part of deck. Built interior cabinets. 1981.
31' whaleboat (ca. 1880s). Rebuilt boat for Whalers Museum, Kaanapali, Hawaii. 1983.
36' ketch SEAWITCH. Rebuilt boat. 1981-'84.
37' MELE MAKANI. Rebuilt boat. 1981-'84.
Metal machining (lathe work).

Yard Information
Retail supplies:
    Teak, fastenings.

IDAHO

HEITMAN BOATS—Herrick Heitman
2185 Glengary Rd.
Sandpoint, ID 83864
208-263-4161

Builder Information
Years in business: 44
Carpenters employed: 1
Shop capacity: Boats to 36'

Recent New Construction
12'6" Marisol dinghy. Plywood lapstrake construction. Gifford Jackson design. Built 1983.

Recent Repair Projects
34' Chris-Craft cruiser (1940). Refinished boat.
32' Monson sloop. Refinished boat.
21' Century Raven (1948). Replaced bottom planking and refinished boat.
26' Blanchard Senior Knockabout-class sloops. Replaced deck canvas and refinished hulls.
26' Folkboat-class sloop. Sistered frames, replaced transom. Renewed upper stem, planking, and cabin. Refinished hull.
33' Chris-Craft cruiser (1939). Completed extensive renovations to hull, renewed power systems.
25' Chris-Craft sedan (1954). Replaced chine and adjacent planking.
32' Jensen cruiser (1934). Replaced bottom planking.

Yard Information
Services:
    Marina facilities
    Launching facilities
    Moorage
Storage:
    Number of boats stored per year: 50
    Percentage of wooden boats: 20
    Inside storage facilities
    Maximum size for hauling and storing:
        Length: 40'
        Draft: 6'
Maintenance:
    Number of boats maintained per year: 10
    Percentage of wooden boats: 100
    Owner maintenance allowed above and below rail.

ILLINOIS

CHAMBERLAIN MARINE—Richard Chamberlain
115 Olive
Carterville, IL 62918
618-985-6119

Builder Information
Years in business: 13
Carpenters employed: 2
Shop capacity: Boats to 28'

Repair Projects
27' Shepherd runabout (1955). Repaired engine and rebuilt transom. Refinished boat.
17' Chris-Craft runabout (1946). Refinished boat.
17' Century runabout (1948). Repaired engine and wiring, renewed brightwork.
14' Speedliner hydroplane (1952). Installed outboard engine, refinished boat.
19' Century runabout (1960). Renewed transom, refinished boat.
18' Chris-Craft runabout (1956). Replaced deck and garboard plank, refinished boat.
19' Century runabout (1964). Renewed transom, refinished boat.
22' Chris-Craft runabout (1947). Recaulked bottom and replaced part of deck. Refinished boat.
14' Lyman runabout (1951). Renewed frames, refinished boat.
21' Century runabout (1962). Renewed bottom planks and caulking.
19' Gar Wood runabout (1935). Replaced deck and refinished boat.
29' Owens cruiser (1962). Refinished boat.
35' Chris-Craft cruiser (1958). Refinished boat.

Yard Information
Services:
  Overland transport
  Gas engine repair
Storage:
  Number of boats stored per year: 6
  Percentage of wooden boats: 100
  Inside storage facilities
  Maximum size for hauling and storing:
    Length: 28'
Maintenance:
  Number of boats maintained per year: 5
  Percentage of wooden boats: 100
  Owner maintenance allowed above and below rail.
Retail supplies:
  Paint, wood accessories, and engine parts.

THE CHICAGOLAND CANOE BASE, INC.—Ralph C. Frese
4019 N. Narragansett Ave.
Chicago, IL 60634
312-777-1489

Builder Information
Years in business: 40
Carpenters employed: 1
Shop capacity: Boats to 34'

Recent New Construction
Platte River-type dugouts. 4 built for TV film "Centennial."

ILLINOIS

Recent Repair Projects
16' Peterborough canoe (ca. 1930). Completely restored boat. 1985.
17' Old Town wood-and-canvas canoes (ca. 1930). Completely restored 2 canoes. 1985.
12' Penn Yan cartopper. Renewed frames and planking. Refinished boat.

Yard Information
Retail supplies:
   Materials for canoe and kayak repair. Books on repair.

THE GREAT RIVER SMALL BOAT CO.—William H. Abel
P.O. Box 1601
Rock Island, IL 61201

Builder Information
Years in business: 5
Carpenters employed: 1
Shop capacity: Boats to 18'

Recent New Construction
Boats designed by William Abel for plywood construction:
   16' kayak. Built 1984.
   14' kayak. 3 built 1985.
   12' kayak. 2 built 1985.
   12' cartop skiff. Built 1985.

FRED NAGELBACH
2748 Ewing Ave.
Evanston, IL 60201

Builder Information
Years in business: 5
Carpenters employed: 1
Shop capacity: Boats to 15'

Recent New Construction
12' lapstrake dory. Traditional design. Built 1982.
14' double-paddle canoe. Lapstrake construction. Walt Simmons design. Built 1983.

Yard Information
Maintenance:
   Number of boats stored per year: 2
   Percentage of wooden boats: 100

ILLINOIS

VAN DELL CANOES—Kenneth Van Dell
481 E. Dayton St.
Galesburg, IL 61401
309-343-1029

Builder Information
Years in business: 5
Carpenters employed: 1
Shop capacity: Boats to 18'
Willing to travel for on-the-site building projects.

Recent New Construction
Strip-planked canoes. 4 built through 1984.

YACHT STANDARD—John Scully
1207 Glenwood Ave.
Joliet, IL 60435
815-725-6849

Builder Information
Years in business: 5
Carpenters employed: 1
Shop capacity: Boats to 100'
Willing to travel for on-the-site building projects.

Recent Repair Projects
45' Chris-Craft power cruiser (1953). Renewed transom framing and planking. Repaired flying-bridge windshield and cabintop. Replaced toerail. Started 1980.
35' Sparkman & Stephens sloop (1956). Refastening decks, renewing toerail, doing general carpentry and maintenance work. Current project.
35' Chris-Craft Sea Skiff (1967). Extensive restoration. Renewed hull, deck, windshield, and interior. Refinished. 1985.
18' Century Resorter (1952). Renewed framing, planking, and transom, refinished boat. 1983.
90' Trumpy motoryacht SEQUIA (1920s). Replaced cowl vent base. 1984.

INDIANA

KING MARINE—Howard A. King
5049 Robison Rd.
Indianapolis, IN 46268
317-872-7845

Builder Information
Years in business: 28
Carpenters employed: 3
Shop capacity: Boats to 30'

Recent New Construction
Boats of molded-plywood construction:
    11'5" Penguin class.
    17' Thistle-class sloop.
    20' Highlander-class sloop.
    Iceboats.

Recent Repair Projects
26' Chris-Craft. Renewed chines. 1985.
17' Thistle-class sloops. Repairs to transom, planking, and centerboard trunks.
Runabouts, racing- or cruising-type sailboats. Minor repairs to complete restorations.

Yard Information
Services:
    Gas engine repair
    Sailmaking
    Rigging
Storage:
    Number of boats stored per year: 25
    Percentage of wooden boats: Varies
Maintenance:
    Number of boats maintained per year: Varies
    Owner maintenance allowed above and below rail.
Retail supplies:
    Sailboat hardware, spars and rigging material. Paint and refinishing supplies. Will order materials on request.

IOWA

BIGFORK CANOE TRAILS—Jack Minehart
Fall and Winter address:
3016 Neola St.
Cedar Falls, IA 50613
319-266-8939
Spring and Summer address:
RR #1
Max, MN 56659
218-798-2735

Builder Information
Years in business: 6
Carpenters employed: 1
Shop capacity: Boats to 37'
Willing to travel for on-the-site building projects.

Recent New Construction
16' and 18' Chippewa "long-nosed" racing canoes. Birchbark construction. Traditional design. 4 built 1984-'85.
26' Rabeska fur-trading-type canoe. Birchbark construction. Development of voyageur-type canoe. Built 1985.

Recent Repair Projects
12' Cree hunting canoe. Replaced ribs and planking. 1985.
15' old-style Algonquin canoe. Renewed gunwales, replaced bindings. 1985.
17' Old Town Traveler canoe. Replaced keel and outwales. 1985.

Yard Information
Services:
    Launching facilities
    Overland transport
Storage:
    Number of boats stored per year: 4-5
    Percentage of wooden boats: 100
    Inside storage facilities
Retail supplies:
    Clear, straight-grained white cedar, split to order or in the log.

OKOBOJI BOATS—Ralph R. Schneider
Box 619
Okoboji, IA 51355
712-332-2144

Builder Information
Years in business: 97
Carpenters employed: 1
Shop capacity: Boats to 30'

Recent Repair Projects
Chris-Craft and Century mahogany sport boats to 30'. Replanking, refinishing, and general maintenance work.

IOWA

Yard Information
Services:
    Marina facilities
    Overland transport
    Launching facilities
    Moorage
    Gas engine repair
    Rigging
Storage:
    Number of boats stored per year: 400
    Percentage of wooden boats: 5
    Inside storage facilities
    Maximum size for hauling and storing:
        Length: 30'
        Draft: 4'
Maintenance:
    Number of boats maintained per year: 1,000
    Percentage of wooden boats: 5
Retail supplies:
    Wood, fastenings, paint.

MAINE

ACADIA CANOE SHOP—Lee K. LaBelle
RFD #5, Box 372
Ellsworth, ME 04605
207-667-9433

Builder Information
Years in business: 2
Carpenters employed: 1
Shop capacity: Boats to 20′

Recent New Construction
18½′ wood-and-canvas canoes. E.M. White guide model. 2 built in 1985.

Recent Repair Projects
17′ Old Town canoe. Recanvased. 1985.
15′ Old Town canoe. Complete restoration. 1985.
15′ E.M. White canoe. New rails. 1985.
13′ Westfield canoe. New rails and deck. 1985.
20′ Old Town canoe. New keel. 1985.
15′ Old Town canoe. New keel. 1985.

EUGENE ALEXANDER
P.O. BOX 133
Orrs Island, ME 04066
207-833-6198

Builder Information
Years in business: 30
Carpenters employed: 1
Shop capacity: Boats to 35′

Recent New Construction
20′ strip-planked lobsterboat. Designed by Eugene Alexander. Has built several since 1975.
8-20′ strip- and carvel-planked skiffs and rowboats. Designs by Eugene Alexander. 25 built during 1984 and 1985.

Repair Projects
22′6″ sloop. Replaced garboards, frames, and floors; refastened and recaulked bottom. 1985.

Yard Information
Services:
    Overland transport
    Temporary moorage

ANDROSCOGGIN BOAT CO.—Jon Capozza
P.O. Box 72, Rte. 133
Wayne, ME 04284
207-685-9925

Builder Information
Years in business: 10
Carpenters employed: 1
Shop capacity: Boats to 25′

MAINE

Recent New Construction
10' plywood dinghies. Jon Capozza design. 3 built in 1985.

Recent Repair Projects
18' Gar Wood runabout (1936). Complete restoration. 1984-'85.
19' Chris-Craft Sportsman (1938). Complete restoration. 1984-'85.
22' Chris-Craft Deluxe Utility (1947). Complete restoration. 1984-'85.
16' Old Town lapstrake runabout (1960). Repaired stem, keelson, and planking. 1984-'85.
14' North Haven dinghy (1895). Complete restoration. 1984-'85.
17' Rangeley Lake boat. Complete restoration. 1984-'85.
   Canoes. Restoration and recanvasing. 11 since 1984.

Yard Information
Storage:
   Number of boats stored per year: 40
   Percentage of wooden boats: 50
   Inside storage facilities
   Maximum size for hauling and storing:
      Length: 22'
Maintenance:
   Number of boats maintained per year: 20
   Percentage of wooden boats: 95

APPRENTICESHOP OF MAINE MARITIME MUSEUM
John Burke, Director
963 Washington St.
Bath, ME 04530
207-443-1316

Builder Information
Years in business: 13
Carpenters employed: 12 apprentices, 2 instructors
Shop capacity: Boats to 45'

Recent New Construction
14'6" carvel and cold-molded North Haven dinghies. 3 built 1984, 1985.
12' lapstrake dory. Chaisson design. 2 built 1984.
40' pinky. Lines from 1832 half model. Built 1982-'85.

Recent Repair Projects
29' Willard Hodgdon fantail launch (1904). Replacing garboards, floors, and keel.
   Current project.

Yard Information
Services:
   Moorage
Maintenance:
   For museum collection only

MAINE

ARIEL BOATWORKS—Gregory Moore
P.O. Box 531
Rockport, ME 04856
207-354-2435

Builder Information
Years in business: 3
Carpenters employed: 1-2
Shop capacity: Boats to 40′
Willing to travel for on-the-site building projects.

Recent New Construction
14′8″ sailing canoe OBOE. Lapstrake construction. Modified R.H. Baker
PICCOLO design. Built 1984-'85.

Recent Repair Projects
14′6″ to 20′ wood-and-canvas canoes and skiffs. Old Town, Chestnut,
Kennebec, Morris, and Penn Yan models. Approximately 15 boats restored
and/or recanvased in past 3 years.
Other repair and maintenance work has been done on dories, peapods, skiffs,
the 50′ racing yacht FIGARO, and the 37′ Spray replica SCUD.

Yard Information
Maintenance:
Number of boats maintained per year: 2-5
Percentage of wooden boats: 100

ARUNDEL SHIPYARD—Arthur Brendze
P.O. Box 434A
Kennebunkport, ME 04046
207-967-5550

Builder Information
Years in business: 10
Carpenters employed: 3-4
Shop capacity: Boats 60+

Recent Repair Projects
30′ K. Aage Nielsen sloop. Completely restored boat. 1980-'81.
24′ Muscongus Bay cutter. Completely restored boat. 1981-'82.
38′ power cruiser CARIBOU. Renewed decks and planking. Refastened hull.
1983-'85.
36′ Hinckley Sou'wester sloop. Completed major restoration work. 1983-'84.
30′ Murray Peterson schooner STORMY. Renewed stem and restored
major portion of hull. Refinished boat. 1983-'85.
30′ yawl. Renewed decks and planking. Refastened hull. 1984-'85.
28′ double-ended power launch. Completely restored boat. 1984-'85.
28′ Kings Cruiser-class sloop. Completed major restoration work. 1983-'85.
21-48′ lobsterboats. Minor repairs to complete restorations. 1976 to present.
Numerous small craft. Minor repairs, refastening and refinishing of hull.
1976 to present.

MAINE

Yard Information
Services:
    Marina facilities
    Launching facilities
    Moorage
    Diesel and gas engine repair
    Rigging
Storage:
    Number of boats stored per year: 50
    Percentage of wooden boats: 20-25
    Maximum size for hauling and storing:
        Length: 50'
        Draft: 7'
        Tonnage: 15-20
Maintenance:
    Number of boats maintained per year: 25-30
    Percentage of wooden boats: 30
    Owner maintenance allowed above and below rail.
Retail supplies:
    Good supply of basic materials. Will order items on request.

BACK RIVER BOAT SHOP—Sam Francis
Star Rte. 2, Georgetown Island
Bath, ME 04530
207-371-2510

Builder Information
Years in business: 14
Carpenters employed: 2
Shop capacity: Boats to 50'

Recent Repair Projects
40' Concordia yawl. Renewed planking, rigging, and brightwork. 1984-'85.
45' seining dory. Replaced deck, trim, and cabintop. 1985.
30' Nielsen yawl. Replaced structural keel and deadwood. Renewed hull planking and stern. 1985.
36' Nielsen yawl. Refinished boat. 1985.
25' Folkboat sloop. Replaced backbone and planking. 1985.

Yard Information
Services:
    Rigging
Maintenance:
    Number of boats maintained per year: 2
    Percentage of wooden boats: 100

MAINE

DON BAMAN, BOATBUILDER
Kansas Rd.
Milbridge, ME 04568
207-546-7473

Builder Information
Years in business: 4
Carpenters employed: 1
Shop capacity: Boats to 21'
Willing to travel for on-the-site building projects.

Recent New Construction
64' schooner JANET MAY. Lines developed by Phil Shelton from Biloxi, Mississippi, freight schooner of 1880. Built by Shelton and Baman, 1982-'84.

Recent Repair Projects
10' lapstrake skiff. Complete restoration. Current project.
16' lapstrake pulling boat. Complete restoration. Current project.
12' Penguin-class sailing dinghy. Complete restoration. Current project.

BILLINGS DIESEL & MARINE SERVICES, INC.
Harlan Billings
Box 67
Stonington, ME 04681
207-367-2328

Builder Information
Years in business: 19
Carpenters employed: 9
Shop capacity: Boats to 115'
Willing to travel for on-the-site building projects.

Recent New Construction
72' passenger ferry PATIENCE. Spencer Lincoln design. Built 1982.
45' lobsterboat. Arno Day design. Built 1978.

Recent Repair Projects
145' Grand Banks schooner SHERMAN ZWICKER. Renewing foredeck and deckbeams, top timbers, and sheer clamps. Replacing lower stem apron. Current project.
100' sail training schooner WESTERN UNION. Renewing deck. Current project.
110' Pilgrim's ship replica MAYFLOWER II. Rebuilt bow area, replanked both topsides with adjacent frame repair. Recaulked weather deck. 1982, 1983, 1985.
40' Sparkman & Stephens/Nevins yawl. Replaced structural keel.
33' L.F. Herreshoff ketch ARAMINTA. Totally reframed and refurbished boat. Built new interior. 1982.
39' Concordia yawl. Installed plywood/Dynel overlay on deck. Renewed backbone fastenings. 1985.
31' Winter Harbor "21" sloops (1907). Renewed cabin and trim. Renewed deck canvas. Refurbished and refinished boats. 2 boats completed 1978.

MAINE

Yard Information
Services:
    Marina facilities
    Launching facilities
    Overland transport
    Moorage
    Diesel and gas engine repair
    Rigging
Storage:
    Number of boats stored per year: 368
    Percentage of wooden boats: 60
    Inside storage facilities
    Maximum size for hauling and storing:
        Length: 100'
        Draft: 12'
        Tonnage: 180
Maintenance:
    Number of boats maintained per year: 1000+
    Percentage of wooden boats: 50
    Owner maintenance allowed above rail.
Retail supplies:
    Ship's chandlery—extensive inventory.

BLEVINS COMPANY—Thomas Blevins
Rte. 27, Box 69
Edgecomb, ME 04556
207-882-6396

Builder Information
Years in business: 15
Carpenters employed: 2-4
Shop capacity: Boats to 44'
Willing to travel for on-the-site building projects.

Recent New Construction
12' Columbia sailing dinghy. Lapstrake construction. N.G. Herreshoff design.
    2 built 1984-'85.
12' cold-molded canoe. T. Blevins design. Built 1985.
12' lapstrake South Bristol flat-iron skiff. Built 1985.

Recent Repair Projects
28' Giles Vertue-class sloop. Complete restoration. Rebuilding house, mast, and hatches.
    Replacing deck canvas, head, exhaust system, engine compartment, and bilge pump.
    Refastening planking and refinishing. Current project.
16' Herreshoff 12½-class sloop. Refastening and recaulking hull. Refinishing boat.
    Current project.

Yard Information
Services:
    Diesel and gas engine repair
    Rigging
Maintenance:
    Number of boats maintained per year: 8
    Percentage of wooden boats: 100
    Owner maintenance allowed above and below rail.
(continues)

MAINE

(Blevins Company, continued)
Retail supplies:
    Paints, varnishes, brushes, fastenings, marine equipment. Wood including teak, cedars, oaks, mahoganies, ash, cherry, cypress, basswood, plywood, and veneer.

BRASS TACKS CANOE SHOP—Steven Van Syckel
RFD #1, Box 844 (Depot St.)
Cornish, ME 04020
207-625-3676

Builder Information
Years in business: 1
Carpenters employed: 1
Shop capacity: Boats to 19'6"

Recent New Construction
20' wood-and-canvas canoe. Built 1985.
17'6" wood-and-canvas canoe. Rollin Thurlow design. Built 1985.

Recent Repair Projects
19' Old Town runabout. Replaced 12 ribs and 20% of the planking. New transom and gunwales. Recanvased and refinished.
Numerous canoe repairs, including 18' Old Towns, a 17' White, a 17' Arnold, 17' OTCAs, and a 10' Corson. Repair work has entailed stem, rib, and plank replacement. Recanvasing and refinishing.

Yard Information
Maintenance:
    Number of boats maintained per year: 20
    Percentage of wooden boats: 100
Retails supplies:
    Cedar planking, ribs (cut to order), $^{11}/_{16}$" brass tacks, #10 canvas.

BROOKLIN BOAT YARD—Joel White
Brooklin, ME 04616
207-359-2236

Builder Information
Years in business: 30
Carpenters employed: 5
Shop capacity: Boats to 50'

Recent New Construction
30' strip-planked auxiliary cutter. Cy Hamlin design. Built 1985.
18' daysailer. Eaton design. 2 built 1984.
50' power cruiser. Joel White design. Built 1982.
7'7" and 9'6" sailing prams. Lapstrake plywood construction. Joel White design. 6 built 1983-'85.
20' Bangor Packet rowing wherries. 10 built 1982-'85.
37' gaff ketch. William Hand design. Built 1981.

Recent Repair Projects
40' Concordia yawl. New deck. 1985.
33' Concordia 33 sloop. New deck. 1984.
43' Herreshoff Fishers Island class. New deck. 1984.

MAINE

Yard Information
Services:
  Launching facilities
  Moorage
  Diesel and gas engine repair
  Sailmaking and repair
Storage:
  Number of boats stored per year: 50
  Percentage of wooden boats: 95
  Inside storage facilities for 45 boats
  Maximum size for hauling and storing:
    Length: 45'
    Draft: 7'
    Tonnage: 12
Maintenance:
  Number of boats maintained per year: 50
  Percentage of wooden boats: 95
Retail supplies:
  Paint, fastenings, rope, hardware.

J.O. BROWN & SON, INC.—Foy W. Brown
North Haven, ME 04853
207-867-4621

Builder Information
Years in business: 97
Carpenters employed: 4
Shop capacity: Boats to 45'

Recent New Construction
32' daysailer. Phil Bolger design. Built 1983.
34', 36', and 38' lobsterboats. J.O. Brown & Son, Inc. design. 4 built 1982-'85.

Recent Repair Projects
30' sloop (1955). Completely rebuilding boat. Renewing bottom and keel.
  Sheathing hull in fiberglass. Current project.

Yard Information
Services:
  Marina facilities
  Launching facilities
  Moorage
  Diesel and gas engine repair
  Sail repair
  Rigging
Storage:
  Number of boats stored per year: 75
  Percentage of wooden boats: 50
  Inside storage facilities
  Maximum size for hauling and storing:
    Length: 45'
    Draft: 7'
    Tonnage: 15
(continues)

MAINE

(J.O. Brown & Son, Inc., continued)
Maintenance:
    Number of boats maintained per year: 75
    Percentage of wooden boats: 50
    Owner maintenance allowed above and below rail.
Retail supplies:
    Complete inventory. Marine store.

CADDIS CANOE—Olga Lange Willmann and Brian Keegstra
Box 245A
Brooksville, ME 04617
207-326-4345

Builder Information
Years in business: 2
Carpenters employed: 2
Shop capacity: Boats to 25'
Willing to travel for on-the-site building projects.

Recent New Construction
Boats of strip-plank construction:
    16'6"tandem canoe. Chestnut Canoe Co. design. 2 built 1984-'85.
    14' solo canoe. Brian Keegstra design. Built 1985.
    10' rowing boat. Hiram Blake design. Built 1985.
Other new construction:
    14' flat-iron skiff. John Gardner design. Current project.

Recent Repair Projects
16' Old Town Charles River canoe (ca. 1930). Replaced gunwales, decks,
    some ribs and planking. 1984.
8' pram. Replaced gunwales, transom, knees, and skeg. 1985.
12' rowing boat. Renewed guardrails and shoe on keel. 1985.

WM. CANNELL BOATBUILDING CO., INC.—Bill Cannell
Box 900, Atlantic Ave.
Camden, ME 04843
207-236-8500

Builder Information
Years in business: 9
Carpenters employed: 9
Shop capacity: Boats to 80'

Recent New Construction
25' fantail launch. Pete Culler design. Built 1985.
9'4" lapstrake tender. N.G. Herreshoff design. 6 built 1980-'85.
16' lapstrake tender. N.G. Herreshoff design. Built 1984.
25' sailing surfboat. U.S. government design. Built 1984.

Recent Repair Projects
45' Murray Peterson/Aage Nielsen schooner. Renewed floors, lower frame ends,
    horn timber, stem knee, centerboard trunk. 1985.

MAINE

Yard Information
Services:
  Marina facilities
  Launching facilities
Retail supplies:
  Imported English copper rivets.

THE CANOE WORKS—Guy A. Cyr
P.O. Box 33
West Sullivan, ME 04689
207-422-9095

Builder Information
Years in business: 25
Carpenters employed: 1
Shop capacity: Boats to 17'

Recent New Construction
17' Rushton Indian Girl canoe. 3 built 1984-'85.

Recent Repair Projects
15-20' canoes and fishing boats. Recanvased and refinished hull. Replaced gunwales, decks, planking, thwarts, seats. 1950-'85.

Yard Information
Storage:
  Number of boats stored per year: 5
  Percentage of wooden boats: 100
  Inside storage facilities
  Maximum size for hauling and storing:
    Length: 20'
Maintenance:
  Number of boats maintained per year: 15
  Percentage of wooden boats: 100
  Owner maintenance allowed.
Retail supplies:
  Materials for canoe construction and repair. Canvas, tacks, planking and rib stock, seats, deck, thwarts, stem bands, and paddles.

THE CARPENTER'S BOATSHOP—Robert E. Ives
Branch Rd.
Pemaquid, ME 04558
207-677-3768

Builder Information
Years in business: 7
Carpenters employed: 7
Shop capacity: Boats to 24'
(continues)

MAINE

(The Carpenter's Boatshop, continued)

Recent New Construction
13'2" Woods Hole spritsail boat. Built 1985.
12' lapstrake dinghy. Herreshoff design. Built 1985.
20' garvey scow. Built 1985.
17½' lapstrake Swampscott dory. Fred Dion design. Built 1985.
13' lapstrake Matinicus Island peapod. Built 1985.
12' lapstrake sailing dory.

Recent Repair Projects
13' sailing dinghy (circa 1880s). Replaced ribs, deck coaming. Refinished. 1985.

Yard Information
Storage:
    Number of boats stored per year: 5
    Percentage of wooden boats: 100
    Inside storage facilities
    Maximum size for hauling and storing:
        Length: 16'
Maintenance:
    Number of boats maintained per year: 6 (those built by shop)
    Percentage of wooden boats: 100

CHEBEAGUE MARINE, INC.—Michael Porter
Chebeague Island, ME 04017
207-846-3145

Builder Information
Years in business: 10
Carpenters employed: 2
Shop capacity: New construction to 35'
Willing to travel for on-the-site repair projects.

Recent New Construction
Boats of lapstrake construction:
    17' sailing Swampscott dory. 2 built 1983.
    14' sailing skiff. M. Porter design. Built 1984.
    16' outboard semi-dory. J. Gardner design. 2 built 1983-'84.
    18' outboard skiff. M. Porter design. Built 1985.
    13'6" Good Little Skiff. R.D. Culler design. 2 built 1983.
Other new construction:
    26' power launch. M. Porter design. Current project.
    35' steamboat. M. Porter design. Current project.
    12' flatiron skiff. M. Porter design. 2 built 1984.

Recent Repair Projects
33' ketch. Did major overhaul. 1984.
30' Mason sloop. Renewed fore-gripe and planking. 1983-'84.
35' lobsterboat. Replaced steering gear. 1985.
38' lobsterboat. Replaced butt blocks, renewed interior. 1984.
35' lobsterboat. Installed flush hatches on deck. 1983.

Yard Information
Services:
    Launching facilities
    Overland transport
    Diesel and gas engine repair
    Rigging

MAINE

Maintenance:
    Number of boats maintained per year: 3
    Percentage of wooden boats: 100
    Owner maintenance allowed.
Retail supplies:
    Complete line of materials.

R.S. COLSON BOATWORKS—James Moores
146 Water St.
Lubec, ME 04652

Builder Information
Years in business: 69
Carpenters employed: 1-3
Shop capacity: Boats to 95'
Willing to travel for on-the-site building projects.

Recent New Construction
27' lapstrake fishing boat. J.P. Moores design. Built 1977.,
18' cold-molded pleasure-type fishing boat. J.P. Moores design. Built 1979.
16' plywood-and-epoxy pleasure-type fishing boat. Built 1981.
30' pleasure-type fishing boat. J.P. Moores design. Built 1980.

Recent Repair Projects
45' workboat. Replaced stem and garboards. 1978.
45' workboat. Replaced stem and adjacent planks. 1979.
54' workboat. Renewed deck, pilothouse, and planking. 1979.
38' lobsterboat. Replaced keel. 1979.
16' lapstrake Deer Island skiff. Totally restored. 1981.
48' charter boat. Replaced keel and garboards. 1982.
30' lobsterboat. Renewed pilothouse. 1982.
40' yacht. Replaced horn timber. 1983.
16' Century runabout. Rebuilt forward deck. 1983.
50' motoryacht. Extensive reconstruction. Renewed planking, frames, cabin sides. 1984.

Yard Information
Services:
    Launching facilities
    Storage
Maintenance:
    Number of boats maintained per year: 8
    Percentage of wooden boats: 50
    Owner maintenance allowed above rail.
Retail supplies:
    Wood, fastenings, paint.

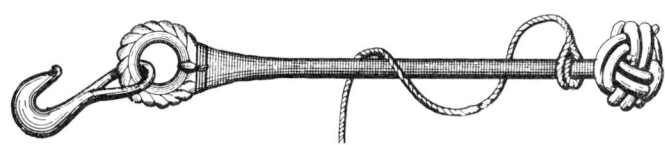

MAINE

CRANBERRY ISLAND BOATYARD—Edward Gray
Cranberry Island, ME 04625
207-244-7316

Builder Information
Years in business: 10
Carpenters employed: 3
Shop capacity: Boats to 55'
Willing to travel for on-the-site building projects.

Recent New Construction
10' plywood punts. In-house design. 2 built 1985.
28' plywood-and-fiberglass barge. Ed Gray design. Built 1985.

Recent Repair Projects
32' power cruiser. Renewed interior, platform, wiring, plumbing. Repaired planking. 1985.
30' power cruiser. Renewed interior, platform, wiring, pilothouse. Complete restoration. Current project.

Yard Information
Services:
    Launching facilities
    Moorage
Storage:
    Number of boats stored per year: 70
    Percentage of wooden boats: 20
    Maximum size for hauling and storing:
      Length: 42'
      Draft: 7'
      Tonnage: 20
Maintenance:
    Number of boats maintained per year: 100
    Percentage of wooden boats: 20
Retail supplies:
    Fastenings, paint, wood, hardware, and rope. Full line of marine supplies.

CUSTOM BUILDING—E. Tyler Proctor
16 Shannon Rd.
Bar Harbor, ME 04609
207-288-3679

Builder Information
Years in business: 30
Carpenters employed: 1
Shop capacity: Boats to 24'

Recent New Construction
10' strip-planked yacht tender. Atkin design. Built 1970.
14' lapstrake Flat-Iron Pod. Proctor design. Built 1969.
8' lapstrake pram. L.F. Herreshoff design. 9 built 1970–'85.
24' lapstrake sharpie. Atkin design. Built 1969.
14' lapstrake skiff. Proctor design. Built 1968.
10' lapstrake sailing pram. John Gardner design. Built 1985.
16' lapstrake peapod (Jonesport model). Lines by H.I. Chapelle. Built 1980.

Recent Repair Projects
18' Old Town canoe (1923). Recanvased hull and sponsons; replaced keel and 3 frames. 1984.

MAINE

DANA CREEK BOATWORKS—Abe Baggins
P.O. Box 694
Camden, ME 04843
207-236-2908

Builder Information
Years in business: 6
Carpenters employed: 1
Shop capacity: Boats to 20'

Recent New Construction
10' lapstrake pram. Traditional Norwegian design. 3 built 1983-'84.
17' lapstrake faering. Traditional Norwegian design. 3 built 1980-'84.

Yard Information
Services:
    Rigging

DARK HARBOR BOATYARD CORP.
Box 1986
Islesboro, ME 04848
207-734-2246

Builder Information
Years in business: 65
Carpenters employed: 3
Shop capacity: Boats to 60'

Recent New Construction
12', 14', and 16' power work skiffs. Plywood construction. W. Rossiter design.
12' tender. Lawley design. Current project.

Recent Repair Projects
45' THREE BELLES. Installed new teak garboards, replaced butt
    blocks. Rebuilt engine, stripped and refinished hull. 1984-'85.

Yard Information
Services:
    Marina facilities
    Launching facilities
    Moorage
    Diesel and gas engine repair
    Rigging
Storage:
    Number of boats stored per year: 120
    Percentage of wooden boats: 30
    Inside storage facilities
    Maximum size for hauling and storing:
        Length: 50'
        Draft: 6'6"
        Tonnage: 20
Maintenance:
    Number of boats maintained per year: 120
    Percentage of wooden boats: 30
Retail supplies:
    Ship's chandlery, complete marine store.

MAINE

DIBBLE & THOMAS—Keith Dibble
Water St.
Blue Hill, ME 04614
Mailing address:
East Blue Hill, ME 04629
207-374-5023

Builder Information
Years in business: 4
Carpenters employed: 2
Shop capacity: Boats to 40′

Recent Repair Projects
32′ Crocker ketch. Replaced several planks. 1982.
24′ sloop. Renewed keel, floors, and structural timbers. 1982.
16′ Luders runabout. Renewed keel. 1985.
30′ launch. Stripping and refinishing hull. Current project.

DION'S YACHT YARD, INC.—Elmer L. J. Dion and Janine Dion Johnson
P.O. Box 600, 48 Bowen Rd.
Kittery, ME 03904
207-439-9582

Builder Information
Years in business: 22
Carpenters employed: 5

Recent Repair Projects
65′ Sutton trawler-yacht SEASENSE. Completely overhauled boat's exterior and interior. Did custom interior joinerwork and fabrication. Renewed wiring, fuel, and water systems. Refinished boat. 1977-'79.
71′ oceangoing yacht FLYING WINGS. Renewed electrical panels and wiring system. Modified interior, fabricated custom hardware, and refitted boat. 1980-'83.
41′ Concordia yawl PENARROW. Replaced stem and some planks. Repowered with diesel, renewed wiring, and refinished boat. 1980-'84.
41′ Concordia yawl OTTER. Replaced maststep, floor timbers, cabin sole, engine and beds. Renewed joinerwork, wiring, and electronics. Rebuilt cockpit. Refastened hull as needed and refinished boat. 1980 to present.
48′ Sparkman & Stephens Seafarer design ECLIPSE. Modified interior and renewed joinerwork, wiring, plumbing, and engine. Refinished hull and replaced railcaps and winches. 1981-'83.
72′ ketch MAYBE. Renewed generator, batteries, plumbing, wiring, and rigging. Refinished hull. 1983.
48′ Alden schooner THIRSTY MAJOR. Total rebuild. Replacing all rotted wood, renewing stem, horn timbers, deckbeams, decking, and rails. 1983 to present.
72′ Jongert motorsailer. Refitted boat with new electrical equipment. Overhauled sea furl, and refinished boat. 1984.

Yard Information
Services:
  Marina facilities
  Launching facilities
  Overland transport
  Moorage
  Diesel and gas engine repair
  Rigging

MAINE

Storage:
    Number of boats stored per year: 61
    Percentage of wooden boats: 17
    Inside storage facilities
    Maximum size for hauling and storing:
        Length: 72'
        Draft: 9'
        Tonnage: 100
Maintenance:
    Number of boats maintained per year: 61
    Percentage of wooden boats: 28
Retail supplies:
    Can supply any and all equipment. Large inventory of hardware and other marine supplies.

THE DORY SHOP—Arnie Smith
Box 619, Indian River
Addison, ME 04606
207-497-2010

Builder Information
Years in business: 10
Carpenters employed: 1
Shop capacity: Boats 20' +

Recent New Construction
17' lapstrake Swampscott dory. Fred Dion design.
10' lapstrake tender. Arnie Smith design.
12' diagonally-planked duckboat. Arnie Smith design.
8' flat-iron skiff. Carvel and plywood planking. Arnie Smith design.

Recent Repair Projects
25' Revelcraft. Replaced bottom.
34' Frost-built lobsterboat. Replaced keel, repaired planking and frames.

Yard Information
Retail supplies:
    Paints, fastenings, tools, cedar.

DOWNEAST PEAPODS—James Steele
Box 82
Brooklin, ME 04616
207-359-8842

Builder Information
Years in business: 20
Carpenters employed: 1
Shop capacity: New construction to 13½'

Recent New Construction
13'6" peapods for oar and sail. J.F. Steele design.
    Over 100 built since 1964.

Recent Repair Projects
28' Rozinante ketch. L.F. Herreshoff design. Renewing cockpit seats
    and floorboards. Current project.

MAINE

DUCK TRAP WOODWORKING—Walter J. Simmons
P.O. Box 88
Lincolnville Beach, ME 04849
207-789-5363

Builder Information
Years in business: 16
Carpenters employed: 1
Shop capacity: Boats to 25'

Recent New Construction
Boats of lapstrake construction (153 built to date):
    16' Lincolnville salmon wherry. Traditional design.
    17' Duck Trap wherry. Walt Simmons design.
    15' lapstrake canoe. Walt Simmons design.
    25' Hutchinson-type power launch. Nelson Zimmer design. (Construction planned for 1986.)

Recent Repair Projects
18' Old Town guide's model canoe (ca. 1913). Completely restored: Renewed ribs, planking, canvas, rails, and finish. 1985.

Yard Information
Retail supplies:
    Planking, fastenings, hardware, and tools. Boat plans, boatbuilding books, and workshops.

EAST/WEST CUSTOM BOATS—Ted Perry
Rte. 236
Eliot, ME 03903
207-439-4769

Builder Information
Years in business: 7
Carpenters employed: 5
Shop capacity: Boats to 50'
Willing to travel for on-the-site building projects.

Recent New Construction
27' cold-molded schooner Energy 27. Arthur Martin design. Built 1982.
48' cold-molded power cruiser Energy 48. Arthur Martin design. Built 1980.
48' cold-molded power yacht. Roger Marshall design. Current project.
16' cold-molded peapod Appledore 16. Arthur Martin design. 60 built between 1979 and 1985.

Recent Repair Projects
22' Star-class sloop. Refinished. 1982-'85.
48' powerboat. New interior. 1984.
26' lobsterboat. New platform.
20' lobsterboat. New transom.

MAINE

FARRIN'S BOATSHOP—Bruce A. Farrin
Sproul Rd.
Walpole, ME 04573
207-563-5506

Builder Information
Years in business: 14
Carpenters employed: 5
Shop capacity: Boats to 50'
Willing to travel for on-the-site building projects.

Recent New Construction
40' diesel yacht for coastal cruising. Murray Peterson Associates design. Current project.

Yard Information
Retail supplies:
   Limited supply of materials for the construction of wooden boats.

FRANKLIN CEDAR CANOES—Charles Grosjean
Box 175
Franklin, ME 04634
207-565-2282

Builder Information
Years in business: 3
Carpenters employed: 1
Shop capacity: Boats to 18'

Recent New Construction
12', 16', and 18' wood-and-canvas fishermen's canoes. A few built each year.

GREAT HERON WORKS—James L. Murdock
P.O. Box 172, States Point Rd.
Tenants Harbor, ME 04860
207-372-8625 or 372-8877

Builder Information
Years in business: 2
Carpenters employed: 1
Shop capacity: New construction to 20'
Willing to travel for on-the-site building projects.

Recent New Construction
12'10" lapstrake peapod. Robert Baker design. Built 1985.
17' lapstrake Swampscott dory. Fred Dion design. Built 1984-'85.
10' lapstrake rowing skiff CHERRY STONE. Design by James L. Murdock. 3 built 1985.

Recent Repair Projects
50' ketch, designed for SORC. Modified interior for charter work, installed watertight bulkhead, extended cabin accommodations. Repaired cabin rot, cockpit coaming, carlin, and deckbeams. 1985.
34' Alden ketch. Built new main saloon and galley. 1985.
28' Herreshoff Rozinante. Renewed spars, cabintop, and cockpit. 1985.

MAINE

HAMILTON CANOE & BOAT SHOP—Daniel W. Hamilton
RFD, Box 1700, Goshen Road
Winterport, ME 04496
207-223-4188
(see MA pg. 122)

H & H BOATWORKS—Cymbrid Hughes
Maquoit Rd.
Brunswick, ME 04011
207-725-5644

Builder Information
Years in business: 8
Carpenters employed: 3
Shop capacity: Boats to 48'
Willing to travel for on-the-site building projects.

Recent Repair Projects
36' Colonial power cruiser (1960). Complete restoration.
28' Rozinante ketch (1975). New cabin, deck, and main bulkhead.
36' Hinckley Pilot (1940s). Complete restoration.
28' Pilot cutter (1907). Complete restoration.
21' Chris-Craft Cadet (1928). Complete restoration, except bottom.
22' triple-cockpit Gar Wood (1936). Complete restoration.
21' Boothbay One-Design (1950s). Complete restoration.

Yard Information
Services:
    Diesel and gas engine repair
Maintenance:
    Number of boats maintained per year: 10-15
    Percentage of wooden boats: 90
    Owner maintenance allowed.
Retail supplies:
    "Everything we use, we sell."

HERITAGE BOATBUILDERS, INC.—William Lowell, Pres.
Rte. 9
Pownal, ME 04069
207-353-2163 or 353-9503

Builder Information
Years in business: 10
Carpenters employed: 3
Shop capacity: Boats to 55'

Recent New Construction
30'8" lobsterboat. Royal Lowell design. Built 1983.

Recent Repair Projects
26' power cruiser. Replaced garboards and transom, installed sister frames. Rewired, refinished. Some replacement of deck, repairs to house and trunk.

MAINE

HODGDON YACHTS, INC.—Timothy Hodgdon
Murray Hill Rd., Box 505
East Boothbay, ME 04544
207-633-4194 or 633-4668

Builder Information
Years in business: 167 under various family names
Carpenters employed: 7
Shop capacity: Boats to 100'
Willing to travel for on-the-site building projects.

Recent New Construction
38' Pilot schooner. G. Stadel design. Built 1975.
85' power cruiser. Double-planked construction. Eldredge-McInnis design. Current project.
42' power cruiser. Double-planked construction. H.A. Scheel design. Built 1982.
32-50' lobsterboat/pleasure cruisers. Nielsen design. 3 built 1971-'77.
36', 42', and 50' lobsterboats. Eldredge-McInnis design. 3 built 1975-'79.
14' sailing dory. John Gardner design. Built 1979.

Recent Repair Projects
85' Fife ketch. Replaced stem. 1984.
104' schooner-yacht AMERICA. Renewed interior. 1979.
55' Alden ketch. Replaced deck, renewed joinerwork. 1975.
42' Frank Paine power cruiser. Remodeled interior. 1982.

IRIS BOAT WORKS—James P. Hanna
HCR 71, Box 165
Machias, ME 04654
207-255-4216

Builder Information
Years in business: 8
Carpenters employed: 1
Shop capacity: New construction to 30'
Willing to travel for on-the-site building projects.

Recent New Construction
16' wood-and-canvas canoe. Mawhinney design. 3 built 1985.
20' wood-and-canvas Grand Laker canoe. Bacon design. Built 1984.
10' lapstrake tender. Chaisson design. Built 1985.
15' Rangeley boat. Barrett design. Built 1984.

Recent Repair Projects
36' lobsterboat. Converted to pleasure craft (raised and enclosed wheelhouse, redesigned and built cabin accommodations). Refinished hull and topsides. 1982.
15' Rangeley Lake boat. Replaced most of the frames and 30% of the planking. Built a new custom backrest, stripped and repainted hull. 1983.
12' Watt's peapod. Renewed keel and floorboards. Refinished hull. 1985.
20' Whalen daysailer. Removed fiberglass sheathing, refastened and recaulked hull. Replaced floor timbers and mast, modified rig, added cuddy Current project.
Continually repairing and restoring wood/canvas canoes.

Yard Information
Services:
    Overland transport
(continues)

MAINE

(Iris Boat Works, continued)
Storage:
    Number of boats stored per year: 10-12
    Percentage of wooden boats: 100
Retail suplies:
    Will order on request.

ISLAND FALLS CANOE—Jerry Stelmok
RFD 3, Box 76
Dover-Foxcroft, ME 04426
207-564-7612

Builder Information
Years in business: 12
Carpenters employed: 1
Shop capacity: Boats to 20'

Recent New Construction
16' wood and canvas guide canoe. F.M. White design. 3 built 1984-'85.
16' Featherweight wood-and-canvas canoe. 3 built since 1981.
18'6" wood-and-canvas canoes. 12 built to date.
20' wood-and-canvas canoe. 3 built since 1984.

Yard Information
Retail supplies:
    Materials for canoe repair—canvas, filler, fastenings.

ISLAND WOODWORKING—M. Chas. Liebow
Cranberry Isles, ME 04625
207-244-7225

Builder Information
Years in business: 12
Carpenters employed: 3
Shop capacity: Boats to 50'
Willing to travel occasionally for on-the-site building projects.

Recent New Construction
12' lapstrake lobster punts. M. Chas. Liebow design. 2 built 1982-'84.

Recent Repair Projects
36' passenger boat. Replaced cabintop and refastened. 1975.
32' passenger boat. Replaced cabintop, installed new engine. 1976.
42' passenger boat. Installed new waterways and engine. 1974.
36' power cruiser. Refinished brightwork, replaced some of the cabin. 1983-'84.
42' power cruiser. Repaired shafts, rebedded windows, stripped and varnished
    brightwork. 1985-'86.

Yard Information
Services:
    Launching facilities
    Engine repair

Storage:
    Number of boats stored per year: 35
    Percentage of wooden boats: 50
    Inside storage facilities for 15 boats
    Maximum size for hauling and storing:
        Length: 42'
        Draft: 5'
        Tonnage: 20
Maintenance:
    Number of boats maintained per year: 40
    Percentage of wooden boats: 60
    Owner maintenance allowed.
Retail supplies:
    Paint, electronics, hydraulics, lumber and milling. Most marine supplies.

T. JASON BOATS—Terence T. Jason
Goods Point Rd.
Steuben, ME 04680
207-546-2066

Builder Information
Years in business: 30
Carpenters employed: 1
Shop capacity: Boats to 50'

Recent New Construction
48' schooner. Current project.
20' plywood skiff. T. Jason design. 310 built to date.

Recent Repair Projects
32' lobsterboat. Replaced deck, planking, tanks, rails. Rebuilt house. 1984.

Yard Information
Services:
    Launching facilities
    Overland transport
    Diesel and gas engine repair
    Rigging
Storage:
    Number of boats stored per year: 3-4
    Percentage of wooden boats: 50
    Maximum size for hauling and storing:
        Length: 30'
        Draft: 3'
        Tonnage: 6
Maintenance:
    Number of boats maintained per year: 2-3
    Percentage of wooden boats: 50
    Owner maintenance allowed.
Retail supplies:
    Marine and commercial fishing supplies.

MAINE

JOHN'S BAY BOAT CO.—Peter H. Kass
P.O. Box 58
South Bristol, ME 04568
207-644-8261

Builder Information
Years in business: 8
Carpenters employed: 2
Shop capacity: Boats to 45'

Recent New Construction
15' peapod. Kass design. Built 1984.
16' skiff. Kass design. 2 built in 1980 and 1983.
18' lobster-style skiff. Kass design. 3 built in 1982-'83.
24' lobsterboat cruiser. Kass design. Built 1983-'84.
22' deep-V lapstrake speedboat. Fred Lyman design. Built 1984.
23' diesel launch. Arno Day design. Built 1985.
13' Whitehall. Mystic Seaport Museum plans. Built 1982.
12' peapod. Kass design. 3 built 1980.

Recent Repair Projects
33' lobsterboat. Replaced a good deal of starboard side. 1981
24' lobster-style yacht. Replaced wheelhouse, Installed new engine. 1980.
22' sloop. Retimbered and replaced deck. 1983.
26' sloop. Refastened and replaced deck. 1983.
34' lobster-style yacht. Replaced deck, house, and transom. 1984-'85.
42' dragger. Replaced shaftlog, fuel tanks, and decks. 1983.
45' sardine carrier. Replaced garboards. 1982.

Yard Information
Services:
    Launching facilities
    Moorage
    Diesel and gas engine repair
    Rigging
Storage:
    Number of boats stored per year: 15
    Percentage of wooden boats: 75
    Inside storage facilities
    Maximum size for hauling and storing:
        Length: 45'
        Draft: 7'
        Tonnage: 15
Maintenance:
    Number of boats maintained per year: 15
    Percentage of wooden boats: 75
    Owner maintenance allowed above and below rail.
Retail supplies:
    Stock all supplies used regularly. Wood, fiberglass, fastenings, paint, compounds, sandpaper.

MAINE

J. ERVIN JONES, BOATBUILDER—J. Ervin Jones
Murray Hill Rd., P.O. Box 37
East Boothbay, ME 04544
207-633-2824

Builder Information
Years in business: 25
Carpenters employed: 1
Shop capacity: Boats to 45'
Willing to travel locally for on-the-site building projects.

Recent New Construction
26' gaff-rigged sloop. George Stadel design. Built 1982.
34' lobsterboat. J.E. Jones design. Built 1983.
36' lobsterboat. J.E. Jones design. Built 1984.
14' strip canoe. Gilbert design. Built 1983.
16' strip canoe. Gilbert design. Built 1985.

Recent Repair Projects
22' lobsterboat. Refinished. 1984.
24' lobsterboat launch. Installed sister frames, refastened, and refinished. 1984.
26' lobsterboat. Installed sister frames, refastened, and refinished. 1985.
    All for the Maine Maritime Museum.

Yard Information
Maintenance:
    Number of boats maintained per year: 40
    Percentage of wooden boats: 60
    Owner maintenance allowed above and below rail.
Retail supplies:
    Lumber, fastenings, paint, some hardware and marine supplies.

CLIFF KEALIHER
Box 24
Greenville, ME 04441
207-695-2484 or 695-2855

Builder Information
Years in business: 15
Carpenters employed: 1
Shop capacity: Boats to 20'

Recent New Construction
16' wood-and-canvas guideboats. Lines taken from 1914 Whitney design.
    4 built to date.
18' wood-and-canvas canoes. Lines taken from Whitney design.
    6 built to date.

Recent Repair Projects
Wood-and-canvas canoes and boats. Morris, Old Town, and E.M. White
    designs. Repairwork has included stem, rib, plank, gunwale, and
    thwart renewal, hull recanvasing and refinishing. Currently restoring
    a Grand Laker square-sterned canoe and a 20' E.M. White guide canoe.

Yard Information
Retail supplies:
    Materials by order only. Cedar planking, fastenings, canvas, and
    canvas filler. Paint and varnish.

MAINE

KONITZKY BOAT WORKS—Gustav A. Konitzky
Rte. 2, Box 85
New Harbor, ME 04554
207-677-3726

Builder Information
Years in business: 12
Carpenters employed: 3
Shop capacity: Boats to 50'

Recent New Construction
32' lobsterboat. Alvin Beal design. Built 1980.
10'6" canoe. Built 1985.
9' lapstrake dinghy. Herreshoff design. Built 1979.

Recent Repair Projects
32' Hinckley sloop (1932). Complete restoration. Keel, hull, deck, frames. 1981-'82.
42' Cheoy Lee yawl (1964). Replaced deck and systems. 1984-'85.
22' Goudy and Stevens launch (1921). Installed new engine. Refastened hull. 1984-'85.
32' Quoddy pilot sloop (1975). Complete overhaul. New mast and rigging. 1985.
32' Arno Day lobsterboat (1972). Replaced stem, forefoot, and some planking. 1979.

Yard Information
Services:
    Launching facilities
    Overland transport
    Moorage
    Diesel and gas engine repair
Storage:
    Number of boats stored per year: 25
    Percentage of wooden boats: 50
    Maximum size for hauling and storing:
        Length: 50'
        Draft: 8'
        Tonnage: 19
Maintenance:
    Number of boats maintained per year: 35
    Percentage of wooden boats: 50
    Owner maintenance allowed above rail.
Retail supplies:
    Milled lumber, marine hardware, paint, sealant.

THE LANDING SCHOOL OF BOATBUILDING AND DESIGN
John T. Burgess, Director
P.O. Box 1490
Kennebunkport, ME 04046
207-985-7976

Builder Information
Years in business: 7
Carpenters employed: 3 instructors, various students
Shop capacity: Boats to 35'

MAINE

Recent New Construction
18'8" Concordia Buzzards Bay sloop. R.D. Culler design. 2 built 1985.
18' catboat. Ron Carter design. 2 built 1985.
17' Swampscott dory for oar and sail. Lapstrake construction. Dion design.
    4 built 1984-'85.
35' cutter. Carvel, chine, and strip construction. Reg Butler design.
    Current project.
13' dory skiff for oar and sail. Lapstrake construction. Chamberlain design.
    Built 1985.
26' Alerion-class sloop. N.G. Herreshoff design. Current project.

LEAVITT QUALITY CANOE—James A. Leavitt
RFD #1, Box 1549
Hampden, ME 04444
207-234-2341

Builder Information
Years in business: 5
Carpenters employed: 1
Shop capacity: Boats to 20'4"

Recent New Construction
Canoes of plank-on-frame construction with canvas or fiberglass sheathing:
    20'4" canoe. Leavitt design. 2 built 1985.
    18'6" canoe. Leavitt design. 11 built 1985.
    16' canoe. Leavitt design. 9 built 1985.
    11'6" canoe. Spaldin design. 13 built 1985.

Recent Repair Projects
Wood-and-canvas or wood-and-fiberglass canoes. Minor repairs to complete restorations.
    Work has included replacing ribs, planking, and hull canvas.

Yard Information
Services:
    Rigging repair
Retail supplies:
    Cedar, ash, and other boatbuilding woods. Brass screws, bolts, and tacks,
    resin, and fiberglass cloth.

D.M. LEIGHT & CO.—Dennis M. Leight
Glenmere Rd.
Tenants Harbor, ME 04860
207-372-6668

Builder Information
Years in business: 30 self-employed, 5 as D.M. Leight & Co.
Carpenters employed: 1-2
Shop capacity: Boats to 32'
Willing to travel occasionally for on-the-site building projects.
(continues)

MAINE

(D.M. Leight & Co., continued)

Recent New Construction
16' lapstrake Swampscott dory. John Gardner design. Built 1985.
17' lapstrake Swampscott dory. D.M. Leight design. 20 built since 1982.
26' lapstrake lobsterboat. Verity & Leight design. Built 1984.
19' plywood Bartender. George Calkins design. Built 1983.
12' lapstrake work skiff. D.M. Leight design. Built 1983.
8' plywood prams. D.M. Leight design. 2 built 1985.

Recent Repair Projects
19' lobsterboat. Replaced decks and transom, reframed hull. 1985.
16' lobster skiff. Renewed transom and refastened hull. 1985.
22' Star-class sloop. Replaced rudder, refastened and recaulked hull. 1984.

Yard Information
Services:
    Overland transport under 20'
    Moorage
    Rigging
    Gas engine repair
Storage:
    Number of boats stored per year: 8
    Percentage of wooden boats: 100
    Maximum size for hauling and storing:
        Tonnage: 15
Maintenance:
    Number of boats maintained per year: 6
    Percentage of wooden boats: 50
Retail supplies:
    No inventory, but will order on request.

DAVID LENOWITZ
P.O. Box 272
Rockport, ME 04856
207-236-9042

Builder Information
Years in business: 1
Carpenters employed: 1

Recent New Construction
12' Catspaw dinghy. N.G. Herreshoff and J. White design. Built 1985.
16' lapstrake Duck Trap wherry. Walt Simmons design. Built 1985.

Recent Repair Projects
34' Hinckley Sou'wester. Replaced 6 keelbolts, installed new pumps.
    Recaulked and refinished hull bottom. 1985.

LONGFIELD DORY CO.
*Main St.
East Blue Hill, ME 04629
207-374-5656*

Builder Information
Years in business: 15
Carpenters employed: 3
Shop capacity: Boats to 100'
May be willing to travel for on-the-site building projects.

Recent New Construction
14' working punts. Plywood construction. Design sponsored by
   Preston Mt. Fish Club. 10 built 1982-'84.
20' dory. In-house design. Built 1984.
14' skiff. In-house design. Built 1985.

Recent Repair Projects
16' Herreshoff $12\frac{1}{2}$ sloop. Completely refastened hull. 1980-'81.
33' Novi cutter. Renewed deadwood and garboard plank. 1985.
26' schooner. Rebuilding hull, renewing engine and rigging. Current project.

Yard Information
Storage:
   Number of boats stored per year: 10
   Percentage of wooden boats: 50
   Inside storage facilities
   Maximum size for hauling and storing:
      Length: 30'
      Draft: 5'
      Tonnage: 3
Maintenance:
   Number of boats maintained per year: 25
   Percentage of wooden boats: 50
Retail supplies:
   Marine hardware, engines, rigging supplies.

MACHIASPORT MARINE RAILWAY CO.—Walter and Karl Kurz
*Rte. 92, P.O. Box 352
Machiasport, ME 04655
207-255-4036 or 207-255-3688*

Builder Information
Years in business: 10
Carpenters employed: 1, part-time
Shop capacity: Boats to 40'

Recent New Construction
12' sneakbox. Perrine design. Built 1983.
18' inboard launch. Built 1984.
12' tender. Lawley design. Built 1982.

Recent Repair Projects
24' Nielsen sloop (1940). Renewed deck, refinished boat. 1985.
45' Dawn power cruiser (1928). Rebuilt backbone, refinished boat. 1981.
(continues)

MAINE

(Machiasport Marine Railway Co., continued)
Yard Information
Services:
    Launching facilities
    Moorage for 1 boat
    Engine repair
    Sail repair
    Rigging repair
Maintenance:
    Number of boats maintained per year: 4
    Percentage of wooden boats: 100
    Owner maintenance allowed above and below rail.
    Maximum size for hauling:
      Length: 40'
      Draft: 6'
      Tonnage: 30
Retail supplies:
    Cedar and oak. Will order other supplies on request.

PETER MacMURRAY
P.O. Box 293
Bath, ME 04530
207-389-2266

Builder Information
Years in business: 10
Carpenters employed: 1
Shop capacity: Boats to 20'
Willing to travel locally for on-the-site building projects.

Recent New Construction
13'6" Melonseed class. 1983.
8' lapstrake Nereia dinghy. L.F. Herreshoff design. 1982-'83.
17' lapstrake double-ended rowing boat. Herreshoff and Gardner design. Current project.

Recent Repair Projects
9'8" Turnabout class (hull #4). New bottom, centerboard and trunk, rub rails. Refinishing. Current project.

MALONE BOATBUILDING CO.—Bruce Malone
Barnstown Rd.
Camden, ME 04843
207-236-8795

Builder Information
Years in business: 7
Carpenters employed: 2
Shop capacity: New construction to 36'

Recent New Construction
18' lapstrake daysailer. John Leather design. Built 1985.
17' lapstrake Rangeley Lake boat. 2 built in 1985.

MAINE

Recent Repair Projects
36' sailboat. Refastened, recovered deck, repaired cockpit. 1985.
43' motorsailer. Refastened and refinished hull. 1985.
28' sailboat. Refinished hull, renewed interior joinery and plumbing. 1985.
45' sailboat. Renewed interior joinery. 1985.

L.A. McCARTHY BOATSHOP—Lucy McCarthy
P.O. Box 409
Belfast, ME 04915
207-338-1786 (evenings)

Builder Information
Years in business: 7
Carpenters employed: 1, part-time
Shop capacity: Boats to 20'
Willing to travel for on-the-site building projects.

Recent New Construction
20' utility launch. Arno Day design. Current project.
10'6" lapstrake dory tender. Chaisson design. 9 built 1980-'84.

Recent Repair Projects
42' sloop. Repaired deck rot, replaced bulwarks. Renewed canvas on decks and cabintop. 1982-'83.
17' Dark Harbor-class sloop. Replaced some deckbeams and repaired transom rot. Renewed canvas on decks and cabintop. 1983.

Yard Information
Storage:
    Number of boats stored per year: 3
    Percentage of wooden boats: 100
    Inside storage facilities
    Maximum size for hauling and storing:
        Length: 15'
        Draft: shallow draft
Maintenance:
    Number of boats maintained per year: 2
    Percentage of wooden boats: 100
    Owner maintenance allowed.
Retail supplies:
    Will order on request.

MIDCOAST MARINE SERVICE, INC.—Robert T. Sylvia
Box 103, Round Pond Rd.
Bristol, ME 04539
207-563-3030

Builder Information
Years in business: 7
Carpenters employed: 3
Shop capacity: Boats to 50'
(continues)

MAINE

(Midcoast Marine Service, Inc.,continued)
Recent Repair Projects
25' Friendship sloop. Completely rebuilt cockpit. 1985.
40' Concordia yawl. Recanvased deck. 1985.
40' Concordia yawl. Renewed maststep and 3 floortimbers. Scarfed in new forefoot section. 1985.
40' Concordia yawl. Renewed keelbolts and electrical panel. Recanvased deck, replaced sheer planks and covering boards. Refinished brightwork and spars. 1984.
31' Concordia sloop. Recanvased deck. 1983.
40' Concordia yawl. Recanvased deck, renewed rudder. 1982.

Yard Information
Services:
    Overland transport
    Diesel and gas engine repair
Storage:
    Number of boats stored per year: 28
    Percentage of wooden boats: 50
    Inside storage facilities for 5 boats
    Maximum size for hauling and storing:
        Length: 46-50'
        Draft: 6-7'
        Tonnage: 18-20
Maintenance:
    Number of boats maintained per year: 28
    Percentage of wooden boats: 50
    Owner maintenance allowed.
Retail supplies:
    Limited inventory. Paint, fastenings, oil, antifreeze, general boat supplies.

MILE CREEK BOAT SHOP—John D. Little
RFD Box 257
Washington, ME 04574
207-845-2708

Builder Information
Years in business: 45
Carpenters employed: 1
Shop capacity: Boats to 45'

Recent New Construction
Boats designed by John Little for lapstrake construction:
    16' catboat. 6 built 1984-'85.
    11' Black Hall River skiff. 4 built 1985.
    8' dinghy. Built 1983.
Other new construction:
    21' catboat. Fenwick Williams design. Built 1981.
    17' Swampscott dory. Lapstrake construction. Bob Pittaway design. Built 1983.

Recent Repair Projects
43' Egg Harbor powerboat. Replaced skeg, bottom planking, and aft end of keel. Renewed structural timbers, shaftlogs, struts, rudder, and though-hull fittings. Recaulked hull. 1984.
25' Crosby Wianno Senior-class sloop. Removed and rehung ballast casting. Renewed deadwood, ballast bolts, and garboard plank. Recaulked hull. 1984-'85.
25' Wm. Morse Friendship sloop. Recaulked hull. 1985.

MAINE

MILL COVE SMALL BOAT WORKS—Roy Jenkins and Jerry St. Clair
153 Commercial St.
Boothbay Harbor, ME 04538
207-633-2787

Builder Information
Years in business: 2
Carpenters employed: 2
Shop capacity: Boats to 16'

Recent New Construction
13'6" sprit-rigged Good Little Skiff. Lapstrake construction. R.D. Culler design. Built 1985.
9'3" lapstrake tender. Lawley design. Built 1984-'85.

NEW HARBOR YACHTS, INC.—David Stimson and Evan Kruger
HC 62, Box 112, Snowball Hill Rd.
New Harbor, ME 04554
207-677-2062

Builder Information
Years in business: 15
Carpenters employed: 1-3
Shop capacity: Boats to 100'
Willing to travel for on-the-site building projects.

Recent New Construction
14' catboat. David Stimson design. Built 1981.
22' lapstrake sharpie. David Stimson design. Built 1985.
13' Good Little Skiff. R.D. Culler design. 2 built 1977 and 1981.
16' lapstrake skiff. R.D. Culler design. Built 1981.
14' lapstrake surf dory. John Gardner design. Built 1981.
13' North Haven dinghy. Built 1984.
16' power skiff. Lapstrake construction. David Stimson design. 2 built 1977 and 1981.
16' lapstrake double-paddle canoe. L.F. Herreshoff design. Built 1977.
13' Banks dory. Lapstrake construction. Built 1981.

Recent Repair Projects
44' schooner SURPRISE. Replaced sternpost, stem, and horn timbers. Renewed transom and transom framing. Replaced 18 planks, some frames, and refastened bottom. 1979.
45' New York 30-class sloop LINNET. Replaced 70 frames, floor timbers, transom, and transom framing. Renewed deck and 20' of keel. 1982.
46' Herreshoff schooner SENECA. Replaced floors, frames, deckbeams, and deck. Renewed transom, cabin houses, and 6 planks. 1985.
72' BARLOVENTO. Renewed interior joinerwork. 1985.
40' KITTIWAKE. Replaced cabin sides and beams, recaulked deck. 1985.

Yard Information
Retail supplies:
   Lumber, paint, and fastenings.

MAINE

NORTH END SHIPYARD—Doug Lee, Linda Lee, and John Foss
Front St., P.O. Box 482
Rockland, ME 04841
207-594-8007

Builder Information
Years in business: 12
Carpenters employed: 6
Shop capacity: Boats to 100′

Recent New Construction
94′ Maine coastal windjammer HERITAGE. Doug and Linda Lee design. Built 1983.
16′ yawlboat for HERITAGE. Doug Lee design. Built 1983.
14′ yawlboat. John Foss design. Built 1977.
14′ yawlboat. Doug Lee design. Built 1978.
18′ pulling boat. Doug Lee design. Built 1983.
16′ seine boat. John Foss design. Built 1985.
12′ lapstrake pulling boat. John Foss design. 2 built 1984.
12′ lapstrake pulling boat. Ed Glaser design. Built 1984.

Recent Repair Projects
98′ Gloucester fishing schooner AMERICAN EAGLE. Completely rebuilt from waterline up. Refastened below waterline, enlarged rig and extended stern. 1985-'86.
64′ coasting schooner LEWIS R. FRENCH. Completely rebuilt from waterline up. Refastened hull below waterline. 1973-'76.

Yard Information
Services:
    Moorage
Storage:
    Number of boats stored per year: 12
    Percentage of wooden boats: 100
    Inside storage facilities
    Maximum size for hauling:
        Draft: 10′
        Tonnage: 100
Maintenance:
    Number of boats maintained per year: 13
    Percentage of wooden boats: 100
    Owner maintenance allowed above and below rail.

NORTHWOODS CANOE SHOP—Rollin Thurlow
RFD #3, Box 118-2A
Dover-Foxcroft, ME 04426
207-564-3667

Builder Information
Years in business: 10
Carpenters employed: 1
Shop capacity: Boats to 20′
Willing to travel for on-the-site building projects.

Recent New Construction
17½′ wood-and-canvas canoe. Rollin Thurlow design. Built 1985.

Recent Repair Projects
16′ Gerrish wood-and-canvas canoe. Completely restored. Installed 18 frames, new stems, rails, and deck. Recanvased and refinished. 1985.

MAINE

Yard Information
Retail supplies:
  Any material necessary for wood-and-canvas construction. Wood, frames, canvas, tacks, brass stem bands, paint, etc.

DAVID NUTT BOATBUILDER—David Nutt
Box 321, Ebenecook Rd.
West Southport, ME 04576
207-633-6009

Builder Information
Years in business: 14
Carpenters employed: 3
Shop capacity: Boats to 55'
Willing to travel locally for on-the-site building projects.

Recent New Construction
38'6" offshore cutter. Bjarne Aäs design.

Recent Repair Projects
45' Herreshoff New York 30 sloop LINNET. Reframing, replacing half of keel, refastening floors. Replacing deck and planking as necessary. Installing new cabinhouse to original design. Current project.
33' Friendship sloop DEPRESSION (1899). Totally reconstructed. Renewed everything but the stem, redesigned house to more traditional lines. Launched 1985.
42' Dickerson ketch. Repaired bottom damage caused by galvanic degradation. Replaced areas around through-hull fittings, sheathed hull below the waterline in fiberglass and epoxy. 1985.
38'9" Rhodes Bounty sloop. Refastened ballast keel.
40' Concordia yawl. Major rebuild. Renewed planking, relaminated mast. 1984-'85.

OAT CANOE CO.—Jeff Hanna
RFD #1, Box 4100
Mt. Vernon, ME 04352
207-293-2694

Builder Information
Years in business: 7
Carpenters employed: 1
Shop capacity: Boats to 25'

Recent New Construction
15' Maine lumberman's bateau. Lapstrake construction. Jeff Hanna design from traditional lines. Built 1984.
18' wood-and-canvas canoes. James and Jeff Hanna design. 8 built 1978-'85.

Recent Repair Projects
Canoes, fishing skiffs, Rangeley Lake boats. Minor repairs to complete restoration. 69 boats repaired to date.

Yard Information
Services:
  Overland transport
(continues)

MAINE

(Oat Canoe Co., continued)
Storage:
    Number of boats stored per year: 10
    Percentage of wooden boats: 100
    Inside storage facilities
    Maximum size for hauling and storing:
        Boats 150-200 lbs
Maintenance:
    Number of boats maintained per year: 6
    Percentage of wooden boats: 100
    Owner maintenance allowed above and below rail.
Retail supplies:
    By order.

OLD TOWN CANOE—Steve Krautkremer
58 Middle St.
Old Town, ME 04468
207-827-5513

Builder Information
Years in business: 80+
Carpenters employed: 3
Shop capacity: Boats to 34'

Recent New Construction
15-20' canoes. 75 built to date.

Recent Repair Projects
Canoes to any length. Any type repair.

MARK OSBORNE
RFD 4, Box 538
Old Limerick Rd.
Arundel, ME 04005
207-282-2879

Builder Information
Years in business: 5
Carpenters employed: 1
Shop capacity: Boats to 30'
Willing to travel within 25 miles for on-the-site building projects.

Recent New Construction
17' sailing Whitehall. John Gardner design. Built 1981.
21' powerboat Long John. Lapstrake sides and splined bottom. R.D. Culler
    design for *National Fisherman*. Built 1985.
17' rowing bateau. Lapstrake sides, splined bottom. R.D. Culler design. Built 1984.

MAINE

Recent Repair Projects
18'1" Alden Biddeford Pool-class sloop. Total restoration. Current project.
40' Colin Archer rescue boat. Replaced sawn frames and floor timbers. New keel, sternpost, and planking. 1985.
13'6" Old Town Whitecap sloop (1950s). Repairing frames, deck, deckbeams, seats, and spars. Current project.
25' Laurent Giles Vertue-class sloop. Repaired frames, bottom planking, deckbeams. Recanvased and refinished. 1983.
40' Pacemaker powerboat. Completely refinished exterior. 1984.

OSMOND'S BOAT SHOP—Osmond M. Beal
Box 177
Beals, ME 04611
207-497-5993

Builder Information
Years in business: 16
Carpenters employed: 1
Shop capacity: Boats to 41'

Recent New Construction
36' power charter boat. Osmond Beal design. 2 built 1984 to present.

HAROLD H. PAYSON
Pleasant Beach Rd.
South Thomaston, ME 04858
207-594-7587

Builder Information
Years in business: 30
Carpenters employed: 1
Shop capacity: Boats to 31'

Recent New Construction
12'3" plywood catboat. Phil Bolger design. Built 1985.
15' plywood utility-type cruiser. Phil Bolger design. Built 1982.
15' plywood kayak. Phil Bolger design. Built 1985.

PEMBROKE BOAT COMPANY—George Gagnon
Union Square
Pembroke, ME 04666
207-726-3920

Builder Information
Years in business: 7
Carpenters employed: 2
Shop capacity: Boats 40-45'
Willing to travel for on-the-site building projects.
(continues)

MAINE

(Pembroke Boat Company, continued)
Recent New Construction
19' lapstrake work skiff. Brett Blanchard design. Built 1985.
10' lapstrake skiff. George Gagnon design. 6 built 1983-'85.
12'6" dory. George Gagnon design. Built 1983.
14'6" dinghy. George Gagnon design. Built 1980.
25' lapstrake seine dory. George Gagnon design. 4 built 1978-'80.

Recent Repair Projects
20' Cape Cod knockabout (1940s). Replaced stem, keel, centerboard trunk, garboards, sheerstrakes, and decks, 1980. Designed and built new cabin. 1985.
31' Casey cutter (1936). Major restoration. Refastened hull, renewed deckbeams, sheer clamp, sheerstrakes, covering boards, rubrails. 1984.
70' seiner CHESTER T. MARSHALL. Refastened bottom and replaced two-thirds of the topside planking and framing. Renewed part of stem and one garboard plank. 1982 and 1984.
67' sardine carrier BETSY & SALLY. Replaced bulwarks, sheerstrake, and rails. Sistered deckbeams. Repaired and extended pilothouse. Fiberglassed fish holds. 1981 to present.

Yard Information
Services:
    Launching facilities
    Overland transport
Storage:
    Number of boats stored per year: Provided for boats under repair only
    Percentage of wooden boats: 100
    Inside storage facilities
    Maximum size for hauling and storing:
        Length: 36'
        Draft: 5'
        Tonnage: 8
Maintenance:
    Number of boats maintained per year: Under 10
    Percentage of wooden boats: 100
    Owner maintenance allowed above and below rail.
Retail supplies:
    Wood. Will order other materials on request.

PETTEGROW BOAT YARD—Richard S. and Nettie J. Pettegrow
Starboard Cove 444
Bucks Harbor, ME 04618
207-255-8740

Builder Information
Years in business: 14
Carpenters employed: 2-5
Shop capacity: Boats 50-60'
Willing to travel occasionally for on-the-site building projects.

Recent New Construction
36' Jonesport lobsterboat.

Recent Repair Projects
42' dragger. Total restoration.

MAINE

Yard Information
Services:
    Launching facilities
    Overland transport
    Moorage
    Diesel and gas engine repair
    Rigging
Storage:
    Number of boats stored per year: 60-70
    Percentage of wooden boats: 75
    Maximum size for hauling and storing:
        Length: 60'
        Tonnage: 100
Maintenance:
    Number of boats maintained per year: 45-60
    Percentage of wooden boats: 75
    Owner maintenance allowed above and below rail outside.
Retail supplies:
    Complete lines of boating supplies and fishing gear.

ROBERT PIERI, INC.—Robert Pieri
U.S. Rte. 1, P.O. Box 50
Lincolnville, ME 04849
207-236-9758

Builder Information
Years in business: 12
Carpenters employed: 6
Shop capacity: Boats to 70'
Recent New Construction
24' plywood rowing shell. Peter Sexton design. 4 built 1985.

Recent Repair Projects
34' Geerd Hendel power cruiser. Rebuilt pilothouse and flying bridge. 1982.
28' Herreshoff Rozinante ketch. Sistered frames, rebuilt cockpit, installed new engine. 1982.
26' lobsterboat. Renewed frames and garboards, refastened. 1983.
32' lobsterboat. Replaced frames, repaired engine. 1983.
24' pleasure-type lobsterboat. Replaced console, installed new outboard and electronics. 1985.
20' Century runabout (1946). Repaired engine, replaced plank, and refinished hull. 1985.
30' pleasure-type lobsterboat. Renewed seats, garboards, and spray rails. 1984-'85.

Yard Information
Services:
    Diesel and gas engine repair
Storage:
    Number of boats stored per year: 8
    Percentage of wooden boats: 25
    Maximum size for hauling and storing:
        Length: 70'
        Draft: 7'
        Tonnage: 35
(continues)

MAINE

(Robert Pieri, Inc., continued)
Maintenance:
    Number of boats maintained per year: 8
    Percentage of wooden boats: 25
Retail supplies:
    All supplies used for construction and repair.

R.S. PULSIFER CO.—Richard S. Pulsifer
RFD #3, Mere Point Rd.
Brunswick, ME 04011
207-725-5457 or 725-2243

Builder Information
Years in business: 10
Carpenters employed: 1
Shop capacity: Boats to 22′

Recent New Construction
22′ Casco Bay Hampton cruising/utility boat. Strip-planked. 22 built to date.

Yard Information
Services:
    Overland transport
Maintenance:
    Number of boats maintained per year: 3
    Percentage of wooden boats: 100
    Owner maintenance allowed above and below rail.

RENAISSANCE YACHT CO.—Douglas Beebe
31 Water St.
Thomaston, ME 04861
207-354-8141

Builder Information
Years in business: 6
Carpenters employed: 7-10
Shop capacity: Boats to 150′
Willing to travel for on-the-site building projects.

Recent New Construction
Boats designed by Bruce King for cold-molded construction:
    90′ sloop WHITEFIN. Built 1979-'83.
    50′ sloop. Built 1984-'85.
    95′ ketch. Current project.

JAMES H. RICH BOAT YARD—James H. Rich
West Tremont, ME 04690
207-244-3208

Builder Information
Years in business: 29
Carpenters employed: 2 +
Shop capacity: Boats to 50′

Repair Projects
15–50′ pleasure boats and fishing boats. Works on several boats each year.

Yard Information
Services:
    Launching facilities
    Diesel and gas engine repair
Storage:
    Number of boats stored per year: 50
    Percentage of wooden boats: 50
    Maximum size for hauling and storing:
        Length: 50′
        Draft: 6′
        Tonnage: 20
Maintenance:
    Number of boats maintained per year: 50
    Percentage of wooden boats: 50
Retail supplies:
    Lumber, fastenings, paint, hardware, marine supplies.

RIVERSIDE BOAT COMPANY—Paul Bryant
Liberty St.
Newcastle, ME 04553
207-563-3398

Builder Information
Years in business: 40
Carpenters employed: 3
Shop capacity: Boats to 40′

Recent New Construction
30′ double-planked cruising sloop. Paul Bryant design. Current project.
24′ lobster-type pleasure boat. Creston Bryant design. 17 built to date.
8′ plywood, flat-bottomed prams. Paul Bryant design. 80 built to date.

Recent Repair Projects
30′ Lash-built Friendship sloop. Replaced cabin in 1981.
30′ Alden schooner. Replaced pine decks with laid teak. 1981.
28′ Murray Peterson schooner. Replaced fir decks with new teak decks. 1982.
34′ cutter. Replaced deck and deckbeams. 1983.
22′ Fred Bates powerboat Pogo. Repowered boat and replaced cabin. 1984.
39′ Cox & Stevens sloop. Replaced deck, cockpit, and bulwarks. 1984.
32′ Marblehead-class sloop. Installed sister frames and new cabin. 1985.
25′ Herreshoff Seafarer sloop. Replaced frames, floors, and some bottom planking. 1985.

Yard Information
Services:
    Launching facilities (railway)
    Moorage
(continues)

MAINE

(Riverside Boat Company, continued)
Storage:
    Number of boats stored per year: 90
    Percentage of wooden boats: 60
    Inside storage facilities
    Maximum size for hauling and storing:
        Length: 40′
        Draft: 5½′
        Tonnage: 12
Maintenance:
    Number of boats maintained per year: 75
    Percentage of wooden boats: 60
    Owner maintenance allowed above and below rail.

RKL BOATWORKS—Bob Lincoln
Pretty Marsh
Mt. Desert, ME 04660
207-244-5997

Builder Information
Years in business: 9
Carpenters employed: 2
Shop capacity: Boats to 35′

Recent New Construction
Boats of strip-plank construction:
    11′ sailing tender. Lawley design. 16 built to date.
    14′ Little Rangeley guideboat. Barrett and RKL design. 30 built to date.
    17′ Rangeley Lake guideboat. Ellis design. 35 built to date.

Recent Repair Projects
12′ Adirondack guideboat. Stripped hull, sealed with epoxy, and
    refinished. Replaced seats and trim. 1985.
16′ Somes pulling boat. Sistered frames, replaced seats. Stripped hull,
    sealed with epoxy, and refinished. 1984.
8′ pram tender. Refinished hull and trim. 1985.

Yard Information
Services:
    Overland transport
    Maintenance
Storage:
    Number of boats stored per year: 10
    Percentage of wooden boats: 60
    Inside storage facilities for 10 boats.
    Maximum size for hauling and storing:
        Length: 25′

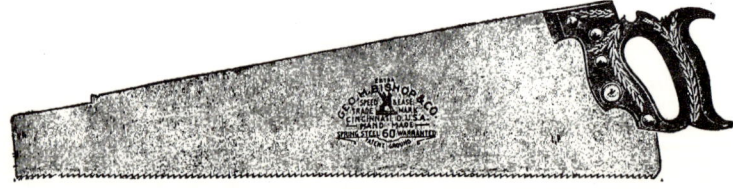

MAINE

THE ROCKPORT APPRENTICESHOP—Lance Lee, Director
Box 539, Sea St.
Rockport, ME 04856
207-236-6071

Builder Information
Years in business: 3
Carpenters employed: 14 apprentices, 2 instructors
Shop capacity: Boats to 36'

Recent New Construction
26' Prospect Marsh pinky schooner. Built 1984.
20' gaff-rigged sloop. Robert Baker design. Built 1985.
16' lapstrake Swampscott dory.
15' lapstrake Washington County peapod.
15' lapstrake Delaware Ducker.
15' lapstrake Swedish rundgatting.
16' Cape Split peapod.
18' Whitehall.
10' lapstrake Norwegian pram.
12' lapstrake dory skiff. Chaisson design.

Recent Repair Projects
26' Norwegian lapstrake launch. Replaced frames and planking. Rebuilt bulkheads, cockpit, engine box, and aft deck.

ROCKPORT MARINE INC.—Taylor Allen
Box 203
Rockport, ME 04856
207-236-9651

Builder Information
Years in business: 23
Carpenters employed: 4
Shop capacity: Boats 60'+

Recent New Construction
43' strip-planked power cruiser. Eldredge-McInnis design. Built 1979.
18' yard workboat. Strip-plank construction. In-house design. Built 1983.
14' peapod. Traditional design. 1 built in 1983, 1 in progress.

Recent Repair Projects
16' Herreshoff 12½-class sloop. Completely restored 3 boats. 1983–'86.
40' Concordia yawl. Renewed deck and cabintop with Dynel overlay. 1984.
36' Ohlson sloop. Overhauled hull structure and refinished boat. 1983–'85.
38' 6-meter sloop. Replaced keel. Renewed framing, deck, and cockpit. 1985.
73' Abeking & Rasmussen ketch. Remodeled stateroom. 1983.
34' power cruiser. Replaced shaftlog. Renewed framing and planking. 1985.
42' Hendel sloop. Replaced sheerstrakes, covering board, and bulwarks. 1984.
40' Concordia yawl. Renewed keelbolts. 1983.
(continues)

MAINE

(Rockport Marine, Inc., continued)
Yard Information
Services:
    Marina facilities
    Launching facilities
    Moorage
    Diesel and gas engine repair
    Sailmaking
    Rigging
Storage:
    Number of boats stored per year: 30
    Percentage of wooden boats: 90
    Inside storage facilities
    Maximum size for hauling and storing:
        Length: 60'
        Tonnage: 40
Maintenance:
    Number of boats maintained per year: 40
    Percentage of wooden boats: 85
    Owner maintenance allowed.
Retail supplies:
    Materials for wooden boat construction and repair.

ROGERS MARINE, INC.—Paul Rogers
5 Park Dr., P.O. Box 684
Rockland, ME 04841
207-594-2215

Builder Information
Years in business: 15
Shop capacity: Boats to 70'

New Construction
26' cold-molded cat-yawl. Phil Bolger design. Built 1975.
37' cold-molded cutter. Henry Scheel design. Built 1974.

RUMERY'S BOAT YARD INC.—Gregory C. Carroll
109 Cleaves St., P.O. Box L
Biddeford, ME 04005
207-282-0408

Builder Information
Years in business: 20
Carpenters employed: 4
Shop capacity: Boats to 50'
Willing to travel for on-the-site repair projects.

Recent Repair Projects
18' Biddeford Pool 18 one-design sloop. Alden design. Complete restoration.
    Replaced frames, decks, deadwood, transom, floorboards, and coaming. 1984–'85.
34' Royal Lowell lobsterboat. Renewed rails, epoxy decks, trunk sides. 1985.
28' Arundel 28 cruiser. Sistered frames and installed new engine. Renewed some
    planking, cabintop, and trunk sides. 1983–'84.
27' Chris-Craft triple-cockpit runabout. Stripped and refinished boat.
    Installed new engine. 1983.

MAINE

Yard Information
Services:
    Marina facilities
    Launching facilities
    Diesel and gas engine repair
Storage:
    Number of boats stored per year: 65
    Percentage of wooden boats: 25
    Inside storage facilities
    Maximum size for hauling and storing:
        Tonnage: 17
Maintenance:
    Number of boats maintained per year: 150
    Percentage of wooden boats: 30
    Owner maintenance allowed above and below rail outside, above rail inside.
Retail supplies:
    PFDs, engine supplies, cordage, hardware, paint, and fasteners. Wood, trailer parts, maintenance supplies, accessories.

SEAL COVE BOATYARD INC.—Robert Vaughan
Box 99
Harborside, ME 04642
207-326-4422

Builder Information
Years in business: 35
Carpenters employed: 3
Shop capacity: Boats to 50'

Recent New Construction
25' strip-planked power launch. Built 1983.

Recent Repair Projects
48'10" Herreshoff yawl (1903). Completely restored boat. Renewed spars, rigging, and hardware. 1982 and 1984.
45' 8-meter-class sloop. Renewed teak deck and trunk house. 1984.
32' Winslow ketch. Replaced frames, planking, and stern. Resheathed deck.
26' Dark Harbor 17$^{1}/_{2}$-class sloop. Completely restored boat. 1984.
13' peapod (ca. 1889). Completely restored boat. 1983.
42' Alden raised-deck yawl. Replacing 6 planks. Renewing stem, transom, and decks. Overhauling engine. Current project.

Yard Information
Services:
    Launching facilities
    Diesel and gas engine repair
    Rigging
Storage:
    Number of boats stored per year: 130
    Percentage of wooden boats: 35
    Inside storage facilities
    Maximum size for hauling and storing:
        Length: 50'
        Draft: 8'
        Tonnage: 25
(continues)

MAINE

(Seal Cove Boatyard, Inc., continued)
Maintenance:
    Number of boats maintained per year: 110
    Percentage of wooden boats: 35
    Owner maintenance allowed above and below rail.
Retail supplies:
    Lumber. Complete inventory of supplies.

SHEW & BURNHAM
Box 131
South Bristol, ME 04568
207-644-8120

Builder Information
Years in business: 21
Carpenters employed: 2
Shop capacity: Boats to 35'

Recent New Construction
28' diesel launch. William Shew design. Current project.
28' workboat. William Shew design. Current project.
8'7" lapstrake dinghy. N.G. Herreshoff design. Built 1985.
18' lapstrake launch. William Deed design. Built 1984.
12' Whitehall skiff. Lapstrake construction. William Shew design. 61 built 1972-'85.
16' lapstrake Adirondack guideboat. Grant design. Built 1985.
16' Whitehall skiff. Lapstrake construction. Plans by H.I. Chapelle. 37 built 1964-'85.

SWANS ISLAND BOATSHOP—James W. Bock
P.O. Box 356
Swans Island, ME 04658
207-526-4368

Builder Information
Years in business: 30 (off and on)
Carpenters employed: 1
Shop capacity: Boats to 45'

Recent New Construction
11'9" Bufflehead-class tender for oar and sail. Lapstrake construction. Built 1985.
14'3" plywood dory TEAL. Built 1974.

Yard Information
Services:
    Marina facilities
    Launching facilities
    Moorage

MAINE

DAVID SWEET
P.O. Box 178
Northeast Harbor, ME 04662
207-276-3272

Builder Information
Years in business: 11
Carpenters employed: 1
Shop capacity: Boats to 50'
Willing to travel occasionally for on-the-site building projects.

Recent New Construction
13' lapstrake peapod. David Sweet design. Built 1983-'84.
10' dinghy. Lapstrake hull with cross-planked bottom. David Sweet design. 4 built 1982-'84.

THAYER'S Y-KNOT BOATYARD—Edwin A. Thayer
Southern Harbor
North Haven, ME 04853
207-867-4701

Builder Information
Years in business: 30
Carpenters employed: 2
Shop capacity: Boats to 50'

Recent New Construction
Boats designed by Edwin Thayer:
    24' and 26' lobsterboats. 3 built 1960, 1965, and 1976.
    31' pleasure-type lobsterboat. Built 1970.
Other new construction:
    Small craft for oar and sail. Designs by John Alden and Edwin Thayer.
      Several built 1950 to present.

Recent Repair Projects
40' lobsterboats to 50' schooners. All types of repair,
    including keel replacements and complete rebuilding of hulls. 1958 to present.

Yard Information
Services:
    Launching facilities
    Moorage
    Diesel and gas engine repair
Storage:
    Number of boats stored per year: 200
    Percentage of wooden boats: Varies
    Inside storage facilities
    Maximum size for hauling and storing:
      Length: 65'
      Draft: 8'
      Tonnage: 30
Maintenance:
    Number of boats maintained per year: 200
    Percentage of wooden boats: 25
    Owner maintenance allowed above and below rail.
Retail supplies:
    All types of wood. Fastenings, paints, and general supplies.

MAINE

TRADITIONAL SHIP CAULKING—Eugene Scalzo
Box 731
Waldoboro, ME 04572
1-800-462-7101 (Maine residents), 1-800-251-2852 (outside Maine)

Builder Information
Years in business: 3 as ship's caulker
Carpenters employed: 1 or more, depending on job
Willing to travel for on-the-site building projects.

Recent New Construction
Caulking work:
    Schooner HERITAGE. 1983.
    Galleon ELIZABETH II. 1983.
    Schooner DAYSPRING. 1984.
    Schooner SPIRIT OF MASSACHUSETTS. 1984.
    Yacht GREBE. 1985.
    Schooner AMERICAN EAGLE. 1985-'86.

Recent Repair Projects
Recaulking work:
    Schooner BOWDOIN (hull, foredeck, and cabintop). 1984.
    Powerboat DIRIGO (below waterline). 1984.
    Schooner CORONET (deck, planking). 1984.
    Power yacht SKAGERAK (below waterline). 1984.
    Schooner J. & E. RIGGIN (cabintop and deck). 1985.
    Ship JOSEPH CONRAD (deck). 1985.

WASHINGTON COUNTY VOCATIONAL TECHNICAL INSTITUTE
Marine Trade Center
Deep Cove
Eastport, ME 04631
207-853-2518

Builder Information
Years in business: 14
Carpenters employed: Approximately 30 students per year
Shop capacity: Boats to 19'

Recent New Construction
17' Buzzards Bay class sloop. L.F. Herreshoff design.
14'9" Whitehall rowing tender.

Yard Information
Services:
    Launching facilities
    Diesel and gas engine repair

MAINE

WAYFARER MARINE CORP.—Stuart Farnham
Sea St.
Camden, ME 04843
207-236-4378

Builder Information
Years in business: 22
Carpenters employed: 5 for repair work
Shop capacity: Boats to 100'

Recent Repair Projects
42' schooner. Replaced aft railcaps and taffrail. 1985.
98' ketch. Replaced stem, resplined hull seams. 1984.

Yard Information
Services:
    Launching facilities
    Marina facilities
    Moorage (for boats worked on only)
    Diesel and gas engine repair
    Rigging
Storage:
    Number of boats stored per year: 160
    Percentage of wooden boats: 15
    Inside storage facilities
    Maximum size for hauling and storing:
        Length: 100'
        Draft: 8'
        Tonnage: 115
Maintenance:
    Number of boats maintained per year: 120
    Percentage of wooden boats: 10
    Owner maintenance allowed above and below rail, space permitting.
Retail supplies:
    Wood, fastenings, paint, hardware, electronics, fuel, rope, Johnson outboard engines, trailers, ice. Extensive inventory of marine supplies.

WELLS BOAT SHOP—Bill Shuman
P.O. Box 682
Sanford, ME 04073
207-324-4577

Builder Information
Years in business: 10
Carpenters employed: 1
Shop capacity: Boats to 50'

Recent New Construction
33' cold-molded trimaran. Chris White design. Built 1985.
21' cold-molded trimaran. Chris White design. Built 1984.
18'6" strip-planked sea kayak. Bill Shuman design. Built 1983.

Yard Information
Retail supplies:
    Will order on request.

MAINE

WEST COVE BOAT YARD—Stephen McMullen
P.O. Box 383
Sorrento, ME 04677
207-422-3137

Builder Information
Years in business: 5
Carpenters employed: Varies
Shop capacity: Boats to 39'

Recent New Construction
30' power cruiser. Ronald Rich design. Current project.

Recent Repair Projects
30' lobsterboat. Replaced garboard and part of #1 plank, port and starboard sides. 1985.

Yard Information
Services:
  Launching facilities
  Moorage
  Diesel and gas engine repair
  Sailmaking
  Rigging
Storage:
  Number of boats stored per year: 94
  Percentage of wooden boats: 10
  Inside storage facilities
  Maximum size for hauling and storing:
    Length: 41'
    Draft: 6'
    Tonnage: 20
Maintenance:
  Number of boats maintained per year: 94
  Percentage of wooden boats: 10

WILLIS ENTERPRISES, INC.—Melvin Willis
Curtis Rd., RD 3, Box 114A
Freeport, ME 04032
207-865-3830

Builder Information
Years in business: 4
Carpenters employed: 1
Shop capacity: Boats to 20'

Recent New Construction
20' canoe-yawl ELVER. Strip-plank construction. Steve Redmond
  design. Current project.

Retail supplies:
  Canoe-building books, canoe accessories, repair parts, and model boats.

MAINE

THE WOODSMITH—Robert Nelson
P.O. Box 248
Jonesport, ME 04649
207-497-2873

Builder Information
Years in business: 1
Carpenters employed: 2

Recent New Construction
9', 10½', and 12' flat-bottomed sea skiffs of cedar and oak, with bottoms of cedar or plywood. Hilson Beal and Robert Nelson design. 25 built to date.

Yard Information
Services:
   Provide custom sawing and milling service for wooden boatbuilders and owners. Will supply replacement toerails, grabrails, guards, washboards, and more.

MARYLAND

CROCKETT BROS. BOATYARD—P. Conner
202 Bank St., P.O. Box 369
Oxford, MD 21654
301-226-5113

Builder Information
Years in business: 8
Carpenters employed: 2
Shop capacity: Boats to 60′

Recent Repair Projects
56′ Sparkman & Stephens design (ca. 1960). Repaired extensive galvanic corrosion damage to planking and fastenings. 1984.
35′ Ohlsen sloop (ca. 1962). Installed large number of laminated frames. 1982.

Yard Information
Services:
    Marina facilities
    Launching facilities
    Diesel and gas engine repair
    Rigging
Storage:
    Number of boats stored per year: 140
    Percentage of wooden boats: 5
    Inside storage facilities
    Maximum size for hauling and storing:
        Length: 55′
        Draft: 6′6″
        Tonnage: 30
Maintenance:
    Number of boats maintained per year: 300
    Percentage of wooden boats: 2
    Owner maintenance allowed above and below rail.
Retail supplies:
    Extensive inventory of marine supplies. Most materials for boat maintenance and repair.

CUTTS & CASE, INC.—Edmund A. Cutts
P.O. Box 9
Oxford, MD 21654
301-226-5416

Builder Information
Years in business: 59
Carpenters employed: 6
Shop capacity: Boats to 65′

Recent New Construction
Boats built by the Cutts method of construction (frameless, double-planked):
    12′ sailing dinghy. F.W. Goeller design. 2 in progress.
    11′ dinghy. N. Herreshoff design. 2 in progress.
    65′ commuter-type motoryacht. Edmund Cutts design. Current project.

Recent Repair Projects
33′ Frederic Lord-designed power cruiser FOTO (Morris Rosenfeld's photo-chase boat). Complete restoration. Current project.

MARYLAND

Yard Information
Services:
  Marina facilities
  Launching facilities
  Overland transport
  Moorage
  Diesel and gas engine repair
  Sailmaking
  Rigging
Storage:
  Number of boats stored per year: 70
  Percentage of wooden boats: 50
  Inside storage facilities
  Maximum size for hauling and storing:
    Length: 60'
    Draft: 7'
    Tonnage: 30
Maintenance:
  Number of boats maintained per year: 70
  Percentage of wooden boats: 50
  Owner maintenance allowed above rail.
Retail supplies:
  Complete line of materials and marine supplies. Cast and forged hardware.
    Engine parts.

GRAHAM ERO WOODEN BOAT SHOP—Graham Ero
Church Street
Still Pond, MD 21667
(see CT pg. 22)

EDWARD FARLEY
Cooper Point Rd.
Bozman, MD 21612
301-745-2717

Builder Information
Years in business: 10-15
Carpenters employed: 1-4
Shop capacity: Boats to 65'
Willing to travel occasionally for on-the-site building projects.

New Construction
12½' strip-planked yawlboats. Edward Farley design. 2 built 1983-'85; 1 in progress.
16' strip-planked Whitehall. Built 1974.
13½' lapstrake peapod. Built 1973.

Repair Projects
48' skipjack STANLEY NORMAN. Replaced decks and beams, stem, staving. 1976-'79.
20' double-ended ketch. Installed new frames and garboard planks. Replaced decks and
    cabintop canvas. 1983.
63' Mower bugeye ketch (1924). Installing new frames and well, replacing transom and decks.
    Converting to schooner rig. Current project.

MARYLAND

LOWERY BOAT YARD—Maynard W. Lowery
Tilghman, MD 21671
301-886-2268

Builder Information
Years in business: 38
Carpenters employed: 2
Shop capacity: Boats to 53′

Recent New Construction
46′ commercial fishing boat. Strip-plank construction.
  Maynard Lowery design. Built 1984.
16′ Cape Cod catboat. Williams design. Built 1983.
21′ Cape Cod catboat. Williams design. Built 1980.
18′7″ open launch. R.M. Steward design. Current project.

Recent Repair Projects
18′ Cape Cod catboat. Stripped hull, reefed and recaulked seams.
  Replaced guardrails, rudder, centerboard, and cabintop. 1985.
18′ Rhodes sloop. Renewing frames. Current project.

MARKS BOAT YARD—Stephen Marks
529 Island Point Rd.
Baltimore, MD 21224
301-284-7038

Builder Information
Years in business: 5
Carpenters employed: 1
Shop capacity: Boats to 30′
May be willing to travel for on-the-site building projects.

Recent New Construction
Boats designed by Stephen Marks for plywood lapstrake construction:
  16′ sloop. Built 1983.
  16′ outboard skiff for fishing and crabbing. 2 built 1982.
Other new construction:
  19′7″ sailing Banks dory. Lapstrake construction. Sam Manning design. Built 1981.
  12′ cold-molded tender. A. Spurling design. Built 1985.

Recent Repair Projects
32′ Chapelle skipjack. Renewed centerboard case, 'midships bulkhead, cockpit, and coaming.
  Replaced bowsprit and canvas on deck and housetop. Renewed bottom planking
  and refastened hull. 1984-'85.

Yard Information
Services:
  Marina facilities
  Launching facilities
  Rigging
Storage:
  Number of boats stored per year: 40
  Percentage of wooden boats: 80
  Maximum size for hauling and storing:
    Length: 35′
    Draft: 3′
    Tonnage: 10

Maintenance:
    Number of boats maintained per year: 4
    Percentage of wooden boats: 100
    Owner maintenance allowed.
Retail supplies:
    Paint, hardware, rope.

JERRY NELSON, WOODWORKER
3513 Decatur Ave.
Kensington, MD 20895
301-946-3319

Builder Information
Years in business: 2
Carpenters employed: 1
Shop capacity: Boats to 20'

Recent New Construction
12'8" sailing canoe PICCOLO. Cold-molded construction.
    R.H. Baker design. Built 1985.
14' plywood catamaran. Jerry Nelson design. Built 1984.
8'6" lapstrake pram. Herreshoff design. Built 1983.

MELBOURNE SMITH
P.O. Box 54
Annapolis, MD 21404
301-268-5804

Builder Information
Years in business: 35
Carpenters employed: 14
Shop capacity: Boats to 180'
Building projects usually on-site.

Recent New Construction
83'4" 1850 revenue cutter CALIFORNIAN. Melbourne Smith design,
    built in San Diego. 1984.
93'6" 1830 brig GLOBE. Melbourne Smith design, built in Sacramento. 1985.
45' commercial skipjacks (for oystering under sail). Melbourne Smith design. 2 built 1982.
86'8" 3-masted schooner. Melbourne Smith design. Planned for 1986.
180' American clipper ship. John W. Griffiths design. Planned for 1988.

Recent Repair Projects
80' oyster buy-boat. Converted for passenger use. Added watertight
    bulkheads and raised bridge to accommodate new shelter deck. 1982.

MARYLAND

SPECTRUM WOODWORK—R.J. Pelasara
4822 Aspen Hill Rd.
Rockville, MD 20853
301-949-3394

Builder Information
Years in business: 5
Carpenters employed: 2
Shop capacity: New construction to 21'
Willing to travel for on-the-site building projects.

Recent New Construction
12'8" Catspaw dinghy. Designed by N.G. Herreshoff and J. White. Built 1984.
17' strip-planked canoe. J.H. Rushton design. Built 1983.
16' strip-planked canoe. J.H. Rushton design. 2 built 1984-'85.
14' strip-planked canoe. J.H. Rushton design. Built 1985.
16' Gloucester light dory. Plywood construction. Phil Bolger design. Built 1984.

Recent Repair Projects
35' lobster/crab fishing boat. Replaced pilothouse. 1983.
29' fishing/utility boat. Replaced seats and coaming. 1984.
37' sailboat. Installed new galley. 1985.

WENZEL BOAT CO.—Jack Wenzel
Rte. 1, Deep Creek Lake
McHenry, MD 21541
301-387-6110

Builder Information
Years in business: 20
Carpenters employed: 1
Willing to travel for on-the-site building projects.
Shop capacity: Boats to 21'

Recent Repair Projects
18' Chris-Craft Riviera (1950). Replaced 2 planks, renewed upholstery, and refinished hull.

Yard Information
Services:
    Overland transport
    Gas engine repair
Maintenance:
    Number of boats maintained per year: 2
    Percentage of wooden boats: 100
    Maximum size for hauling:
      Length: 22'

MARYLAND

WIKANDER YACHT YARD—Stuart Wikander
P.O. Box 38, Collins Wharf Rd.
Allen, MD 21810
301-749-9521

Builder Information
Years in business: 5
Carpenters employed: 1
Shop capacity: Boats to 40′

Recent New Construction
15′9″ plywood rowing boats. Stuart Wikander design. 2 built 1985.

Recent Repair Projects
40′ Owens cabin cruiser. Repaired deteriorated portions of transom and topsides. Installed new butt block under rudderpost, completely refinished exterior hull. 1985.

Yard Information
Services:
    Launching facilities
    Marina facilities
    Overland transport
    Moorage (dockage)
    Diesel and gas engine repair
    Rigging
Storage:
    Number of boats stored per year: 50
    Percentage of wooden boats: 50
    Inside storage facilities
    Maximum size for hauling and storing:
        Length: 50′
        Draft: 6′3″
        Tonnage: 25
Maintenance:
    Number of boats maintained per year: 70
    Percentage of wooden boats: 65
    Owner maintenance allowed above and below rail.
Retail supplies:
    Limited amounts of lumber. Bronze and stainless fastenings, paint. Rope, cleaners, and parts for engine repair.

YACHT MAINTENANCE CO., INC.—Philip W. McKee
101 Hayward St.
Cambridge, MD 21613
301-228-8878

Builder Information
Years in business: 10
Carpenters employed: 3
Shop capacity: Boats to 80′
(continues)

MARYLAND

(Yacht Maintenance Co., Inc., continued)
Recent Repair Projects
"We do the routine maintenance of many of the remaining skipjacks on Chesapeake Bay, and have restored and maintained some of the log canoes. We have completely restored two 1930s sailboats, and, being a full-service yard, routinely do extensive repairs and maintenance on other wooden vessels. Repair projects have included both sail and power boats, used commercially or for pleasure."

Yard Information
Services:
    Marina facilities
    Launching facilities
    Engine repair
    Rigging
Storage:
    Number of boats stored per year: 120
    Percentage of wooden boats: 15
    Inside storage facilities
    Maximum size for hauling and storing:
        Length: 60-120'
        Draft: 14'
        Tonnage: 60 on Travelift, 200 on rail
Maintenance:
    Number of boats maintained per year: 25
    Percentage of wooden boats: 20
    Owner maintenance allowed above and below rail.
Retail supplies:
    Standard supplies, including sandpaper, paint, and solvents. Will order other materials and equipment on request.

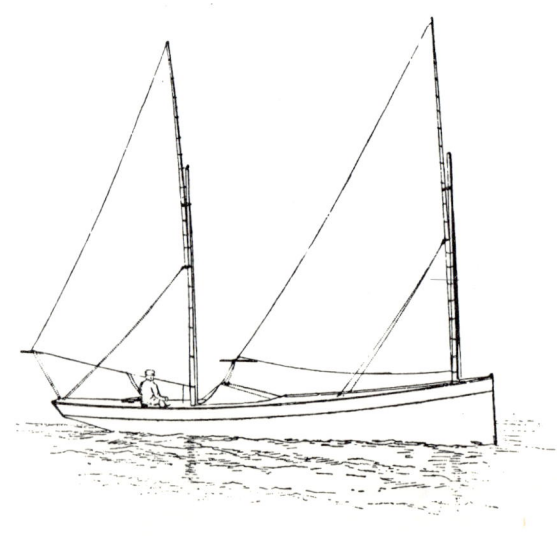

MASSACHUSETTS

R.H. BAKER BOAT & LAUNCH WORKS—Anne W. Baker
29 Drift Rd.
Westport, MA 02790
617-636-3272

Builder Information
Years in business: 40
Carpenters employed: 2
Shop capacity: New construction to 25'
Willing to travel for on-the-site building projects.

Recent New Construction
11' lapstrake North Shore sailing dinghy. R.H. Baker design. Built 1985.
12'10" lapstrake dinghy. Lines taken by R.H. Baker. Built 1984.
14'10" lapstrake sailing Whitehall. Designed by R.H. Baker. Built 1983.
15' Whitehall (1890s). Lines taken by R.H. Baker, 2 built 1982 and 1984.
10' duckboat. Lines taken by Julia Ferguson. Built 1983.

Recent Repair Projects
17'6" Georgian Bay wherry. Replaced keel, frames, and planking. Took lines. 1984.
29' whaleboat for New Bedford Whaling Museum. Repaired stem, replaced ceiling and thwarts. 1982.
12' sharpies. Replaced frames and planking, refinished. Repaired 3. 1983-'84.
16' Crosby cat. Renewed kingplank, deck, and centerboard. 1983.
15' Belgrade Lake boat. Refinished. 1984.
18' Alden O-boat. Installed new frames, replaced part of deck. 1983.
12' Beetle Cat. Refinished. 1984.

Yard Information
Services:
    Diesel and gas engine repair
    Sail repair
    Rigging repair
Storage:
    Number of boats stored per year: 2
    Percentage of wooden boats: 100
    Maximum length for hauling and storing:
        Length: 15'
        Draft: 8'
        Tonnage: 4
Maintenance:
    Number of boats maintained per year: 3
    Percentage of wooden boats: 100
Retail supplies:
    Bronze swivel oarlocks and outriggers. Robert H. Baker plans (write for catalog).

BALLENTINE'S BOAT SHOP, INC.—Stephen Ballentine
Box 457
Cataumet, MA 02534
617-563-2800

Builder Information
Years in business: 11
Carpenters employed: 3-4
Shop capacity: Boats to 40'

(continues)

MASSACHUSETTS

(Ballentine's Boat Shop, Inc., continued)

Recent New Construction
22' double-ended yawl JENNY WREN. Charles G. Davis design. Current project.
10' yacht tender. Lawley design. Built 1980.
11' flat-bottomed skiff. Asa Thomson design. Built 1983.

Recent Repair Projects
16' Herreshoff 12½ sloops. Has restored about 24 of these boats since 1978.
  Many are total rebuilds.

Yard Information
Services:
  Rigging
Storage:
  Number of boats stored per year: 45-50
  Percentage of wooden boats: 75
  Maximum size for hauling and storing:
    Length: 45'
    Draft: 7'
Maintenance:
  Number of boats maintained per year: 45-50
  Percentage of wooden boats: 75
Retail supplies:
  Wood, fastenings, paint. Limited inventory.

LESLIE BEAVAN
607 Setucket Rd., RR 2
South Dennis, MA 02660
617-385-3470

Builder Information
Years in business: 10
Carpenters employed: 1
Shop capacity: Boats to 26'

Recent New Construction
17'6" lapstrake daysailer. R.D. Culler design. Built 1982.
10'6" lapstrake clam skiff. Built 1985.
13'5" rowing skiff. Leslie Beavan design. Built 1985.
6'6" plywood punts. 2 built 1984.

Recent Repair Projects
* 57' ketch. Replaced 30% of teak decking. Reefed and recaulked deck. 1984.
* 34' Owens power cruiser. Replaced cockpit coaming, starboard side of house. 1985.
  14' Marblehead skiff. Spliced 4' section on broken mast. 1985.

* Work done for Falmouth Marine, Inc., Falmouth, Massachusetts.

MASSACHUSETTS

BETULA CANOE—Jay B. Parsons
243 Hendrick St.
Easthampton, MA 01027

Builder Information
Years in business: 2
Carpenters employed: 1
Shop capacity: Boats to 16'
Willing to travel for on-the-site building projects.

Recent New Construction
16' birchbark canoe. Chippewa type. 3 built 1983.
15'6" birchbark canoe. Chippewa and Cree. Built 1983.

R. BIGELOW AND CO., INC.—Myron C. Bigelow
140 MacArthur Blvd.
Bourne, MA 02532
617-759-4026

Builder Information
Years in business: 86
Carpenters employed: 2
Shop capacity: Boats to 40'

Recent New Construction
13'6" Wenaumet Kitten catboats. R. Bigelow design. 80 built 1935 to present.

Recent Repair Projects
Catboats and other craft. Minor repairs to complete rebuilding.
  Frame renewal, hull refastening, and spar repairs.

Yard Information
Services:
  Launching facilities
  Overland transport
  Moorage
  Diesel and gas engine repair
  Rigging
Storage:
  Number of boats stored per year: 30
  Percentage of wooden boats: 80
  Inside storage facilities
  Maximum size for hauling and storing:
    Length: 30'
    Draft: 5'
    Tonnage: 7
Maintenance:
  Number of boats maintained per year: 40
  Percentage of wooden boats: 82
  Owner maintenance allowed.
Retail supplies:
  Cedar, oak, mahogany, ash, pine, and marine plywood. Stainless steel
    fastenings, paint.

MASSACHUSETTS

WILLIAM CLEMENTS, BOATBUILDER
18 Mt. Pleasant St., P.O. Box 87
North Billerica, MA 01862
617-663-3103

Builder Information
Years in business: 5
Carpenters employed: 1
Shop capacity: Boats to 18'
May be willing to travel for on-the-site building projects.

Recent New Construction
14'8" sailing canoe. Plywood lapstrake construction. J.H. Rushton design. 3 built 1984.
18' sailing canoe. Plywood lapstrake construction. W.P. Stephens design. Planned for 1986.

Recent Repair Projects
11-18' wood-and-canvas canoes and powerboats. Work ranges from minor repairs to major restorations. Hull recanvasing. 1984-'85.

CONCORDIA CO., INC.—Alden Trull
South Wharf, P.O. Box P-203
South Dartmouth, MA 02748
617-999-1381

Builder Information
Years in business: 45 in repair, 22 in new construction
Carpenters employed: 10
Shop capacity: Boats to 58'

Recent New Construction
12'4" Beetle-class catboats. C. Beetle design. 25-30 built each year.
38' cold-molded trimaran. Newick design. Built 1983.
32'6" Buzzard Bay 25-class sloop. Cold-molded construction. N.G. Herreshoff design. Built 1983.

Recent Repair Projects
39' Concordia yawl. Renewed sternposts and maststeps. 4 boats repaired 1982-'83.
45' Concordia ketch. Renewed planking, rebuilt transom. 1983.
7-meter-class sloop. Applied cold-molded overlay to hull. 1983.

Yard Information
Services:
    Launching facilities
    Moorage
    Diesel and gas engine repair
    Sailmaking
    Rigging
Storage:
    Number of boats stored per year: 80
    Percentage of wooden boats: 45
    Inside storage facilities for 15 boats
    Maximum size for hauling and storing:
        Length: 50'
        Draft: 8'
        Tonnage: 25

Maintenance:
    Number of boats maintained per year: 100
    Percentage of wooden boats: 45
    Owner maintenance allowed above rail.
Retail supplies:
    Wood, fastenings, paint, rope, wire, hardware, engine parts.
    Everything needed to maintain or repair boats stored and serviced.

CHESTER A. CROSBY AND SONS—David Anderson
P.O. Box 490, Bridge St.
Osterville, MA 02541
617-428-2017

Builder Information
Years in business: 50
Carpenters employed: 5-10
Shop capacity: Boats to 45'

Recent New Construction
16' Wianno Junior-class sloop. Crosby design. Built 1984.
36' schooner. Wm. Daniel Knott design. Built 1979.
18' lapstrake rowing shell. Built 1984.

Recent Repair Projects
36' Elco Cruiser. Renewed garboard, decks, and house.
    Refastened hull and rechromed hardware. 1983-'84.
26' Crosby catboat. Replaced frames and planking. Renewed house and decks.
    Refastened hull. 1982-'83.

Yard Information
Services:
    Marina facilities
    Launching facilities
    Moorage
    Diesel and gas engine repair
    Rigging
Storage:
    Number of boats stored per year: 200+
    Percentage of wooden boats: 25
    Inside storage facilities
    Maximum size for hauling and storing:
        Length: 45'
        Draft: 6'
        Tonnage: 50
Maintenance:
    Number of boats maintained per year: 300+
    Percentage of wooden boats: 25
    Owner maintenance allowed above rail.
Retail supplies:
    Marine plywood, lumber, fastenings, paint, hardware, and engine parts.

MASSACHUSETTS

DAVIS CUSTOM BOATS—Tony Davis
1493 Beacon St.
Brookline, MA 02146
617-277-8099

Builder Information
Years in business: 3
Carpenters employed: 1
Shop capacity: New construction to 30'
Willing to travel for on-the-site building projects.

Recent New Construction
11' lapstrake rowing skiff. Arno Day design. 2 built 1984-'85.

Recent Repair Projects
44' Rhodes 27. Repaired leaking seams, renewed interior joinerwork. 1984.

Yard Information
Services:
  Diesel engine repair
  Rigging
Maintenance:
  165' schooner SPIRIT OF MASSACHUSETTS

FRED J. DION YACHT YARD—Frederick J. Atkins
23 Glendale St.
Salem, MA 01970
617-744-0844

Builder Information
Years in business: 71
Carpenters employed: 4
Shop capacity: Boats to 75'

Recent Repair Projects
48' Abeking & Rasmussen yawl. Replacing garboard planks and refastening bottom. Renewing teak decks, bulwarks, covering board, railcaps. Rebuilding housetop, port side of trunk cabin, cockpit, and much of interior. Replacing spars, mast partners, chainplates, and rudder. Installing new engine, replacing plumbing and wiring. Current project.
67' Alden sloop. Replaced keelbolts and some floor timbers. Sistered frames and renewed planking. Cast new rudder-heel fittings. 1984.
53' English cutter SHIRIS. Cast and installed bronze floor timbers. Renewed paneling and interior joinerwork. Built curved bulkhead for spiral stairway. 1983.

Yard Information
Services:
  Launching facilities
  Moorage
  Diesel and gas engine repair
  Rigging
Storage:
  Number of boats stored per year: 90
  Percentage of wooden boats: 50
Inside storage facilities
  Maximum size for hauling and storing:
    Length: 75'
    Draft: 9'
    Tonnage: 50

Maintenance:
    Number of boats maintained per year: 150
    Percentage of wooden boats: 30
Retail supplies:
    Limited supply of lumber, fastenings, and paint.

ESSEX BAY BOAT CO., INC.—David Condino
15 Rock Neck Ave., P.O. Box 520
Gloucester, MA 01930
617-281-2189

Builder Information
Years in business: 6
Carpenters employed: 2-3
Shop capacity: Boats to 100'
Willing to travel for on-the-site building projects.

Recent New Construction
26' strip-planked Muscongus Bay lobster smack. Lines by H.I. Chapelle. Built 1985.
32' cold-molded cutter. Design by David Condino. Built 1983-'84.
26' strip-planked Crotch Island pinky. Lines by H.I. Chapelle. Built 1983.
15' plywood-and-epoxy rowing dory. David Condino design. 5 built 1983 to present.
12' cold-molded dinghy for oar and sail. Charles Wittholz design. Built 1984.

Recent Repair Projects
35' Friendship sloop. Refastened, replaced engine and garboard. Extensive rebuilding on decks and cockpit. 1984.
45' Murray Peterson schooner MORNING STAR. Refastened, replaced garboards, interior joinerwork. 1984.
40' SPRAY reproduction, MISS RACHEL. Complete restoration, including new engine, shaftlog, engine beds, interior joinerwork. 1985.
31' Rice Brothers lake launch (1927). Complete restoration. Current project.
16' runabout LAY STABLE. Complete restoration. 1985.

Yard Information
Services:
    Launching facilities
    Overland transport
    Diesel and gas engine repair
    Sail repair
    Rigging
Storage:
    Number of boats stored per year: 10
    Percentage of wooden boats: 80
    Maximum size for hauling and storing:
        Length: 45'
        Draft: 6'
        Tonnage: 15
Maintenance:
    Number of boats maintained per year: 15-20
    Percentage of wooden boats: 95
    Owner maintenance allowed above and below rail.
Retail supplies:
    Dealer for WEST System epoxy. Also carry paint, fastenings, lumber, engine parts, rigging supplies, and hardware. Custom millwork available.

MASSACHUSETTS

FLYER'S BOAT SHOP—Francis Santos
131A Commercial St.
Provincetown, MA 02657
617-487-0518

Builder Information
Years in business: 41
Carpenters employed: 3
Shop capacity: Boats to 60'

Recent New Construction
25' daysailer. In-house design. 2 built 1970.
31' sportfisherman. In-house design. Built 1983.
16' outboard skiffs. In-house design. 6 built 1980.

Recent Repair Projects
Commercial fishing craft to 60'. Repairs as needed.

Yard Information
Services:
　　Marina facilities
　　Launching facilities
　　Moorage
　　Diesel and gas engine repair
　　Rigging
Storage:
　　Number of boats stored per year: 35
　　Percentage of wooden boats: 40
　　Maximum size for hauling and storing:
　　　　Length: 60'
　　　　Draft: 10'
　　　　Tonnage: 50
Maintenance:
　　Number of boats maintained per year: 220
　　Percentage of wooden boats: 50
　　Owner maintenance allowed above rail.
Retail supplies:
　　Outboard engines. Fully stocked marine store.

GANNON & BENJAMIN, INC. MARINE RAILWAY—Nat Benjamin
P.O. Box 1095, Beach Rd.
Vineyard Haven, MA 02568
617-693-4658

Builder Information
Years in business: 15
Carpenters employed: 3
Shop capacity: Boats to 60'

Recent New Construction
Boats designed by Nat Benjamin:
　　25'6" centerboard sloop. 3 built 1980, 1982, and 1983.
　　20' catboat. Built 1981.
　　23'6" keel sloop. Built 1984.
　　45' keel schooner. Current project.
　　10' yacht tender. 2 built 1984 and 1985.

Other new construction:
   12′8″ Catspaw dinghy. Herreshoff and Joel White design. 3 built 1980, 1983, and 1984.

Recent Repair Projects
12′ Beetle Cats to 60′ racing sloops to 50-ton fishing boats.
   Repair work has included replacing keels, stems, transoms, frames, planking, decks, spars, and engines. Dozens of boats rebuilt to date.

Yard Information
Services:
   Marina facilities
   Launching facilities
   Moorage
   Engine repair
   Sailmaking
   Rigging
Storage:
   Number of boats stored per year: 8
   Percentage of wooden boats: 100
   Maximum size for hauling and storing:
     Length: 60′
     Draft: 8′
     Tonnage: 50
Maintenance:
   Number of boats maintained per year: 15
   Percentage of wooden boats: 100
   Owner maintenance allowed above and below rail.
Retail supplies:
   Wood, fastenings, paint, bronze hardware, T-shirts.

BILL GILES
626 School St.
North Dighton, MA 02764
617-823-5653

Builder Information
Years in business: 25
Carpenters employed: 1
Shop capacity: Boats to 12′

Recent New Construction
Plywood hydroplanes. Giles design. 150 built 1960-'85.

Recent Repair Projects
Hydroplane. Repaired damages from an accident while in competition.

MASSACHUSETTS

GREAT CANADIAN CANOE—John Berg
65-45 Water St.
Worcester, MA 01604
1-800-343-3432 or 617-755-5237

Builder Information
Years in business: 143
Carpenters employed: 5
Shop capacity: Boats to 30'

Recent New Construction
13'8" to 18' cedar-strip canoes. Traditional Huron Indian design. 315 built 1985.

Recent Repair Projects
15-19' canoes. Repairs to planking, ribs, gunwales, thwarts, canvas, and fiberglass sheathing.

Yard Information
Services:
    Overland transport.

HAMILTON CANOE & BOAT SHOP—Daniel W. Hamilton

1732 Monument St.		*RFD, Box 1700, Goshen Road*
Concord, MA 01742	*NEW ADDRESS*	*Winterport, ME 04496*
617-369-2325		*207-223-4188*

Builder Information
Years in business: 10
Carpenters employed: 1
Shop capacity: Boats to 20'
Willing to travel for on-the-site building projects.

Recent New Construction
17' Stripper canoes. David Hazen design. 2 built 1979-'80.

Recent Repair Projects
Rangeley Lake boats. Total restoration. Planking, frames, transom. 2 in 1985.
17' Old Town Charles River canoe. New decks, some frames, new canvas. 1985.
19' Lightning class. New planking and decks, refastened and refinished. 1985.
15-20' Old Town canoes. Restoration and rebuilding. 5 in 1985.
15-18' Chestnut canoes. Restoration and rebuilding. 3 in 1985.
15-18' miscellaneous canoes. Restoration and rebuilding. 4 in 1985.
15' Amesbury skiff. Recaulked seams, replaced planks. 1985.

Yard Information
Services:
    Overland transport
Maintenance:
    Number of boats maintained per year: 10
    Percentage of wooden boats: 100
    Owner maintenance allowed above and below rail
Retail supplies:
    Supplies for canoe building and repair. Fillers, paints, etc. Paddles, seats, and other canoeing accessories.

MASSACHUSETTS

HINGHAM BOAT WORKS, INC.—Robert E. Murray
349 Lincoln St., Building 40
Hingham, MA 02043
617-749-8868

Builder Information
Years in business: 6
Carpenters employed: 2

Repair Projects
25' Eldredge-McInnis bassboat (1954). Renewing cockpit, planks, frames, in an ongoing restoration. Current project.
42' Wheeler sportfisherman. Replaced stem and planking.
34' Hinkley Sou'wester (1948). Installed 7 new frames, replaced 5 planks, rebuilt galley.
36' Novi lobsterboat. Rebuilt cabinhouse.
26' pocket cruiser (1947). Replaced deck canvas and mahogany trim.

PERT LOWELL CO., INC.—Ralph F. Johnson, Jr.
Lane's End
Newbury, MA 01950
617-462-7409

Builder Information
Years in business: 260
Carpenters employed: 2
Shop capacity: Boats to 30'

Recent New Construction
16'6" Town-class sloop. Lapstrake construction. Pert Lowell design. 2 built 1984.
18' Fleet-O-Wing sloop. Sparkman & Stephens design. Built 1985.
14' Brutal Beast-class catboat. Hard-chined with ship-lap planking. W. Starling Burgess design. 5 built 1985.
10' skiff. Pert Lowell design. 2 built 1985.

Recent Repair Projects
26' strip-planked sailboat. Replaced 20' of planking. 1985.
16'6" Town-class sloops. Replaced planking. 1985. Several other "Townies" repaired to date.

Yard Information
Services:
    Launching facilities
    Rigging
Storage:
    Number of boats stored per year: 20
    Percentage of wooden boats: 90
    Maximum size for hauling and storing:
        Length: 30'
        Draft: 4'
        Tonnage: 6
Maintenance:
    Number of boats maintained per year: 4
    Percentage of wooden boats: 75
    Owner maintenance allowed above and below rail.
Retail supplies:
    Wood, fastenings, paint, rope, hardware, special-order items.

MASSACHUSETTS

LOWELL'S BOAT SHOP, INC.—Jim Odell
459 Main St.
Amesbury, MA 01913
617-388-0162

Builder Information
Years in business: 192
Carpenters employed: 5
Shop capacity: Boats to 26'

Recent New Construction
Boats of dory-type construction (with epoxy-coated bottoms):
    24' sailing surf dory. Jim Odell design. Built 1985.
    18' sailing surf dory. Odell modification. Built 1985.
    17' and 18' Salisbury Point sailing skiffs. Lowell design. 2 built 1985.
    18' Atlantic rowing and sailing skiff. Odell design. Built 1985.
    15' Amesbury sailing skiff. Lowell/Odell design. Built 1985.
    14' Atlantic Amesbury power skiff. Lowell/Odell design. Built 1985.
    15' and 17' Atlantic rowing skiffs. Odell design. 4 built 1985.
    15' Salisbury Point rowing skiff. Lowell design. Built 1985.
    12' Merrimack rowing skiff. Lowell design. 3 built 1985.
    11' sailing tender. Odell design. 2 built 1985.
    8'9" rowing tender. Odell design. Built 1985.

Recent Repair Projects
16' Truscott runabout (1948). Restored hull, rebuilt engine and reupholstered. 1985.
16' White lapstrake outboard runabout (1954). Restored interior and decks, repaired stem and transom. 1985.
12' Merrimack rowing skiffs. Repaired 2 for town of Weymouth. 1985.
12' Lawley tender (1921). Restored. 1982.
20' carvel-planked Swampscott dory. Replaced rotted sections of hull and completed construction begun in 1908! Installed decks, single-cylinder engine, and power steering. 1984.

Yard Information
Services:
    Overland transport
    Moorage and docking
Storage:
    Limited number of boats stored per year
    Maximum size for hauling and storing:
        Length: 20'
        Draft: 1'
Retail supplies:
    Very limited. Bronze hardware and fastenings, paint, and epoxy.

MARTHA'S VINEYARD SHIPYARD—Thomas Hale
Beach Rd.
Vineyard Haven, MA 02568
617-693-0400

Builder Information
Years in business: 120
Carpenters employed: 2
Shop capacity: Boats to 45'

MASSACHUSETTS

Recent New Construction
14' lapstrake pulling boats. 2 built in 1985.

Recent Repair Projects
34' Fife-designed and -built auxiliary sloop. Replaced aft end of keel, stem, sternpost, and horn timber. 1982 and 1985.
18' Manuel Schwartz catboat. Replaced entire keel. 1985.

Yard Information
Services:
    Launching facilities
    Moorage
    Diesel and gas engine repair
    Sailmaking and sail repair
    Rigging
Storage:
    Number of boats stored per year: 140
    Percentage of wooden boats: 15
    Inside storage facilities
    Maximum size for hauling and storing:
        Length: 45'
        Draft: 6'
        Tonnage: 16
Maintenance:
    Number of boats maintained per year: 140
    Percentage of wooden boats: 20
    Owner maintenance allowed above rail (inside and outside storage), below rail (outside storage only).

Retail supplies:
    Everything except electronics.

DAMIAN McLAUGHLIN JR. CORPORATION—Damian McLaughlin
294 Sam Turner Rd., P.O. Box 538
North Falmouth, MA 02556
617-563-3075

Builder Information
Years in business: 15
Carpenters employed: 6-10
Shop capacity: Boats to 55'

Recent New Construction
38' cold-molded trimarans. Dick Newick design. 2 built 1983.
45' cold-molded trimaran. Dick Newick design. Built 1983.
35' cold-molded trimaran. Damian McLaughlin design. Built 1984.
50' cold-molded catamaran. Chris White design. Current project.

MASSACHUSETTS

MEADS BOATBUILDING CO.—Charles E. Meads
#16, 1112 Main St.
Osterville, MA 02655
617-428-7789

Builder Information
Years in business: 2
Carpenters employed: 2
Shop capacity: Boats to 38'
Willing to travel for on-the-site building projects.

Recent New Construction:
21' V-bottomed powerboat. Edwin Monk design. Built 1985.
12' lapstrake tender. Pete Culler design. Built 1985.

Recent Repair Projects
46' Dawn cruiser. Repaired fire damage to saloon. Installed new cabinets. 1985.
12' Beetle Cats. Refastens, replaces deck canvas, and renews coamings. Repairs 3-4 per year.
36' pleasure-type lobsterboat. Installed interior cabinets, doors, shelving. 1983.
20' powerboat. Replaced stern, refastened. 1985.

Yard Information
Services:
    Rigging for small boats
Maintenance:
    Number of boats maintained per year: 6-8
    Percentage of wooden boats: 100
Retail supplies:
    Lumber, marine plywood, fastenings, paint, some hardware.

MOLLYS COVE BOAT WORKS INC.—Daniel C. Briggs
22 Harbor Rd.
Mattapoisett, MA 02739
617-758-6630

Builder Information
Years in business: 5
Carpenters employed: 2-6
Shop capacity: Boats to 65'
Willing to travel for on-the-site building projects.

Recent Repair Projects
The following boats were given a cold-molded overlay to their existing
    hulls and underwent total restoration between 1983 and 1985:
    57' motoryacht.
    29' bassboat.
    22' catboat.
    36' Sparkman & Stephens Weekender-class sloop.
    15' Herreshoff 12½ sloop.
    24' bassboat.
    10' Herreshoff dinghy (1909).

Yard Information
Services:
    Overland transport
    Diesel and gas engine repair

Storage:
    Number of boats stored per year: 6
    Percentage of wooden boats: 50
    Maximum size for hauling and storing:
        Length: 65'
        Draft: 8'
Maintenance:
    Number of boats maintained per year: 4
    Percentage of wooden boats: 100
    Owner maintenance allowed above and below rail.

MONTGOMERY BOAT YARD—David Montgomery
Ferry St.
Gloucester, MA 01930
617-283-0262

Builder Information
Years in business: 85
Carpenters employed: 2
Shop capacity: Boats to 40'
Willing to travel for on-the-site building projects.

Recent New Construction
15' Fish-class catboat. N.W. Montgomery and Harry Friend design.
    5 built 1982-'85.
31' Manchester I-boat. Small Bros. design. Built 1983.
15' Whitehall. John Gardner design. Built 1979.
17' Swampscott dory. Lapstrake construction. John Gardner design. Built 1981.
21' cat-yawl. L.F. Herreshoff design. Built 1985.
Boats designed by Phil Bolger:
    17' English cutter. Current project.
    24' raised-deck power cruiser. Built 1978.
    28' lobsterboat. Built 1984.
    32' lobsterboat. Built 1983.
    15' plywood light dory. 5 built 1978-'79.
    11' and 15' plywood pirogues. 2 built 1983 and 1985.
    15' pulling boat CRYSTAL. Built 1984.

Recent Repair Projects
21' Indian. Replaced frames and deck. 1985.
16' Gloucester Midget (small Tancook Whaler, ca. 1918). Completely rebuilt.
    Renewed frames and planking. 1985.

Yard Information
Services:
    Launching facilities
Storage:
    Number of boats stored per year: 35
    Percentage of wooden boats: 90
    Inside storage facilities
    Maximum size for hauling and storing:
        Length: 32'
        Draft: 5'
        Tonnage: 10

(continues)

MASSACHUSETTS

(Montgomery Boat Yard, continued)
Maintenance:
    Number of boats maintained per year: 12
    Percentage of wooden boats: 80
    Owner maintenance allowed.

NANTUCKET SHIPYARD—Mark W. Barber
Washington St.
Nantucket, MA 02554
617-228-0263

Builder Information
Years in business: 60
Carpenters employed: 4
Shop capacity: Boats to 50'

Recent New Construction
26' cold-molded Alerion sloop. N.G. Herreshoff design. 20 built 1980-'83.
13' plywood Nantucket sharpies. Doug Alvord design. 3 built 1984.

Recent Repair Projects
42' 30-square-meter. Major restoration. New frames, keel, deadwood. 1984-'85.
32' Vineyard Sound Interclub sloop. Extensive restoration. New frames, coaming, cockpit. 1984-'85.
19' Bristol 19. Composite reconstruction. New deck and frames. 1984.

Yard Information
Services:
    Launching facilities
    Overland transport
    Moorage
    Diesel and gas engine repair
    Sailmaking
    Rigging
Storage:
    Number of boats stored per year: 350
    Percentage of wooden boats: 30
    Inside storage facilities
    Maximum size for hauling and storing:
        Length: 50'
        Draft: 7'
        Tonnage: 20
Maintenance:
    Number of boats maintained per year: 350
    Percentage of wooden boats: 30
    Owner maintenance allowed above rail.
Retail supplies:
    Extensive inventory. Fastenings, paint, hardware, wood, moorings, sails, engines. We sell everything!

MASSACHUSETTS

OLD WHARF DORY CO.—Walter Baron
Box W/Old Chequessett Neck Rd.
Wellfleet, MA 02667
617-349-2383

Builder Information
Years in business: 8
Carpenters employed: 1
Shop capacity: Boats to 36' (shallow draft)

Recent New Construction
34'6" shallow-draft yawl of plywood with fiberglass sheathing. Designed by Phil Bolger. Built 1985.
14', 16', and 18' plywood flat-bottomed work skiffs. Walter Baron design. 4 built 1982-'84.
17' Swampscott dory, lapstrake plywood construction. Lines from Mystic Seaport collection. 4 built through 1984.

Recent Repair Projects
16' Amesbury skiff. Repaired planks, installed sheer planks. Refastened bottom, installed new deck framing and plywood/canvas deck. Replaced rails, coaming, and hardware. 1984.
18' Old Town sailing canoe. Rebuilt stems and one end deck. Recanvased hull and sponsons, replaced rails. 1984.

Yard Information
Retail supplies:
    Wood, fastenings, hardware.

OPUS YACHTS—Gary L. Ungarean
P.O. Box 1701
Framingham, MA 01701

Builder Information
Years in business: 10
Shop capacity: Boats to 62'

Recent New Construction
23' cold-molded sloop. Kirby design.
40' cold-molded sloop. In-house design. Current project.

SOUTH COVE BOAT SHOP—Robert Barker
P.O. Box 10, 9 S. Main St.
Montague, MA 01351
413-367-2424

Builder Information
Years in business: 5
Carpenters employed: 1
Shop capacity: Boats to 24'
Willing to travel in southern New England for on-the-site building projects.
(continues)

MASSACHUSETTS

(South Cove Boat Shop, continued)

Recent New Construction
16′ Thomaston Galley for sail or oar. Plywood construction. Phil Bolger design. Built 1985.
14′9″ lapstrake sailing skiff. John Atkin design. Built 1985.
10′6″ lapstrake sailing tender. Walt Simmons design. Built 1984.
16′ strip-planked runabout. Sam Rabl design. Built 1983–'84.
12′ plywood kayak. Phil Bolger design. Built 1982.
18′ sliding-seat pulling boat. Plywood construction. Robert Barker design.
   2 built 1983 and 1985.

Recent Repair Projects
22′ cruising sloop. Recaulked hull, replaced floors and frames.
   Rebuilt interior and fiberglassed cabintop. 1979–'83.
14′ plywood daysailer. Refinished hull. 1985.

STORY SHIPYARD—D. Bradford Story
Main St.
Essex, MA 01929
617-768-6291

Builder Information
Years in business: 172
Carpenters employed: 2
Shop capacity: Boats to 50′

Recent New Construction
Boats designed by Phil Bolger:
   20′ Chebacco 20 cat yawls. Cold-molded construction. 3 built 1984–'85.
   15′ catboat HARBINGER. Built 1984.
   36′ cruising cat PALO DE AGUA. Carvel and strip-plank construction. Built 1984.
   26′ lobsterboat. Built 1983.
   20′ plywood sharpie. Built 1983.
   11′6″ multi-chined skiff for oar and sail. Plywood construction. Built 1985.
Other new construction:
   36′6″ double-ended ketch. Herreshoff design. Built 1985.
   10′ hard-chined skiff for oar and sail. Plywood construction. Bob Parlee design.
      Built 1984.

Recent Repair Projects
28′ Herreshoff daysailer. Renewed frames and keel. Refastened hull. 1983.
30′ fin-keeled sloop. Replaced keel, repaired planking. 1984.
48′ Bolger lugger. Installed new engine, replaced masts. 1985.

SUN JUNCTION BOATWORKS—Bill Plettner
Box 322
West Falmouth, MA 02574
617-540-0729

Builder Information
Years in business: 6
Carpenters employed: 1
Shop capacity: Boats to 40′

Recent New Construction
16–22′ plywood skiffs. Sun Junction Boatworks design. 140 built since 1979.

WINNIPESAUKEE CANOE CO.—John Fiske
58 Linden St.
Needham, MA 02192
413-449-8966

Builder Information
Years in business: 4
Carpenters employed: 1
Shop capacity: Boats to 18'
Willing to travel for on-the-site building projects.

Recent New Construction
16' and 18' wood-and-canvas canoes. John Fiske design. 2 built 1982 and 1985.

Recent Repair Projects
17' Chestnut Cruiser canoe. Replaced 18 ribs, decks, thwarts, canvas, and outwales. 1984.
18' Peterborough canoe. Replaced 8 ribs, decks, canvas, and gunwales. 1985.
15' Quebec Indian canoe. Replaced hull canvas. 1985.
18' Old Town Charles River canoe (1916). Replaced outwales. 1985.

Yard Information
Services:
   Overland transport
Retail supplies:
   Parts for wooden canoes. Custom-made ribs, gunwales, decks, thwarts, planking.

YACHTCRAFT—Emerson Dahmen
94 Ocean Ave.
Salem, MA 01970
617-744-3180

Builder Information
Years in business: 13
Carpenters employed: 2
Shop capacity: Boats to 32'
Willing to travel for on-the-site building projects.

Recent New Construction
18' sloop. L.F. Herreshoff design. 2 built 1981-'82.
16' plywood outboard skiff. Phil Bolger design. Built 1985.
14' cold-molded rowboat. John Marples design. Built 1985.
10' plywood pram. Emerson Dahmen design. Built 1983.

Recent Repair Projects
20' Casey catboat. Replaced 6 planks, sistered 20 frames. Replaced main bulkhead, stem knee, and house sides. 1985.
Miscellaneous small repair projects have included building new rudders and centerboards, replacing coaming, hatches, planking, frames. Also rigging repairs, electrical and plumbing repairs, and hardware installation. 1982-'85.

Yard Information
Services:
   Rigging
Retail supplies:
   Wood, paint, fastenings, rope, caulking materials, adhesives, and some hardware.

MICHIGAN

BINGHAM BOAT WORKS—Joseph Bingham, Jr.
Star Rte. 550, Box 58
Marquette, MI 49855
906-225-1427

Builder Information
Years in business: 55
Carpenters employed: 2
Shop capacity: Boats to 45'
Willing to travel for on-the-site building projects.

Recent New Construction
28' V-bottomed cutter. Strip-plank construction. Bill Jackson design. Built 1983.

Recent Repair Projects
16' Carver runabout. Renewed transom. 1985.
25' Chris-Craft Sea Skiff. Replaced decks. 1985.
19' Thompson runabout. Renewed decks and vinyl. 1985.
18' runabout. Replaced bottom and transom planking, installed new engine and shaft. 1985.
26' Carver inboard/outboard. Renewed decks and cabin roof with plywood and fiberglass overlay. 1985.
22' Bingham cat-rigged boat (1956). Replaced frames, renewed cabin and deck. Converted to ketch rig. 1985.

Yard Information
Services:
  Gas engine repair
  Rigging
Storage:
  Number of boats stored per year: 8
  Percentage of wooden boats: 3
  Inside storage facilities
Maintenance:
  Number of boats maintained per year: 25
  Percentage of wooden boats: 50
Retail supplies:
  Wood, fastenings, hardware, and paint by special order.

CANOESPORT—Ned Sharples
940 N. Main St.
Ann Arbor, MI 48104
313-996-1393

Builder Information
Years in business: 7
Carpenters employed: 1-3
Shop capacity: Boats to 20'

MICHIGAN

Recent Repair Projects
15′ Carleton canoe (ca. 1920). Renewed outwales and caprails. Refinished interior.
15′ Peterborough skiff (1949). Rebuilt stem and deck. Renewed frames, planking, and gunwales. Recanvased hull.
16′ Chestnut canoe (1955). Renewed plank, yoke, and peaks.
18′ White canoe. Removed fiberglass sheathing. Rebuilt and recanvased hull.
16′ Old Town canoe (1936). Restored and recanvased hull.
13′ Rice Lake canoe (1913). Renewed ribs and seats, refinished hull.
16′ Cedar Craft canoe. Patched hull canvas, refinished gunwales.
16′ Old Town canoe (1954). Removed sponsons, repaired peaks and frames. Recanvased and refinished hull.
18′ Old Town canoe (1939). Recanvased and refinished hull.
16′ Peterborough canoe. Repaired bow deck, recanvased hull.

Yard Information
Services:
    Launching facilities for canoes
    Overland transport
    Rigging for canoes
    Sailmaking for canoes
Storage:
    Number of boats stored per year: 120
    Percentage of wooden boats: varies
    Inside storage facilities
    Maximum size for hauling and storing:
        Length: Rowing shells to 48′
Retail supplies:
    Materials for repair and refinishing of wood canoes. Some fiberglass, resin, and epoxy.

JERRY CASSELL
1516 Romence
Portage, MI 49081
616-327-7999

Builder Information
Years in business: 5, part-time
Carpenters employed: 1
Shop capacity: Boats to 20′

Recent Repair Projects
Wood-and-canvas canoes. All types of repair. About 20 canoes restored in last 5 years.

FAERING DESIGN—Chip Stulen
Rte. 1, Box 223
Suttons Bay, MI 49682
616-271-6729

Builder Information
Years in business: 10
Carpenters employed: 1
Shop capacity: Boats to 25′
(continues)

MICHIGAN

(Faering Design, continued)
Recent New Construction
Boats designed by Chip Stulen for lapstrake construction:
   19'6" Fjording 19.5 cuddy sloop. Built 1983.
   16' and 18' faerings for sail. 4 built 1984-'85.
   18' power launch. Built 1979.
   8' and 10' prams. 4 built 1984-'85.
   14'6" faering for oar. Built 1984.

Recent Repair Projects
Custom spar work:
   80' hollow oval mast for N-boat SERENADE. 1985.
   40' hollow oval mast for Rhodes Swiftshore-class sloop. 1985.
   40' hollow oval mast for Rhodes sloop. 1985.

GRAND CRAFT—Dick Sligh
446-448 W. 21st St.
Holland, MI 49423
616-396-5450

Builder Information
Years in business: 5
Carpenters employed: 10
Shop capacity: Boats to 30'

Recent New Construction
Boats of double-planked mahogany:
   20' sport runabout. Grand Craft design. Built 1985.
   23' luxury sport runabout. Grand Craft design.
   24' and 27' classic runabouts. Chris-Craft designs. 6 built to date.

Recent Repair Projects
Chris-Crafts. Minor repairs to complete restorations.

Yard Information
Services:
   Gas engine repair
Retail supplies:
   Mahogany, hardware.

KLONDIKE WOOD WORKS—Elmer L. Johnson
Rte. #1, Box 19
Lake Linden, MI 49945
906-296-0691

Builder Information
Years in business: 10
Carpenters employed: 1
Shop capacity: Boats to 20'

Recent New Construction
14'6" and 16' wood-and-canvas canoes. Elmer Johnson design. 18 built 1978-'85.

Recent Repair Projects
16' lapstrake boats. Several repaired for Isle Royale rental service. 1984-'85.

MICHIGAN

LEELANAU BOAT REPAIR—Bob Pierce and Gretchen Sauvage
Box 111
Northport, MI 49670
616-386-7497

Builder Information
Years in business: 7
Carpenters employed: 2
Shop capacity: Boats to 35'
Willing to travel for on-the-site building projects.

Recent New Construction
12'6" plywood Yankee Tender skiff. WoodenBoat design. Current project.

Recent Repair Projects
16' Dispro (1953). Plank and stem repair.
10' Old Town dinghy (1935). Recanvased hull.
16' Herreshoff 12½ (1938). Restoration work.
62' N-class sloop. Assisted Chip Stulen in building new 80' spar.
11'6" Penguin class. Restoration work.
Chris-Craft runabout. Restoration work.

Yard Information
Services:
    Rigging
Storage:
    Number of boats stored per year: 10
    Percentage of wooden boats: 80
    Maximum size for hauling and storing:
        Length: 35'
        Draft: 5'
Maintenance:
    Number of boats maintained per year: 50
    Percentage of wooden boats: 20
    Owner maintenance allowed above and below rail.
Retail supplies:
    Will order on request.

MACKIE'S BOAT REPAIR—Alan Mackie
P.O. Box 219
Algonac, MI 48001
313-794-3261

Builder Information
Years in business: 13
Carpenters employed: 1
Shop capacity: Boats to 35'
Willing to travel for on-the-site building projects.

Recent New Construction
17' Whitehall. John Gardner design. Built 1980.

Recent Repair Projects
18-38' Chris-Craft cruisers and sea skiffs (1900-'65). Bottom planking, deck, and cabin renewal. Dry-rot repair as needed. Hull refinishing.
Chris-Craft, Greavette, Century, and other antique runabouts. Restoration work.

(continues)

MICHIGAN

(Mackie's Boat Repair, continued)
Yard Information
Services:
    Marina facilities
    Launching facilities
    Moorage
    Diesel and gas engine repair
Storage:
    Number of boats stored per year: 20
    Percentage of wooden boats: 50
    Maximum size for hauling and storing:
      Length: 45'
      Draft: 6'
Maintenance:
    Number of boats maintained per year: 25
    Percentage of wooden boats: 100

MARSHALL MARINE & WOODWORKING—Thomas F. Marshall
5599 Scenic Dr.
Sault Ste. Marie, MI 49783
906-635-9106

Builder Information
Years in business: 3
Carpenters employed: 2
Shop capacity: Boats to 25'
Willing to travel for on-the-site building projects.

Recent New Construction
7'2" skiff, Cabin Boy. John Atkin design. Built 1985.
13'6" wood-and-canvas kayak. T. Marshall design. Built 1983.

Recent Repair Projects
23' Sea Bird yawl (1932). Complete restoration. Renewed cockpit and
    canvas decks. Replaced spars, rigging, and rudder. Installed new engine and
    refitted interior. 1984–'85.
16' Chris-Craft Rocket (1947). Refastened and recaulked hull. Renewed upholstery
    and refinished boat. 1985.
16' Wayfarer-class dinghy (1966). Replaced trim, seats, boom, and floorboards.
    Refinished boat. 1985.
17' Dean canoe (1901). Complete restoration. Replaced several ribs and planks.
    Renewed stem, knees, decks, and gunwales. Refinished boat. 1985.
16' Old Town canoe (1922). Replaced seats, decks, and gunwales. Recanvased
    and repainted hull. 1985.

Yard Information
Services:
    Marina facilities (dockage on Lower St. Mary's River)
    Overland transport
    Limited moorage
    Engine repair
    Rigging
Maintenance:
    Number of boats maintained per year: 3
    Percentage of wooden boats: 100
    Owner maintenance allowed.

Retail supplies:
  Fastenings, paint, WEST System epoxy, varnishes, brushes, fittings, and rigging materials. Very limited inventory.

MAYEA BOAT WORKS—Larry Mayea
8679 Dixie Hwy.
Fair Haven, MI 48023
313-725-6111

Builder Information
Years in business: 76
Carpenters employed: 3
Shop capacity: Boats to 65'

Recent New Construction
31' twin-screw offshore cruiser. Mayea design. 400 built to date; currently builds approximately 1 new boat each year.

Recent Repair Projects
Chris-Crafts, Huckins, and others. Repair and refinishing.

Yard Information
Services:
  Launching facilities
  Engine repair
Storage:
  Number of boats stored per year: 118
  Percentage of wooden boats: 70
  Inside storage facilities
  Maximum size for hauling and storing:
    Length: 50'
    Tonnage: 40
Maintenance:
  Number of boats maintained per year: 200+
  Percentage of wooden boats: 90
Retail supplies:
  Bronze and stainless steel fastenings, varnish, and paints.

MENTHA WOODEN BOAT CO.—Marv King
12485 E.D. Ave.
Richland, MI 44083
616-629-4280

Builder Information
Years in business: 6
Carpenters employed: 2
Shop capacity: Boats to 30'
Willing to travel for on-the-site building projects.
(continues)

MICHIGAN

(Mentha Wooden Boat Co., continued)
Recent New Construction
21'8" single scull. Plywood construction. Steve Lewis and Marv King
 design. Built 1985.
18' single scull. Plywood construction. Ken Bassett and Marv King design.
 11 built 1983-'85.
17' lapstrake Rangeley Lake boat. Ellis design. Built 1984.
14' strip-planked Rangeley Lake boat. Steve Lewis and Marv King design. Built 1984.
14'6" solo canoe. Strip-plank construction. Marv King design. 15 built 1982-'85.

Recent Repair Projects
Chris-Crafts, Centurys, Lymans, Penn Yans, canoes, 210s, and other
 sailing boats. Repairwork ranges from refinishing boats to completing major
 structural repairs. Plank renewal, dry rot repairs, and more.

Yard Information
Services:
  Marina facilities
  Launching facilities
  Overland transport for boats built by company
  Gas engine repair
  Rigging
Storage:
  Number of boats stored per year: 150
  Percentage of wooden boats: 15
  Inside storage facilities
  Maximum size for hauling and storing:
   Length: 30'
   Draft: 10'
Maintenance:
  Number of boats maintained per year: 10
  Percentage of wooden boats: 100
  Owner maintenance allowed.
Retail supplies:
  Lumber, fastenings, hardware, cordage. Good inventory of supplies.

NOAH BOATWORKS/PLANECAT CATAMARANS—Richard Rogala
P.O. Box 717
Houghton, MI 49931
906-296-0451

Builder Information
Years in business: 15
Carpenters employed: 2-4
Shop capacity: Boats to 60'
Willing to travel for on-the-site building projects.

Recent New Construction
Boats designed by R. Rogala:
  16' planing catamaran sloop PLANECAT. Composite construction.
   1 built 1972, 1 in progress.
  29' planing catamaran sloop PLANECAT. Composite construction.
   Built 1982.
  11' and 15' dories for oar and sail. Plywood construction. 2 built 1980-'81.

MICHIGAN

Recent Repair Projects
26' ex-Navy whaleboat. Converted to sailing cutter. Sistered frames, renewed planks and floor timbers. Raised sheer 8" and replaced deck. 1974.
26' ex-Navy whaleboat. Converted to sailing fisherman. Built spars and pilothouse. 1983.

PATRICK'S LANDING—Bruce W. Patrick
Park Ave. Box 28, Rte. 1
Cedarville, MI 49719
906-484-3398

Builder Information
Years in business: 55
Carpenters employed: 1
Shop capacity: Boats to 26'

Recent New Construction
16' lapstrake rowing shell. Bruce W. Patrick design. Built 1985.
12' flat-bottomed skiff. Bruce W. Patrick design. Built 1985.
Inboard motor launches to 26'. Bruce W. Patrick design.

Recent Repair Projects
23' ferry boat. Complete rebuild—hull, cabin, deck. 1985.
15' lapstrake outboard. New transom, some new planking.
15' strip-planked outboard. New transom and some new planking.

Yard Information
Services:
　Gas engine repair
　Moorage
Storage:
　Number of boats stored per year: 40
　Percentage of wooden boats: 75
　Inside storage facilities
　Maximum size for hauling and storing:
　　Length: 26'
　　Draft: 3'
　　Tonnage: 5
Maintenance:
　Number of boats maintained per year: 50
　Percentage of wooden boats: 75

ST. CLAIR FLATS MARINA & SCRIPPS MARINE ENGINE
Peter Henkel Inc.
7650 S. Channel
Harsens Island, MI 48028
313-748-3600

Builder Information
Years in business: 13
Carpenters employed: 2
Shop capacity: Boats to 20'
(continues)

MICHIGAN

(St. Clair Flats Marina & Scripps Marine Engine, continued)
Recent New Construction
16′ and 19′ barrelback runabouts. Chris-Craft design. 2 built 1981 and 1984.

Recent Repair Projects
20′ Chris-Craft Sportsman (ca. 1955). Renewed plywood bottom and planked deck.
20′ Chris-Craft Custom (1947). Renewed forefoot and $1/3$ of bottom framing.
    Replaced bottom planking with cold-molded veneers.
16′ Chris-Craft runabout (1941). Renewed frames, planking, and decks.

Yard Information
Services:
    Marina facilities
    Launching facilities
    Overland transport
    Moorage
    Gas engine repair
Storage:
    Number of boats stored per year: 65
    Percentage of wooden boats: 60
    Inside storage facilities
    Maximum size for hauling and storing:
      Length: 30
      Tonnage: 4
Maintenance:
    Number of boats maintained per year: 65
    Percentage of wooden boats: 60
    Owner maintenance allowed.
Retail supplies:
    Paint, varnish, sealants, new and used custom hardware, engines.

SALT RIVER BOAT WORKS—Arthur E. Teutsch
48747 Salt River Dr.
New Baltimore, MI 48047
313-725-4450

Builder Information
Years in business: 25
Carpenters employed: 1
Shop capacity: New construction to 12′
Willing to travel for on-the-site building projects.

Recent New Construction
12′ DN 60 iceboats. Plywood-and-epoxy construction. Design sponsored by *Detroit News*.
    Approximately 6-10 boats built per year.

Recent Repair Projects
12-50′ power or sailing boats. Work has included mast and dry-rot repairs, interior rebuilding,
    laying vinyl decks, varnishing and refinishing hulls. 1980-'85.

Yard Information
Services:
    Gas engine repair
    Rigging

MICHIGAN

Maintenance:
   Number of boats maintained per year: 2-10
   Percentage of wooden boats: 90
   Owner maintenance allowed above and below rail.
Retail supplies:
   Hardware, masts, booms, and planking stock for DN iceboats.

TASSIER BOATWORKS—Marvin and Gary Tassier
Rte. #1, Box 5
Cedarville, MI 49719
906-484-2573

Builder Information
Years in business: 4, under present ownership
Carpenters employed: 2

Recent Repair Projects
22' Chris-Craft (1927). Replaced topside and deck planking as needed, refinished boat, and rechromed hardware. 1985.
Chris-Craft. Replaced 3 topside planks, refinished boat, and rechromed hardware. 1984-'85.
Chris-Craft (1935). Replaced stern planks. Refinished boat, rechromed hardware, and replaced upholstery. 1983.

Yard Information
Services:
   Marina facilities
   Launching facilities
   Moorage
   Engine repair
   Rigging
Storage:
   Number of boats stored per year: 190
   Percentage of wooden boats: 66
   Inside storage only
   Maximum size for hauling and storing:
      Length: 30'
Maintenance:
   Number of boats maintained per year: 190
   Percentage of wooden boats: 66
Retail supplies:
   Paint, hardware, rope, gas, oil, and supplies for motor tune-up and repair. Crusader and Chrysler engines.

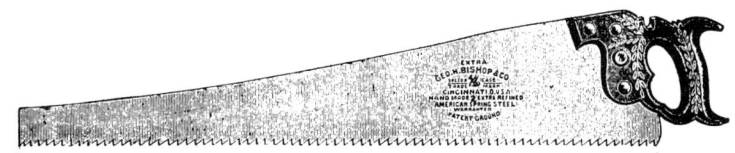

MICHIGAN

THUNDER BAY CANOES—J.W. Brown
2684 Lake Winyah Rd.
Alpena, MI 49707
517-354-8179

Builder Information
Years in business: 40
Carpenters employed: 3
Shop capacity: Boats to 18'

Recent New Construction
18' Tandem canoe. Cedar with fiberglass sheathing.
15' Trapper canoe. Cedar with fiberglass sheathing.

Yard Information
Maintenance:
    Number of boats maintained per year: 5-6
    Percentage of wooden boats: 100
    Owner maintenance allowed.

VAN DAM WOOD CRAFT—Stephen Van Dam
200 Franklin St.
Harbor Springs, MI 49740
616-526-6144

Builder Information
Years in business: 15
Carpenters employed: 3
Shop capacity: Boats to 80'

Recent New Construction
25' cold-molded sloop. Henry Scheel design. Built 1984-'85.
33' cold-molded ketch. Wycoff design. Built 1984.
36' cold-molded IOR sloop. Nelson/Morek design. Built 1983.
21' plywood recreational rowing shell. Ford design. 4 built 1985.

Recent Repair Projects
40' sloop. Restored strip-planked hull by cold-molded overlay and laid new teak decks. 1985.

Yard Information
Services:
    Overland transport

J.W. BELTMAN WOODWORKING—John Beltman
Box 406
Ely, MN 55731
218-365-5952

Builder Information
Years in business: 5
Carpenters employed: 1
Shop capacity: Boats to 40'
Willing to travel for on-the-site building projects.

Recent New Construction
14'8" ketch-rigged sailing canoe. Lapstrake construction. Based on design by R.H. Baker. Built 1985.
18' wood-and-canvas canoe. John Beltman design. Current project.

Recent Repair Projects
8-20' skiffs and wood-and-canvas canoes. Structural repairs including rib, plank, stem, rail, and deck replacements. Recanvasing and refinishing hull. Restores about 12 boats per year.

Yard Information
Services:
    Rigging
Retail supplies:
    Traditional paddles and oars.

BIGFORK CANOE TRAILS—Jack Minehart
Spring and Summer address:
RR #1
Max, MN 56659
218-798-2735
Fall and Winter address:
3016 Neola St.
Cedar Falls, IA 50613
319-266-8939

Builder Information
Years in business: 6
Carpenters employed: 1
Shop capacity: Boats to 37'
Willing to travel for on-the-site building projects.

Recent New Construction
16' and 18' Chippewa "long-nosed" racing canoes. Birchbark construction. Traditional design. 4 built 1984-'85.
26' Rabeska fur-trading-type canoe. Birchbark construction. Development of voyageur-type canoe. Built 1985.

Recent Repair Projects
12' Cree hunting canoe. Replaced ribs and planking. 1985.
15' old-style Algonquin canoe. Renewed gunwales, replaced bindings. 1985.
17' Old Town Traveler canoe. Replaced keel and outwales. 1985.

(continues)

MINNESOTA

(Bigfork Canoe Trails, continued)
Yard Information
Services:
    Launching facilities
    Overland transport
Storage:
    Number of boats stored per year: 4-5
    Percentage of wooden boats: 100
    Inside storage facilities
Retail supplies:
    Clear, straight-grained white cedar, split to order or in the log.

CEDAR BOAT WORKS—Archie Tobias
9225 Highway 2 East
Grand Rapids, MN 55744
218-326-3314

Builder Information
Years in business: 3
Carpenters employed: 2
Shop capacity: Boats to 18'

Recent New Construction
16-18' outboard fishermen. Strip-plank construction. Built 1984.
8-16' Whitehall-type skiffs. Strip-plank construction.

HAFEMAN BOAT WORKS—Ray Boessel, Jr.
RR #1, Box 187
Bigfork, MN 56628
218-743-3709

Builder Information
Years in business: 64
Carpenters employed: 1
Shop capacity: Boats to 37'
Willing to travel for on-the-site building projects.

Recent New Construction
16' and 17' birchbark canoes. Chippewa Indian and French voyageur models.
    14 built 1985.

LAURENTIAN BOATWORKS—Larry J. Ronning
N. Star 230-B
Two Harbors, MN 55616
218-834-3249

Builder Information
Years in business: 8
Carpenters employed: 1
Shop capacity: Boats to 20'
Willing to travel for on-the-site building projects.

MINNESOTA

Recent New Construction
12' lapstrake tender. Herreshoff design. Built 1981.
16' strip-planked Adirondack guideboat. Design by Grant and Durant. 4 built 1984 to present.
12'3" Yankee Tender skiff. Lapstrake construction. WoodenBoat design. Built 1985.

Recent Repair Projects
17' Lake Superior fishing boat. Sistered frames, renewed stem and knees. 1979.
16' outboard skiff. Replaced all frames, renewed transom and seats. Refastened hull. 1978.
14' Finnish lapstrake rowing boat. Replaced garboard planks and seats. Repaired checks in transom and stem, refinished hull. 1985.
12' lapstrake skiff. Refinished hull. 1985.

MARTIN'S—Ted Dullum
Box 540
Nisswa, MN 56468
218-963-2341

Builder Information
Years in business: 30
Carpenters employed: 1
Shop capacity: Boats to 21'

Recent Repair Projects
19' Chris-Craft. Replaced bottom and topside planks. Recanvased deck. 1984.
20' Chris-Craft. Refinished hull and overhauled engine. 1985.
Century, Gar Wood, and Chris-Crafts. Generally replanks about 6 boats each year.

Yard Information
Services:
    Marina facilities
    Launching facilities
    Moorage
    Gas engine repair
Storage:
    Number of boats stored per year: 200
    Percentage of wooden boats: 10
    Maximum size for hauling and storing:
      Length: 21'
      Tonnage: 2
Maintenance:
    Number of boats maintained per year: 300
    Percentage of wooden boats: 10
    Owner maintenance allowed.
Retail supplies available.

MINNESOTA

STEWART RIVER BOATWORKS—Alex Comb
Rte. #1, Box 203B
Two Harbors, MN 55616
218-834-5037

Builder Information
Years in business: 5
Carpenters employed: 1
Shop capacity: Boats to 30'
Willing to travel for on-the-site building projects.

Recent New Construction
13' lapstrake canoe. R.D. Culler design. 3 built 1982-'85.
15' lapstrake canoe. J.H. Rushton design. 2 built 1982.
16' flush-lap canoe. Peterborough design. 2 built 1983 and 1985.
17' wood-and-canvas canoe. Chestnut design. 10 built 1984 and 1985.
18' wood-and-canvas canoe. Chestnut design. Built 1985.

Repair Projects
Canoes, rowboats, and sailboats. All types of reconstruction.

MISSISSIPPI

WILLIAM HOLLAND, MASTER BOATBUILDER
100 Central Ave.
Biloxi, MS 39532
601-392-5314

Builder Information
Years in business: 30
Carpenters employed: 1
Shop capacity: Boats to 65'
Willing to travel for on-the-site building projects.

Recent New Construction
Designs by William Holland:
    20' catboats. 2 built 1984.
    40', 45', 50', and 54' Biloxi luggers. 8 built 1975–'85.

Yard Information
Services:
    Marina facilities
    Launching facilities
    Moorage
    Engine repair
    Rigging
Storage:
    Number of boats stored per year: 4
    Percentage of wooden boats: 100
    Owner maintenance allowed.

MISSOURI

NIANGUA BOAT AND CANOE CO.—Bill Pierce
Rte. #1, Box 69
Eldridge, MO 65463
417-426-5273

Builder Information
Years in business: 22
Carpenters employed: 1
Shop capacity: Boats to 65'
Willing to travel for on-the-site building projects.

Recent New Construction
20' sailing canoe. Bill Pierce design. 2 built 1984.

Recent Repair Projects
45' Chris-Craft Commander. Renewed transom and deck framing. Replanked bottom and replaced deck canvas. Refinished boat. 1985.
33' Chris-Craft Capitan sports sedan. Renewed transom and interior, rebuilt engine, and sheathed bottom in WEST System. 1985.

Yard Information
Services:
    Overland transport
    Engine repair
    Rigging
    Sailmaking

MORLEY CEDAR CANOES—Greg Morley
P.O. Box 147
Swan Lake, MT 59911
406-886-2242

Builder Information
Years in business: 13
Carpenters employed: 1
Shop capacity: Boats to 30'

Recent New Construction
Boats designed by Morley for strip-plank construction:
- 18' recreational rowing shell. Built 1985.
- 16' recreational rowing shell. 2 built 1985.
- 16' dory. Built 1985.
- 13' whitewater canoe. 2 built 1985.
- 14' solo canoe. Built 1985.
- 16', 17', and 18' canoes. 6 built 1985.
- 16' motor canoe. Built 1985.

Recent Repair Projects
Wood-and-canvas or strip-planked canoes. Restores approximately 4 boats per year.

SUNRISE DESIGNS—BOATBUILDING AND REPAIR
Joe Frechette
Tin Cup Creek Rd.
Darby, MT 59829
406-821-3846

Builder Information
Years in business: 2
Carpenters employed: 1
Shop capacity: Boats to 35'
Willing to travel for on-the-site building projects.

Recent New Construction
Boats of plywood and epoxy construction:
- 16' Windmill-class sloop. Built 1985.
- 12' McKenzie dory drift boats. Joe Frechette design. 4 built 1984-'85.
- 12' sharpie skiff. Sam Devlin design. Built 1985.

Other new construction:
- 22'6" recreational rowing shell. Plywood and cold-molded construction. Ken Bassett design. Built 1985.

Recent Repair Projects
Various daysailers. Work has included hull repair and refinishing.

NEVADA

THE DRYDOCK—Manual Mundschenk
3756 Gross Circle
Carson City, NV 89450
702-885-7040

Builder Information
Years in business: 45
Carpenters employed: 3
Shop capacity: Boats to 50′

Recent New Construction
26′ cold-molded speedboat. Phil Bolger design. Built 1985.

Recent Repair Projects
Antique and contemporary wooden boats. Repairwork has involved
   hull restorations, engine and wiring replacement, and seat upholstering.
   Approximately 15 boats repaired per year.

Yard Information
Services:
   Overland transport
   Diesel and gas engine repair
   Rigging
Storage:
   Number of boats stored per year: 30
   Percentage of wooden boats: 75
   Inside storage facilities
   Maximum size for hauling and storing:
      Length: 35′
      Draft: 6′
      Tonnage: 5-6
Maintenance:
   Number of boats maintained per year: 50
   Percentage of wooden boats: 75
Retail supplies:
   Paint, varnish, and fastenings. Full line of supplies for
   wooden boat construction and repair.

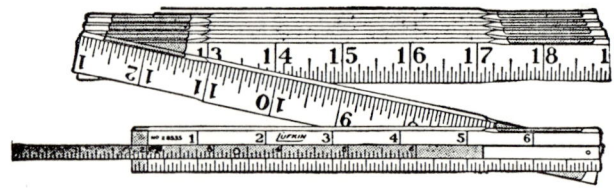

NEW HAMPSHIRE

GEOFFREY BURKE, BOATBUILDER
Box 212
Chocorua, NH 03817
603-323-8702

Builder Information
Years in business: 4
Carpenters employed: 1
Shop capacity: Boats to 20'
Might consider traveling for on-the-site building projects.

Recent New Construction
15' lapstrake, ketch-rigged double-paddle canoe. Walt Simmons design. Built 1982.
13', 15', and 17' lapstrake double-paddle canoes. Walt Simmons design. 7 built 1982-'85.

Recent Repair Projects
14' Rangeley-type wood-and-canvas pulling boat. Replaced keel and floorboard.
15' wood-and-canvas canoe. Replaced keel, repaired canvas.
15' lapstrake canoe. Repaired planking.

Yard Information
Retail supplies:
    White cedar, custom-made single and double paddles, oars.

CUSTOM BOATS—Edward D. (Ned) McIntosh
192 Silver St.
Dover, NH 03820
603-742-1985

Builder Information
Years in business: 60
Carpenters employed: 1
Shop capacity: Boats to 25'

New Construction
13'6" plywood catboat Merry Mac. E.D. McIntosh design. 190 built 1953-'84.
17'6" plywood sloop. E.D. McIntosh design. 16 built between 1960 and 1968.
9' wood-and-canvas dinghy for oar and sail. E.D. McIntosh design. 100 built between 1945 and 1984.

JEFFREY R. FOGMAN YACHT BUILDER, INC.—Jeff Fogman
Swain Rd.
Barrington, NH 03825
603-664-9752

Builder Information
Years in business: 14
Carpenters employed: 2-3
Shop capacity: Boats to 60'
Willing to travel for on-the-site building projects.

Recent New Construction
49'11" schooner. L.F. Herreshoff design. Launched June 1985.
40' schooner. David C. McIntosh design. Current project.

NEW HAMPSHIRE

GALLANT CUSTOM YACHTS—Peter Gallant
80 Winnicut Rd.
Stratham, NH 03885
603-772-2847

Builder Information
Years in business: 4
Carpenters employed: 1
Shop capacity: Boats to 55'
Willing to travel for on-the-site building projects.

Recent New Construction
28' H-28 ketch. L.F. Herreshoff design. Built 1984.

Recent Repair Projects
30' Harvey Gamage motorsailer. Replaced cockpit. 1983.
39' Concordia yawl. Replacing floors and deck sheathing. Repairing rudder, refinishing hull. Current project.
40' Nevins yawl. Renewing centerboard and copper flashing. Resheathing cabintop. Current project.

HARPER'S BOAT RESTORATION—Jerry W. Harper, Sr.
RFD 2, Rte. 3
Meredith, NH 03253
603-279-8841

Builder Information
Years in business: 15
Carpenters employed: 1
Shop capacity: Boats to 40'

Recent Repair Projects
35' Hacker runabout (1926). Replaced ¾ of the keel and bottom. New transom, deck, seats, and engine bed. Completely refinished.
33' Hacker runabout (1925). Complete restoration, new upholstery.
26' Hacker. Replaced windshield, dash, and wooden steering wheel. Replaced section of deck. Completely refinished and reupholstered.
Have rebuilt a number of classic runabouts and speedboats. Designs by Chris-Craft, Hacker, Gar Wood, Shepherd, Dodge, Century, and Dart dating from 1917 to 1965.

Yard Information
Services:
 Overland transport
 Gas engine repair
Storage:
 Number of boats stored per year: 50
 Percentage of wooden boats: 75
 Maximum size for hauling and storing:
  Length: 40'
Maintenance:
 Number of boats maintained per year: 30
 Percentage of wooden boats: 80

NEW HAMPSHIRE

IRWIN MARINE—Jack Irwin
Box 6145, Union Ave.
Laconia, NH 03246
603-524-6661

Builder Information
Years in business: 69
Carpenters employed: 5
Shop capacity: Boats to 46'

Recent Repair Projects
Total repair and restoration services available for Chris-Crafts, Gar Woods, Hacker Crafts, Penn Yans, Centurys, Rivas.

Yard Information
Services:
 Marina facilities
 Launching facilities
 Overland transport within 100 miles
 Moorage: 136 slips
 Gas engine repair
 Rigging
Storage:
 Number of boats stored per year: 600
 Percentage of wooden boats: 30
 Inside storage facilities: Wet and dry
 Maximum size for hauling and storing:
  Length: 46'
  Draft: No restriction
  Tonnage: 25
Maintenance:
 Number of boats maintained per year: 800
 Percentage of wooden boats: 30
Retail supplies:
 Ship's store—complete inventory.

PHILIP A. KENDALL
Middle Rd.
North Sandwich, NH 03259
603-284-7058

Builder Information
Years in business: 38
Carpenters employed: 1
Shop capacity: Boats to 45'

Recent New Construction
14' Whitehall. Current project.

Recent Repair Projects
23' Chris-Craft Continental. Replaced transom and refinished. 1982.
22' outboard-powered gillnetter. Renewed starboard side, pilothouse, and keel. 1983.
23' Cruisers Inc. Installed new windshield, rewired, and refinished. 1983.
17' Penn Yan. Replaced keel. 1983.
34' Post power cruiser. Replaced keel, bottom planking, and cabinsides. 1984-'85.

NEW HAMPSHIRE

KEVIN MARTIN
4 Windsor Lane
Epping, NH 03042
603-679-5153

Builder Information
Years in business: 5
Carpenters employed: 1
Shop capacity: Boats to 20'
Willing to travel for on-the-site building.

Recent New Construction
14'3" Rushton Princess sailing canoe. Built 1983.
13' Rob Roy canoe for sail and paddle. McGregor design. 2 built 1985.
16' Adirondack guideboat. Grant design. Built 1984.
10½' Rushton WEE LASSIE lightweight solo canoe. Built 1985.
12' Rushton solo canoe. Built 1985.

Recent Repair Projects
13-18' wood-and-canvas canoes. Repaired frames, planks, and gunwales, recanvased hull. 1985.
12' Penn Yan (car-topper). Renewed frames and rails, repaired transom. Recanvased hull and refinished boat. 1985.
17' Rangeley rowboat. Replaced frames, stem, outer keel, some planks. Refinished boat. 1985.

Yard Information
Retail supplies:
  Materials for canoe repair. Canvas, filler, tacks, some lumber.

NEW ENGLAND BOAT & MOTOR, INC.—Mark Mason
28 Center St., P.O. Box 1283
Laconia, NH 03247
603-528-3411

Builder Information
Years in business: 6
Carpenters employed: 2
Shop capacity: Boats to 40'

Recent New Construction
27'6" replica of MISS COLUMBIA (1924 Gold Cup Race contestant). George Crouch design. Current project.

Recent Repair Projects
33' Gar Wood speedboat (1931). Complete restoration. Replaced bottom, keel, frames, chines, and transom. Refastened planking, refinished and reupholstered. Repowered with a 1927 Curtiss Aero Plane V-12 engine. 1985.

Yard Information
Services:
  Overland transport
  Gas engine repair
Storage:
  Number of boats stored per year: 45 antique speedboats and launches
  Percentage of wooden boats: 100
  Inside storage facilities
  Maximum size for hauling and storing:
    Length: 40'

NEW HAMPSHIRE

Maintenance:
  Number of boats maintained per year: 75-100
  Percentage of wooden boats: 100
Retail supplies:
  Materials for antique classic boats. Wood, fastenings, paint, varnish, engine parts, instruments, hardware, leather.

SWIFT CUSTOM BOATS—Gordon Swift
RFD #2
Exeter, NH 03833
603-772-5557

Builder Information
Years in business: 35
Carpenters employed: 1
Shop capacity: Boats to 40'

Recent New Construction
34' ketch. Winthrop Warner design. Built 1978.
34' cutter. Winthrop Warner design. Built 1980.
34' cutter. David C. McIntosh design. Built 1982.
33' cutter. Joel White design. Built 1983.
35' cutter. Joel White design. Built 1985.
32' lobsterboat type. Joel White design. Current project.

WOLFEBORO RESTORATION CENTER—Donald A. Benjamin
P.O. Box 1794, Lehner St.
Wolfeboro, NH 03894
603-569-1869

Builder Information
Years in business: 8
Carpenters employed: 1
Shop capacity: Boats to 24'

Recent Repair Projects
19' Pembroke runabout. Replaced transom and reinforced with additional knees. Sistered 5 ribs and added 6 intermediate ribs. 1985.
26' Lyman lapstrake inboard. Completely stripped and refinished. 1985.
17' Correct Craft inboard speedboat. Refastened bottom, repaired keel. 1985.
18' Old Town canoe (1920). Replaced planks and keel. Recanvased and refinished. 1985.
18' canoe (1915). Rebuilt gunwales, repaired and reinforced stems. Replaced and recanvased mahogany deck, refinished entire boat. 1985.
16-18' wood-and-canvas canoes. Refinishing, recanvasing, and repairs. 1985-'86.
24' Chris-Craft. Varnish work. 1985-'86.
22' Chris-Craft. Refastening bottom. 1985-'86.
22' Shepard. Refinishing brightwork. 1985-'86.
17' Correct Craft. Varnish work. 1985-'86.
14' Penn Yan. Recanvasing and refinishing. 1985-'86.

Yard Information
Services:
  Overland transport
(continues)

NEW HAMPSHIRE

(Wolfeboro Restoration Center, continued)
Storage:
  Number of boats stored per year: 17
  Percentage of wooden boats: 100
  Inside storage facilities
Maintenance:
  Number of boats maintained per year: 8-10
  Percentage of wooden boats: 100
  Owner maintenance allowed above and below rail.

THE WOODEN BOAT SHOP—Ivan Phelps
P.O. Box 400
Melvin Village, NH 03850
603-544-7330

Builder Information
Years in business: 15
Carpenters employed: 1
Shop capacity: Boats to 38'
Willing to travel for on-the-site building projects.

Recent Repair Projects
38' Chris-Craft commuter (1930). Completely restored hull and interior. Replaced hardware and installed new engine. 1984-'85.

Yard Information
Services:
  Launching facilities
  Overland transport
  Engine repair
Storage:
  Inside storage facilities for boats undergoing restoration.
  Maximum size for hauling and storing:
    Length: 30'
Maintenance:
  Offered for antique and classic wooden boats.

ZEBCRAFT—Harvard Forden
87 Gold St.
Lakeport, NH 03246
603-524-7189

Builder Information
Years in business: 10
Carpenters employed: 2
Shop capacity: Boats 30-35'

Recent New Construction
23' stepped hydroplane. Cold-molded construction. Heavily modified Elliot Gardner design.

Yard Information
Services:
  Launching facilities
  Gas engine repair

NEW HAMPSHIRE

Storage:
    Number of boats stored per year: 15
    Percentage of wooden boats: 100
    Inside storage facilities
    Maximum size for hauling and storing:
        Length: 30′
Maintenance:
    Number of boats maintained per year: Varies
    Percentage of wooden boats: 100

NEW JERSEY

BARNEGAT BAY BOATWORKS—Glenn Schroeder
362 W. 4th St.
Ship Bottom, NJ 08008
609-494-5814

Builder Information
Years in business: 6
Carpenters employed: 1
Shop capacity: Boats to 25'
Willing to travel for on-the-site building projects.

Recent New Construction
17'2" sailing garvey. Lines by H.I. Chapelle. Current project.
12'8" Catspaw dinghy. Lapstrake construction. Design by N.G. Herreshoff and Joel White. Built 1984.
10'6" lapstrake canoe. Wee Lassie design by J.H. Rushton. Current project.

Recent Repair Projects
18' Barnegat Bay catboat. Renewed frames, floors, inner hull, seats, and some planking. Replaced deck canvas, recaulked and refinished hull. Scarfed mast. 1983-'85.
12' Barnegat Bay racing sneakbox. Renewed frames, deck and deck frame, floorboards, and cockpit coaming. Replaced kingplank, maststep, and toerails. Refastened, recaulked, and refinished hull. 1984-'85.
25' Wianno Sr.-class sloop. Total restoration. Current project.
28' Barnegat Bay catboat KITTY (1875). Complete rebuild to start in 1986.

Yard Information
Services:
   Rigging repair

BARNEGAT BAY SNEAKBOXES—William (Bill) Kelly
5 Silver Lake Dr.
West Creek, NJ 08092
609-296-3389

Builder Information
Years in business: 20
Carpenters employed: 1
Shop capacity: Boats to 18'
Willing to travel for on-the-site building projects.

Recent New Construction
12' sailing sneakbox. Bill Kelly design. 2 built 1985.
18' Barnegat Bay power garveys, skiffs, and runabouts. Bill Kelly designs.
12-14' sneakboxes, rowing boats, and garveys. Bill Kelly designs. 3 built 1985.

Recent Repair Projects
16-18' Barnegat Bay garveys. Renewed stern boards, planking, and fiberglass sheathing. Replaced deck frames, rubrails, and coamings. Renewed skegs, keelsons, shaftlogs, struts, and rudders. 1984-'85.
12' Barnegat Bay sneakboxes. Renewed frames, planking, fiberglass sheathing, and trim. Replaced maststeps, centerboard trunks, rudders, oarlocks. Rebuilt transoms to accommodate outboard engines. 1984-'85.

Yard Information
Services:
   Overland transport
   Engine repair

NEW JERSEY

Storage:
    Number of boats stored per year: 8-10
    Percentage of wooden boats: 50
    Maximum size for hauling and storing:
        Length: 18'
        Draft: 2'
        Tonnage: 2
Maintenance:
    Number of boats maintained per year: 20-30
    Percentage of wooden boats: 90
    Owner maintenance allowed above and below rail.

CHARLES HANKINS, BOATBUILDERS
Lavallette, NJ 08735
201-793-7443

Builder Information
Years in business: 75
Carpenters employed: 1-3
Shop capacity: Boats to 40'

Recent New Construction
16' and 18' Jersey Sea Bright-design surfboats for oar and sail. Lapstrake construction.
    Charles Hankins design.
22-40' powerboats. Lapstrake construction.
Approximately 4,000 boats built to date.

Repair Projects
Jersey Sea Bright surfboats. Planking, framing, and other repairs.

Yard Information
Retail supplies:
    Materials for wooden boat construction and repair.

ERIC KINDERVATER
P.O. Box 2, North St.
West Creek, NJ 08092

Builder Information
Years in business: 30
Carpenters employed: 1 + seasonal helpers
Shop capacity: New construction to 34'
Willing to travel for on-the-site building projects.

Recent New Construction
18-28' garveys. Plywood construction with fiberglass sheathing. 14 built to date,
    2 under construction.
12' sneakboxes. Cedar planking over oak frames. 2 built to date.
(continues)

(Eric Kindervater, continued)
Recent Repair Projects
33' Chris-Craft double-cabin cruiser (1939). Renewed aft cabin and deck, sistered frames and replaced 3 planks. 1985.
46' Egg Harbor sportfisherman (1974). Renewed cockpit decking and supports, installed saloon bulkhead. 1985.
50' bugeye ketch (1921). Replaced centerboard and trunk. Renewed planking, framing and cabin, covered decks with plywood and fiberglass. 1985.
48' Starling Burgess cruising ketch (1927). Renewed mainmast, rigging, and maststep. Replaced stern section, cockpit, and coaming. 1985.

Yard Information
Services:
    Overland transport
    Diesel and gas engine repair
    Rigging
Storage:
    Number of boats stored per year: 15-20
    Percentage of wooden boats: 100
    Maximum size for hauling and storing:
        Length: 32'
Maintenance:
    Number of boats maintained per year: Varies
    Percentage of wooden boats: 100

NAU'S BOAT WORKS—Warren Nau
Highway 35
South Amboy, NJ 08879
201-721-0116

Builder Information
Years in business: 55
Carpenters employed: 1
Shop capacity: Boats to 20'

Recent New Construction
17'6" lifeguard dories for oar and sail. Lapstrake construction. Warren Nau design. 8 built 1984-'85.

OLSEN'S BOAT WORKS—John Olsen
73 East Front St.
Keyport, NJ 07735
201-264-4198

Builder Information
Years in business: 38
Carpenters employed: 2
Shop capacity: Boats to 42'

Recent New Construction
Boats designed by Olsen:
    32' sportfisherman. Built 1984.
    22' and 24' power skiffs. 2 built 1985.

Other new construction:
   31'6" cold-molded sloop. Tom Wylie design. Built 1983.
   12' strip-planked Barnegat Bay sneakbox. 2 built 1985-'86.

Recent Repair Projects
16' Chris-Craft runabout (1936). Renewed bottom planking, decks, and upholstery. Refinished topsides. 1983.

Yard Information
Services:
   Launching facilities
   Moorage
Storage:
   Number of boats stored per year: 140
   Percentage of wooden boats: 20
   Maximum size for hauling and storing:
      Length: 30'
      Draft: 5'
      Tonnage: 2
Maintenance:
   Number of boats maintained per year: 10
   Percentage of wooden boats: 100
   Owner maintenance allowed above and below rail.
Retail supplies:
   Paint, fastenings, wood.

HANS PEDERSEN & SONS, INC.—Wade Pedersen
165 West Front St.
Keyport, NJ 07735
201-264-0971

Builder Information
Years in business: 50
Carpenters employed: 2
Shop capacity: Boats to 50'

Recent New Construction
26' lapstrake powerboat. I. Pedersen design. Built 1985.

Recent Repair Projects
26' Mihm lapstrake power skiff (1955). Completely restored boat for local yacht club.
16' Cape Cod catboat (1937). Completely restored boat.

Yard Information
Services:
   Marina facilities
   Launching facilities
   Overland transport
   Diesel and gas engine repair
Storage:
   Number of boats stored per year: 200
   Percentage of wooden boats: 60
   Maximum size for hauling and storing:
      Length: 50'
      Draft: 6'
      Tonnage: 30
(continues)

NEW JERSEY

(Hans Pedersen & Sons, Inc., continued)
Maintenance:
  Number of boats maintained per year: 75
  Percentage of wooden boats: 60
  Owner maintenance allowed above and below rail.
Retail supplies:
  Complete line of supplies.

PERLOWSKI BROS. BOATWORKS—Walter Perlowski
671 Meyersville Rd.
Gillette, NJ 07933
201-647-2237

Builder Information
Years in business: 3
Carpenters employed: 1
Shop capacity: Boats to 19'

Recent New Construction
14'8" strip-planked canoe. W. Perlowski design. 3 built 1984.
18'3" strip-planked canoe. W. Perlowski design. Built 1985.
15' strip-planked canoe. W. Perlowski design. Current project.

NEWTON S. STERLING PRODUCTS—Newton S. Sterling
Bates Lane
Port Republic, NJ 08241
609-652-1950

Builder Information
Years in business: 18
Carpenters employed: 1
Shop capacity: New construction to 30'
Willing to travel for on-the-site building projects.

Recent New Construction
14'6" power garvey. Newton Sterling design. Built 1985.
14' power sneakbox. Strip-plank construction. Newton Sterling design. Built 1983.

Recent Repair Projects
32' classic speedboat. Totally rebuilding. Current project.
70' commercial fishing boat. General maintenance work. Current project.
Pleasure craft, sportfishermans, and commercial fishing boats. Repairs have included plank, frame, and deck renewal, bottom refastening, hull refinishing, and interior cabinetwork.

Yard Information (as sub-contracted through local yard)
Services:
  Marina facilities
  Launching facilities
  Overland transport
  Diesel and gas engine repair

NEW JERSEY

Storage:
    Number of boats stored per year: 100
    Percentage of wooden boats: 50
    Inside storage facilities
    Maximum size for hauling and storing:
      Length: 45'
      Beam: 13'6"
Maintenance:
    Number of boats maintained per year: Varies
    Percentage of wooden boats: 50
    Owner maintenance allowed above and below rail.
Retail supplies:
    Complete line of supplies.

WAYNE'S MARINE INC.—Wayne A. Mocksfield
Henderson Cove
Lake Hopatcong, NJ 07849
201-663-3214

Builder Information
Years in business: 13
Carpenters employed: 2
Shop capacity: Boats to 30'

Recent Repair Projects
16-30' runabouts (1930s to 1950s). Chris-Crafts, Gar Woods, and Fay & Bowens. Minor repairs to complete restorations. Work has included keel, chine, frame, plank, and deck renewals, hull refinishing, and seat upholstering.

Yard Information
Services:
    Marina facilities
    Launching facilities
    Dockage
    Gas engine repair
Storage:
    Number of boats stored per year: 200
    Percentage of wooden boats: 50
    Inside storage facilities
    Maximum size for hauling and storing:
      Length: 30'
      Draft: 3'
      Tonnage: 2½
Maintenance:
    Number of boats maintained per year: 200
    Percentage of wooden boats: 50
Retail supplies:
    Complete line of marine supplies. Hardware, paint, waterskiing equipment, life jackets.

NEW YORK

THE ADIRONDACK GUIDE BOAT SHOP—John B. Spring
Thomas Edison Rd.
Blue Mountain Lake, NY 12812
518-352-7667

Builder Information
Years in business: 6
Carpenters employed: 2
Shop capacity: Boats to 20'

Recent Repair Projects
Adirondack guideboats, wood-and-canvas canoes, and lapstrake skiffs (Rushton, St. Lawrence, Peterborough). Complete restorations involving plank and frame renewal and refinishing of hulls. Approximately 240 boats restored since 1979.

ALDER CREEK BOAT WORKS—Michael R. Hanna
RD #3, Inkawich Rd.
Remsen, NY 13438
315-831-5321

Builder Information
Years in business: 12
Carpenters employed: 1
Shop capacity: Boats to 20'

Recent New Construction
16' canoe. Peterborough design. 4 built 1985.
13'10" canoe. Peterborough design. Built 1985.
16' wood-and-canvas canoe. Peterborough design. Built 1985.
16' wood-and-canvas double-ended rowing boat. Built 1985.

Recent Repair Projects
16' Rushton guideboat (c. 1890). Replaced cutwater and planking as needed. Refinished hull. 1985.
14' Peterborough outboard Aquaflyer (1949). Replaced transom and rails, refinished hull.
12' outboard cartopper. Completely restored. Renewed transom and planking.
15' and 16' wood-and-canvas canoes. Completely restored.

Yard Information
Services:
  Gas engine repair
Storage:
  Number of boats stored per year: 6
  Percentage of wooden boats: 100
  Maximum size for hauling and storing:
    Length: 22'
    Draft: 18"
    Tonnage: 2½
Retail supplies:
  Bronze, brass, and stainless steel fastenings. Wood and milled lumber, most marine accessories.

NEW YORK

BEDELL MARINE CARPENTRY—Chester S. Bedell
1 Dove Lane
Southtown, Long Island, NY 11787
516-979-9096

Builder Information
Years in business: 3
Carpenters employed: 2
Willing to travel for on-the-site building projects.

Recent Repair Projects
20′ sailing boat (1965). Renewed 15 frames, 3 planks. Repaired leaking centerboard trunk. 1985.
25′ Chris-Craft skiff (1957). Refastened bottom and replaced railcap. 1985.
42′ Pacemaker cabin cruiser (1954). Recaulked bottom and replaced rubrails. 1985.
39′ Ulrichsen cabin cruiser (1957). Replaced plank and windshield. 1985.
33′ Egg Harbor 33 cabin cruiser. Renewed 27 frames, 2 planks, and splash rail. 1985.
32′ Broadwater express cruiser (1958). Replaced transom and frames, recaulked bow area. 1985.
32′ Pacemaker express cruiser (1968). Renewed 42 frames, 3 planks, and refastened bottom. 1985.
35′ Richardson cabin cruiser (1965). Renewed 12 frames and 2 planks. 1985.
38′ Viking cabin cruiser (1967). Renewed 18 frames and 2 planks. 1985.
36′ Pacemaker express cruiser (1969). Renewed starboard side of cabin, repaired deck. 1985.
36′ Owens cabin cruiser (1957). Replaced planks and outer chine. 1985.

BLACK BOTTOM RUNABOUTS, INC.—Patrick Carney
P.O. Box 1552
Rocky Point, NY 11778
516-744-8844

Builder Information
Years in business: 6
Carpenters employed: 2
Shop capacity: Boats 16-21′

Recent New Construction
16′ mahogany runabouts. Batten-seam construction, replica of 1939 Gar Wood.
10′ lapstrake tender. Lawley design. 1 built to date.
18′ Kootenay stem canoe. Strip-planked construction. 1 built to date.

WALTER L. BRIGHAM
12 & 26 Winthrop Rd.
Shelter Island Heights, NY 11965
516-749-0465

Builder Information
Years in business: 50
Carpenters employed: 1
Shop capacity: Boats to 24′

Recent New Construction
13′6″ Wood Pussy-class catboat. Strip-planked. Philip Rhodes design. 5 built 1968-'70.
12′ strip-planked yacht tender. Replica of 70-year-old round-bottomed rowboat. Built 1982.
(continues)

(Walter L. Brigham, continued)

Recent Repair Projects
16′ Herreshoff 12½-class sloop. Renewed frames and refinished hull. 1984–'85.

Yard Information
Services:
  Overland transport
  Rigging
Storage:
  Number of boats stored per year: 5
  Percentage of wooden boats: 50
  Inside storage facilities
  Maximum size for hauling and storing:
    Length: 18′
Maintenance:
  Number of boats maintained per year: 15
  Percentage of wooden boats: 30
  Owner maintenance allowed above and below rail.
Retail supplies:
  Paint, fastenings, hardware.

CARTER BOAT BUILDING CO.—Spencer Jenkins
Star Rte. 2
Tupper Lake, NY 12986
518-359-2498

Builder Information
Years in business: 1
Carpenters employed: 9
Shop capacity: Boats to 40′

Recent New Construction
18′6″ Buzzards Bay sloop. L.F. Herreshoff design. Built 1984.
22′ high-speed inboards for racing or waterskiing. Spencer Jenkins design. 19 built 1985.
16′ wood-and-canvas Indian Girl canoe. J.H. Rushton design. 3 built 1984.
14′ Whitehall tender. Lines by John Gardner. Built 1983.

Recent Repair Projects
16′ guideboat. Repaired planks and replaced ribs. 1983.
16′ Rushton canoe. Renewed ribs, planking, recaulked and refinished hull. 1983.
18′ Hampton One-Design sloop. Repaired planking, recaulked and refinished hull. 1983.
18′ Chris-Craft runabout. Total restoration. Rebuilt engine, refinished hull. Rechromed hardware and reupholstered. 1984.

Yard Information
Services:
  Launching facilities
Maintenance:
  Number of boats maintained per year: 5
  Percentage of wooden boats: 100
Retail supplies:
  WEST System products.

NEW YORK

H. CHALK & SON, INC.—Duane J. Chalk
Box 35
Fishers Landing, NY 13641
315-686-5622

Builder Information
Years in business: 40
Carpenters employed: 2
Shop capacity: Boats to 26′

Recent Repair Projects
22′, 24′, and 26′ Hutchinson utility runabouts ('30s and '40s vintage). Refinished boats.
40′ Herreshoff launch CORSAIR. Renewed engine, hull bottom, and brightwork.
28′ Couch runabout ROSILAND (1916). Renewed hull bottom, refinished boat.
23′ Fitzgerald & Lee triple-cockpit runabout (1935). Refinished boat.
26′ Hacker triple-cockpit runabout (1945). Refinished boat.
20′ Lyman runabout (1959). Refinished boat.
24′ Century runabout (1964). Refinished boat.
23′ Rushton pulling boat. Refinishing boat. Current project.

Yard Information
Services:
    Marina facilities
    Launching facilities
    Overland transport
    Moorage
    Gas engine repair
Storage:
    Number of boats stored per year: 350–400
    Percentage of wooden boats: 10
    Inside storage facilities
    Maximum size for hauling and storing:
      Length: 24′
      Tonnage: $2\frac{1}{2}$
Maintenance:
    Number of boats maintained per year: 600
    Percentage of wooden boats: 15
    Owner maintenance allowed above and below rail.
Retail supplies:
    Lumber and paint. Full line of marine supplies.

COECLES HARBOR MARINA & BOATYARD, INC.
—Peter Needham & Family
Shelter Island, NY 11964
516-749-0700

Builder Information
Years in business: 15
Carpenters employed: 4–6
Shop capacity: New construction to 45′
Willing to travel for on-the-site building projects.

Recent New Construction
40′ cruising yawl. Composite construction. Tripp design. Current project.
21′ launch. Nelson Zimmer design. Built 1984.
(continues)

NEW YORK

(Coecles Harbor Marina & Boatyard, Inc., continued)

Recent Repair Projects
47′ oyster sloop (1875). Replaced frames and floor timbers. 1975-'82.
36′ Nielsen sloop. Renewed trim, toerails, cockpit seats, and coaming. Replaced engine, boom, and spinnaker poles. Renewed deck sheathing. 1982-'84.
36′6″ Baltzer Voyager cabin cruiser. Renewed deck sheathing, cabin sides, and trunk cornerposts. 1979-'84.
75′ commercial ferry boat. Designed and built pilothouse interior. 1985.
36′ Hinckley yawl. Replaced garboard planks. Renewed mizzenmast and spreaders. 1985.
45′ Friendship sloop. Renewed rudderpost, cockpit seats, and coaming. Replaced planks and recaulked hull.
37′ Richie Maine Picnic boat. Designed and built flying bridge. Replaced cockpit floor, modified interior, and installed new cabinets. 1980-'84.

Yard Information
Services:
    Marina facilities
    Launching facilities
    Moorage
    Diesel and gas engine repair
    Rigging
Storage:
    Number of boats stored per year: 130
    Percentage of wooden boats: 20
    Inside storage facilities
    Maximum size for hauling and storing:
        Length: 50′
        Draft: 6′6″
        Tonnage: 30
Maintenance:
    Number of boats maintained per year: 500
    Percentage of wooden boats: 25
    Owner maintenance allowed above rail.
Retail supplies:
    Complete line of marine supplies. Lumber, fastenings, paints, epoxy. Evinrude motors and outboard motor parts.

CUSTOM CANOES—Gerald Borland
RD #1 West St. Rd., Box 216
Carthage, NY 13619
315-493-1964

Builder Information
Years in business: 10
Carpenters employed: 1
Shop capacity: Boats to 20′

Recent New Construction
Boats of strip-plank construction:
    16′ canoe. 67 built 1975-'85.
    16′ Adirondack guideboat. 13 built 1978-'85.

Recent Repair Projects
16-18′ wood-and-canvas canoes and cedar canoes. Structural repairs and recanvasing of hulls.

NEW YORK

CUSTOM WOOD SERVICES—Barry K. Foster
RD 1, Box 398
Chenango Forks, NY 13746
607-648-3196

Builder Information
Years in business: 4
Carpenters employed: 1
Shop capacity: Boats to 16'
Willing to travel for on-the-site building projects.

Repair Work
Complete rebuilding of antique wood-and-canvas canoes, some dating back to 1920.

THE EVERETT BOAT WORKS—F. Everett Smith
RFD 2, Box 321, Boyden Rd.
Canton, NY 13617
315-386-2817

Builder Information
Years in business: 12
Carpenters employed: 2
Shop capacity: Boats to 30'
Willing to travel for on-the-site building projects.

Recent New Construction
20' electric-powered fantail launch. F.E. Smith design. Current project.
16' Adirondack guideboat. Lapstrake construction. Cole design. Built 1985.
15'6" sailing canoe TWILIGHT. Lapstrake construction. J.H. Rushton VESPER design. Built 1975.

Recent Repair Projects
14' Rushton Ugo canoe. Replaced planking and ribs, caned seats, and refinished hull. 1985.
16' Cole guideboat. Replaced planking and ribs, installed new decks and seat. Refinished hull. 1985.
15' Rushton Indian Girl canoe. Recanvased and refinished hull. 1985.
26', 1922 Gold Cup raceboat SCOTTY TOO. Replaced gussets and engine bed. Renewed double-diagonal bottom planking and some topside planking. Installed new engine. 1983.

Yard Information
Services:
    Overland transport
    Gas engine repair

NEW YORK

DOUGLAS FOWLER SAILMAKER—Douglas Fowler
1182 East Shore Dr.
Ithaca, NY 14850
607-277-0041

Builder Information
Years in business: 8
Carpenters employed: 1
Shop capacity: Boats to 20'

Recent Repair Projects
18' decked sailing canoe (1905). Restored boat.
15' decked sailing canoe. (1893). Restored boat.

Yard Information
Services:
    Sailmaking
Retail supplies:
    Sailcloth and canvas.

THE GAR WOOD BOAT CO.—Thomas R. Turcotte
129 Columbia St.
Cohoes, NY 12047
518-235-9041

Builder Information
Years in business: 2
Carpenters employed: 3
Shop capacity: Boats to 33'

Recent Repair Projects
Runabouts and utility cruisers (1900-'50 vintage). Gar Wood boats are a specialty. Have restored several boats to date.

Yard Information
Services:
    Launching facilities
    Overland transport
    Gas engine repair
Storage:
    Number of boats stored per year: 25
    Percentage of wooden boats: 100
    Inside storage facilities
    Maximum size for hauling and storing:
        Length: 35'
        Draft: 2'6"
Maintenance:
    Number of boats maintained per year: 25
    Percentage of wooden boats: 100

NEW YORK

HALL'S BOAT CORPORATION—Mary D. Hall
Box 312
Lake George, NY 12845
518-668-5437

Builder Information
Years in business: 57
Carpenters employed: 3

Recent Repair Projects
Chris-Crafts, Gar Woods, and other antique powerboats. Minor repairs to complete restorations. Approximately 50 boats repaired a year.

Yard Information
Services:
- Marina facilities
- Launching facilities
- Engine repair
- Rigging

Storage:
- Number of boats stored per year: 125
- Percentage of wooden boats: 60
- Inside storage facilities
- Maximum size for hauling and storing:
  - Length: 30'

Maintenance:
- Number of boats maintained per year: 125
- Percentage of wooden boats: 60

Retail supplies:
- Paint, sandpaper, fittings, and other marine supplies.

HATHAWAY BOAT SHOP—Carl Hathaway
70 Algonquin Ave.
Saranac Lake, NY 12983
518-891-3961

Builder Information
Years in business: 22
Carpenters employed: 3
Shop capacity: Boats to 18'

Recent New Construction
12-16' guideboats. Modified Hamner design. 2 built 1983.
14' guideboat. Will Martin design. 2 built 1983.

Recent Repair Projects
Guideboats, canoes, St. Lawrence rowing skiffs, and daysailers. Repairwork has included frame, plank, stem, and centerboard renewal.

Yard Information
Maintenance:
- Number of boats maintained per year: 100
- Percentage of wooden boats: 30
- Owner maintenance allowed above rail.

Retail supplies:
- Limited stock. Paint and varnish.

NEW YORK

KORTCHMAR & WILLNER, INC.
Michael Kortchmar and Andrew Willner
135 Edgewater St.
Staten Island, NY 10305
718-448-5563

Builder Information
Years in business: 5
Carpenters employed: 3
Shop capacity: Boats to 65-70'
May be willing to travel for on-the-site building projects.

Recent New Construction
24' cold-molded powerboat (press boat for *Yachting* magazine). Built 1980-'81.

Recent Repair Projects
62' Herreshoff sloop VENTURA (1922). Renewed frames, planking, and chainplates.

42' Wheeler powerboat (1940). Sistered frames. Renewed keelbolts, floors, planking, and joinerwork. Installed machinery.

38' 7-meter sloop (1917). Replaced keel, keelbolts, and portions of stem and horn timber. Renewed planking and covering board on starboard quarter. Installed engine and replaced standing rigging, refinished hull.

58' oyster dredger/charter schooner (1902). Rebuilt aft third of hull. Renewed sternpost, transom, framing, planking, ceiling, and house. Installed machinery.

28' Controversy sloop (1956). Replaced transom and floors. Renewed joinerwork, companionway hatch, and bowsprit. Refinished boat.

Yard Information
Services (in cooperation with Narrows Marina, Inc.):
   Marina facilities
   Launching facilities
   Overland transport
   Engine repair
   Rigging

KRETZER BOAT WORKS, INC.—Mike O'Connor
459 City Island Ave.
City Island, NY 10464
212-885-2600

Builder Information
Years in business: 79
Carpenters employed: 3
Shop capacity: New construction to 55'

Recent New Construction
42' sloop. Built 1978.
33' lapstrake sportfisherman. 3 built 1977-'81.

Recent Repair Projects
Various types of powered and sailing vessels. Repair projects have involved replacing frames and planking, renewing teak decks, recanvasing decks and housetops, and remodeling interiors. Currently rebuilding a 65' Dutch-built motoryacht.

NEW YORK

Yard Information
Services:
  Marina facilities
  Launching facilities
  Diesel and gas engine repair
  Rigging
Storage:
  Number of boats stored per year: 55
  Percentage of wooden boats: 25
  Inside storage facilities
  Maximum size for hauling and storing:
    Length: 65'
    Tonnage: 60

KUHN'S MARINE SERVICE—Chester Kuhn
8081 Briggs Ave.
Wolcott, NY 14590
315-594-2459

Builder Information
Years in business: 11
Carpenters employed: 1
Shop capacity: Boats to 30'

Recent Repair Projects
30' Lyman cruiser. Replaced 5 planks, 2 frames, bilge stringer, aft deck, and hatches. Renewed vinyl and refinished brightwork.

Yard Information
Services:
  Overland transport
  Gas engine repair
Maintenance:
  Number of boats maintained per year: 2
  Percentage of wooden boats: 100
  Maximum size for hauling:
    Length: 30'
    Draft: 5'
    Tonnage: 8

McGREIVEY'S CANOE SHOP—John McGreivey
1379 Old State Rd.
Cato, NY 13033
315-626-6635

Builder Information
Years in business: 12
Carpenters employed: 1

Recent Repair Projects
Wooden canoes, Adirondack guideboats, and other small craft. All types of repair and restoration. Works on 50-60 boats per year.

(continues)

NEW YORK

(McGreivey's Canoe Shop, continued)
Yard Information
Services:
   Overland transport
Storage:
   Number of boats stored per year: 25
   Percentage of wooden boats: 100
   Inside storage facilities
Maintenance:
   Number of boats maintained per year: 50
   Percentage of wooden boats: 100
Retail supplies:
   Hardware and materials for boat repair. Canvas, paint, filler.

MILLS BOATBUILDING—Jeff Mills
7 Pleasant Hollow
Freeville, NY 13068
607-539-7661

Builder Information
Years in business: 4
Carpenters employed: 1
Shop capacity: Boats to 20'

Recent New Construction
12' lapstrake sailing tender. Traditional design. 5 built 1983-'85.
13' and 15' lapstrake sailing canoes. Rushton designs. 3 built 1984-'85.
16' Adirondack guideboat. Lapstrake construction, traditional design. 2 built 1980-'81.

Recent Repair Projects
16' St. Lawrence skiff. Totally restored boat. 1984.
10' Bisby rowboat. Totally restored boat. 1985.

MORROWS BOAT SHOP—Ralph Morrow
46 Duprey St.
Saranac Lake, NY 12983
518-891-0432

Builder Information
Years in business: 20
Carpenters employed: 1
Shop capacity: Boats to 20'

Recent New Construction
Adirondack guideboats. Vassar design. 22 built to date; 1 in progress.

Recent Repair Projects
All types of small-boat repairs.

NEW YORK

NORTH RIVER BOATWORKS—Howard Mittleman
6 Elm St.
Albany, NY 12202
518-434-4414

Builder Information
Years in business: 7
Carpenters employed: 3
Shop capacity: Boats to 25'

Recent New Construction
19' lapstrake double-ended sloop. Gerr Marine design. Current project.
11' plywood garvey tender. Gerr Marine design. Built 1984.
17' lapstrake Swampscott dory. Fred Dion design. 2 built 1982-'83.
14' lapstrake double-ended pulling boat. J.H. Rushton design. Current project.
15' double-ended North River skiff. Lapstrake construction. H. Mittleman design. 2 built 1983-'84.
18' recreational rowing shell Half-Moon. Plywood construction. H. Mittleman design. Current project.

Recent Repair Projects
21' Chris-Craft Cadet (1928). Replaced deck, transom, and bottom planks. Refinished hull. 1982.
22' Belgrade Lake launch (ca. 1910). Renewed half the planking and 90% of the framing. Installed new trim. 1983.
19' Thistle-class sloop. Repaired transom. 1983.
19' Century Sea Maid runabout. Renewed decks, framing, transom, clamp, and washboards.
18' Old Town canoe (ca. 1910). Renewed stems and planking, recanvased hull. 1985.
17' Adirondack guideboat. Replaced worn planks and refinished hull. 1985.
16-20' Lymans, Thompsons, and Chris-Crafts. Plank, stem, and transom repairs. 1982-'85.

PARKER MARINE ENTERPRISES—Reuel B. Parker
408 Peters Blvd.
Brightwaters, NY 11718

Builder Information
Years in business: 27
Carpenters employed: 3
Shop capacity: Boats to 150'
Willing to travel for on-the-site building projects.

Recent New Construction
63' centerboard schooner SARAH. Cold-molded construction. R.B. Parker design. Built 1984.
44' cold-molded sharpie. R.B. Parker design. Built 1985.

Recent Repair Projects
55' Broward luxury cabin cruiser STARSHIP. Replanked and refastened double-planked hull. Replaced triple-planked transom and transom framing. Renewed paint and brightwork. 1984.
42' Nevins yawl. Repaired keel, replaced shaftlog and some planking. 1983-'84.
30' Alden sloop. Major restoration. Refastened floors and frames. Renewed planking, cockpit, deckbeams, and deck. Refinished hull and spars, replaced rigging. 1982.

Yard Information
Services:
    Diesel and gas engine repair
    Rigging

NEW YORK

JOHN ROGERS
4465 Lake Dr.
Canandaigua, NY 14424
716-394-6855

Builder Information
Years in business: 5
Carpenters employed: 1
Shop capacity: Boats to 20′

Recent New Construction
20′ Shark catamaran. Cold-molded construction. J.R. MacAlpine-Downie design. Built 1981.

Recent Repair Projects
Shark catamarans. Complete redecking and refurbishing. 5 boats since 1982.

Yard Information
Services:
  Overland transport
Retail supplies:
  Fittings for Shark catamarans.

SAG HARBOR YACHT YARD—Jim Ritter
Bay St., P.O. Box 1199
Sag Harbor, NY 11963
516-725-3838

Builder Information
Years in business: 7
Carpenters employed: 1
Shop capacity: Boats to 40′
Willing to travel occasionally for on-the-site building projects.

Recent New Construction
12′ DN and Gambit iceboats. Plywood and solid wood/epoxy construction. 3 built 1984–'85.
16′ plywood tugboat. William Garden design. Current project.
15′ strip-planked canoe. Wilbur & Wheelock design; lines taken by Jim Ritter. Current project.

Recent Repair Projects
25′ Cheoy Lee Frisco Flier sloop. Totally restored boat. Sistered frames, replaced bulkheads, rebuilt decks, cockpit, and cabintop. Refinished hull. 1985.
42′ sharpie schooner. Refastened hull, recaulked and refinished hull. 1985.
40′ Matthews cruiser. Replaced garboard. 1985.
40′ catboat. Replaced part of stem. 1985.
17′ Old Town canoe. Refinished. 1985.

Yard Information
Services:
  Launching facilities
  Overland transport
  Moorage
  Diesel and gas engine repair
  Rigging

Storage:
    Number of boats stored per year: 110
    Percentage of wooden boats: 10
    Inside storage facilities
    Maximum size for hauling and storing:
        Length: 50'
        Draft: 8'
        Tonnage: 30
Maintenance:
    Service provided on request
Retail supplies:
    Materials on hand; will provide as needed.

SAGMAN'S—Ted Charles
435 City Island Ave.
City Island, NY 10464
212-885-1000

Builder Information
Years in business: 25
Carpenters employed: 3
Shop capacity: Boats to 75'

Recent Repair Projects
50' Elco. Repaired hull and deck, struts, and shafts. 1983.
80' Thames sailing barge. Replaced stem, decks, yard, and rails. 1985.
33', 42', and 46' Aldens. Major hull work, laid new teak decks.
U.S. Merchant Marine Academy—8 Monomoy-type pulling boats. Repaired
    hull, planking, rails, steering bars.

Yard Information
Services:
    Marina facilities
    Launching facilities
    Moorage
    Diesel and gas engine repair
    Rigging
Storage:
    Number of boats stored per year: 200
    Percentage of wooden boats: 35
    Inside storage facilities
    Maximum size for hauling and storing:
        Length: 60'
        Draft: 10'
        Tonnage: 40
Retail supplies:
    Sandpaper, paint and varnish, sealants, waxes, wire, rope and rigging
    supplies. Gas and oil filters, pumps, outboard engines and parts.

NEW YORK

SHIPSKILLS, INC.—Andre Mele
1 Rondout Landing
Kingston, NY 12401
914-338-2361

Builder Information
Years in business: 10
Carpenters employed: 6
Shop capacity: Boats to 80'
Willing to travel for on-the-site building projects.

Recent New Construction
36' cold-molded catamaran. Andre Mele and Jim Brown design. Current project.
25' cold-molded power boat RIVERKEEPER. Andre Mele design. Built 1984.
18'6" plywood/epoxy skiff for shad fishing. Andre Mele design. Built 1983, 1985.

Recent Repair Projects
39' Rhodes Bounty-class sloop. Major restoration. Renewed hull, framing, deck, and interior. 1984–'85.
45' Alden yawl. Major restoration of hull, framing, deck, and interior. Current project.
47' Alden ketch. Repairing and renewing floors, frames, planking. Current project.
103' Hudson River sloop CLEARWATER. Doing miscellaneous repairs, including bowsprit and decking. Current project.
25' Wianno Sr.-class sloop. Ongoing restoration work. Current project.

Yard Information
Services:
    Marina facilities
    Diesel engine repair
    Rigging
Storage:
    Number of boats stored per year: 3
    Percentage of wooden boats: 100
Maintenance:
    Number of boats maintained per year: 2
    Percentage of wooden boats: 100
    Owner maintenance allowed.

SILL'S MARINA, INC.—Stewart Sill, Jr.
Rte. 14
Sodus Point, NY 14555
315-483-9102

Builder Information
Years in business: 30
Carpenters employed: 6
Shop capacity: Boats to 50'

Recent New Construction
30' cold-molded IOR sloop. Bruce Kirby design. 2 built 1982.
20' cold-molded sloop. Sill design. Built 1984.

Recent Repair Projects
48' 8-meter sloop. Renewed frames, deck, rig, and rudder. Cast new keel. 1984.
44' 8-meter sloop. Renewed frames, deck, and transom, modified keel. 1985.

Yard Information
Services:
    Marina facilities
    Launching facilities
    Moorage
    Diesel and gas engine repair
    Sailmaking
    Rigging
Storage:
    Number of boats stored per year: 200
    Percentage of wooden boats: 10
    Inside storage facilities
    Maximum size for hauling and storing:
        Length: 50'
        Draft: 10'
        Tonnage: 30
Maintenance:
    Number of boats maintained per year: 100 +
    Percentage of wooden boats: 10
    Owner maintenance allowed above and below rail.
Retail supplies:
    Marine store. Complete inventory of supplies.

SLINGERLAND CLASSIC BOATS—Jack Slingerland
4535 Rte. 89
Seneca Falls, NY 13148
315-549-8737

Builder Information
Years in business: 10
Carpenters employed: 1
Shop capacity: Boats to 20'

Recent New Construction
18' plywood rowing wherry. Ken Bassett design. Built 1985.
16' strip-planked Peterborough canoe. Built 1985.
20' cold-molded rowing wherry BANGOR PACKET. Joel White design. Current project.

Recent Repair Projects
16' runabout. Complete restoration. New decks, planks, frames, seats.
18' canoe. New canvas, seats, ribs.

SPRUCE KNEE BOATBUILDING—Robert W. Frenette
9 High St.
Tupper Lake, NY 12986
518-359-3228

Builder Information
Years in business: 7
Carpenters employed: 1
Willing to travel for on-the-site building projects.
(continues)

NEW YORK

(Spruce Knee Boatbuilding, continued)

Recent New Construction
15' lapstrake canoe for sail, oar, and paddle. Walt Simmons design. Current project.
13' lapstrake double-paddle canoe. Pete Culler design. Built 1981.
16' strip-planked guideboat. J.H. Rushton design. 3 built 1983–'85.
16' guideboat. Plywood lapstrake construction. Modified Rushton design. Current project.

Recent Repair Projects
65' schooner FREEDOM. Helped remove interior joinerwork and lay new sole. 1983.
Canoes, guideboats, and other small craft 16' and under. Repairs have included rib, plank, and stem replacement and hull refinishing. 20 boats were in for repair this year.

Yard Information
Services:
   Overland transport
   Sail repair

TRADITIONAL WOODEN CRAFT—Paul R. White
5794 Clover Meadow Dr.
Canandaigua, NY 14424
716-398-2088

Builder Information
Years in business: 3
Carpenters employed: 1
Shop capacity: Boats to 16'

Recent New Construction
14' strip-planked sailing skiff. 2 built 1984–'85.
9'6" cold-molded tender. Lawley design. 3 built 1984–'85.

WILLIAMS WOOD BOAT SHOP—C. Williams
1916 Union Rd.
West Seneca, NY 14224
716-674-7455

Builder Information
Years in business: 40
Carpenters employed: 3
Shop capacity: Boats to 55'
Willing to travel for on-the-site building projects.

Recent New Construction
36' lapstrake sportfisherman. In-house design. Built 1980.
28' power sedan cruiser. Glen-L Marine design. Built 1979.
16' lapstrake pram Spider. 4 built 1976.

Recent Repair Projects
31' Chris-Craft sedan (1952). Completely rebuilt boat. 1985.
38' Trojan tri-cabin cruiser (1968). Renewed decks, repainted entire boat. 1985.
38' Chris-Craft sedan (1958). Repaired rot. 1985.
36' Chris-Craft Connie (1962). Repaired hull and renewed cabin joinery. 1985.
18' Shepherd (1956). Completely restored boat. 1985.
18'6" hydroplane, 1 Roquie Chief (1954). Rebuilt hull and sponson. 1985.

NEW YORK

Yard Information
Services:
    Overland transport
    Gas engine repair
    Rigging
Storage:
    Number of boats stored per year: 3
    Percentage of wooden boats: 50
    Inside storage facilities
    Maximum size for hauling and storing:
        Length: 42'
        Draft: 3'
        Tonnage: 18
Maintenance:
    Number of boats maintained per year: 7
    Percentage of wooden boats: 80
    Owner maintenance allowed above rail.
Retail supplies:
    Fastenings, wood, millwork, and paint.

NORTH CAROLINA

BISCAYNE BAY BOAT WORKS—Michael Matheson
Rte. 4
Murphy, NC 28906
704-644-5325 or 644-5714

Builder Information
Years in business: 7
Carpenters employed: 1
Shop capacity: Boats to 45′
Willing to travel for on-the-site building projects.

Recent Repair Projects
38′ Chris-Craft Commuter (1929). Complete restoration. Renewed decks, engine, wiring, steering, transom, etc. 1982-'84.
28′ Gar Wood runabout (1928). Complete restoration. 1983.
26′ Chris-Craft runabout (1928). Complete restoration. Renewed decks and transom, refastened bottom, installed new engine. 1984.
30′ Elco launch (1909). Complete restoration. Repairing hull, renewing decks, refinishing. Current project.
17′ Chris-Craft runabout (1938). Replacing decks, bottom, chine, frames, transom. Current project.

Yard Information
Services:
    Overland transport
Storage:
    Number of boats stored per year: 12-30
    Percentage of wooden boats: 60 (boats undergoing repair)
    Inside storage facilities
    Maximum size for hauling and storing:
        Length: 45′
        Draft: 4′
        Tonnage: 10
Maintenance:
    Number of boats maintained per year: 8
    Percentage of wooden boats: 4
Retail supplies:
    Materials for restoration of antique boats.

BLAKE BOATWORKS—Bryan Blake
P.O. Box 41
Gloucester, NC 28528
919-729-8021

Builder Information
Years in business: 9
Carpenters employed: 2-3
Shop capacity: Boats to 60′
Willing to travel for on-the-site building projects.

Recent New Construction
Boats designed by Bryan Blake for strip-plank construction:
    25′ gaff sloop. Built 1984.
    38′ skipjack. 2 built 1983-'85.
    20′ round-sterned inboard. Built 1985.
    36′ trawler. Built 1985.

NORTH CAROLINA

Other new construction:
    20' plywood sloop. E.G. Van de Stadt/Scheepswerf design. Built 1985.
    21' sailing skiff. Earl Rose design. Built 1985.

Recent Repair Projects
32' Herreshoff Meadow Lark. Installed new engine, rebuilt and reglassed deck. 1984.
20-55' boats. Repairs have included frames and plank replacement, as well as interior and exterior modifications.

Yard Information
Services:
    Overland transport
    Diesel engine repair
    Rigging
Maintenance:
    Number of boats maintained per year: 20-30
    Percentage of wooden boats: 100
    Owner maintenance allowed above and below rail.
    Maximum size for hauling:
      Length: 50'
      Draft: 5'
      Tonnage: 25
Retail supplies:
    Wood, fastenings, paint, glue, engines and parts, marine supplies.

CAPE FEAR TECHNICAL INSTITUTE—Bruce MacKenzie
411 North Front St.
Wilmington, NC 28401
919-343-0481

Builder Information
Years in business: 12
Carpenters employed: 13 students
Shop capacity: Boats to 20'
May be willing to travel for on-the-site building projects.

Recent New Construction
14' catboat. Alford design. Built 1985.
22' lapstrake surfboat. MacKenzie design. Built 1984.
12' lapstrake dinghy. Bolger design. Built 1985.
16' plywood dory. Bolger design. Built 1985.

CROWN POINT MARINE—Emerson Willard
745 Masonboro Sound Rd.
Wilmington, NC 28403
919-791-4056

Builder Information
Years in business: 15
Carpenters employed: 1
Shop capacity: Boats to 38'

Recent New Construction
22', 26', 30' ketch-rigged dories. Plywood construction, fiberglass sheathed. Emerson Willard design. 2 30-footers built 1984-'85.
17' inboard net skiff. Plywood construction. Emerson Willard design. Built 1984.
(continues)

NORTH CAROLINA

(Crown Point Marine, continued)

Recent Repair Projects
36′ ketch. Repaired hull damage. 1985.

Yard Information
Services:
  Rigging
Maintenance:
  Number of boats maintained per year: 2
  Percentage of wooden boats: 100

EAST BAY BOAT WORKS—Vance Gillikin
P.O. Box 220
Harkers Island, NC 28531
919-728-2004

Builder Information
Years in business: 30
Carpenters employed: 6
Shop capacity: Boats to 90′
Willing to travel for on-the-site building projects.

Recent New Construction
Boats of strip-planked construction, designed in-house:
  65′ head boat. 8 built 1972-'78, 1 in progress.
  62′ head boat. Built 1985.
  78′ lobsterboat. Built 1980.
  45′ charter boat. 2 built 1983.
  77′ riverboat. Built 1984.

Repair Projects
Company is equipped to do most types of repair. Can handle boats to 75′ on railway, any size in water.

Yard Information
Services:
  Launching facilities
  Diesel and gas engine repair
  Rigging
Maintenance:
  Number of boats maintained per year: 30
  Percentage of wooden boats: 75
  Some owner maintenance allowed above rail.
  Maximum size for hauling:
    Length: 75′
    Draft: 5′
    Tonnage: 50
Retail supplies:
  Marine supplies. Lumber, paint, engines, etc.

NORTH CAROLINA

SCOTT BOATYARD—Michael Scott
Tolson Rd.
Buxton, NC 27920
919-995-5023 or 995-4331

Builder Information
Years in business: 8
Carpenters employed: 2-4
Shop capacity: New construction to 39′

Recent New Construction
26′ and 27′ Roanoke Island sport boats. Design evolved from local use. 91 built 1984-'85.

Recent Repair Projects
20-50′ inboard powerboats. Minor repairs to complete restorations. Approximately 50 wooden boats repaired each year.

Yard Information
Services:
    Marina facilities
    Launching facilities
    Overland transport
    Diesel and gas engine repair
Maintenance:
    Number of boats maintained per year: 150
    Percentage of wooden boats: 50
    Owner maintenance allowed above and below rail.
Retail supplies:
    Paint, zinc, shaft nuts, brushes, rollers, resins, fiberglass.

N.L. SILVA & CO.—Nelson L. Silva
7980 Market St.
Wilmington, NC 28405
919-686-4356

Builder Information
Years in business: 15
Carpenters employed: 1-2
Shop capacity: Boats to 40′

Recent New Construction
25′ strip-planked double-ended sharpie. N.L. Silva design. 2 built 1983-'85.
15′2″ plywood catboat. Charles Wittholz design. Built 1985.
16′ strip-planked lobsterboat skiff. N.L. Silva design. Built 1982.
12′ dinghy for oar and sail. Constant Camber construction. John Marples design. Built 1985.

Recent Repair Projects
36′ lapstrake Chris-Craft cabin cruiser. Replaced trunk cabin and pilothouse roof.
    Renewed deck, 11 frames, cockpit floor, and door trim. 1982-'84.

Yard Information
Maintenance:
    Number of boats maintained per year: 10
    Percentage of wooden boats: 30
    Owner maintenance allowed above and below rail.
Retail supplies:
    Lumber, including teak, mahogany, and ash. WEST System epoxies and fiberglass resin.

NORTH CAROLINA

SLEEPY CREEK BOAT WORKS—Gary Davis
Harbor Rd.
Marshallberg, NC 28553
919-729-8181

Builder Information
Years in business: 8
Carpenters employed: 5
Shop capacity: Boats to 65'
Willing to travel for on-the-site building projects.

Recent New Construction
31' cold-molded yawl, Malabar Jr. John Alden design (modified). Built 1983-'84.
19' gaff-rigged sharpie. Gary Davis design. 2 built 1983-'84.
36' strip-planked lobsterboat for sportfishing. G. Davis design. Built 1984-'85.
54' strip-planked crab boat for sportfishing. G. Davis design. Built 1985.
35' strip-planked trawler. G. Davis design. Built 1985.
60' strip-planked head boat. G. Davis design. Current project.
19' cold-molded speedboat. G. Davis design. Current project.

Recent Repair Projects
36' trawler. Replaced rudder, bottom plank, 1985.
35' sportfisherman. Laid new teak cabin sole, renewed cockpit and gunwales. Replaced engines and steering system. 1985.

Yard Information
Services:
  Marine facilities
  Launching facilities
  Moorage
  Diesel and gas engine repair
  Rigging
Maintenance:
  Number of boats maintained per year: 5
  Percentage of wooden boats: 90
  Owner maintenance allowed above and below rail.
Retail supplies:
  Lumber, paint, fastenings, hatches, hardware, supplies for maintenance.

OHIO

CASSELL MARINE—Charles Cassell
115 W. Liberty St.
Hubbard, OH 44425
216-534-9388

Builder Information
Years in business: 16
Carpenters employed: 2
Shop capacity: Boats to 40'
Willing to travel for on-the-site building projects.

Current Repair Projects
30' Owens Flagship (1965). Restoring hull and engine.
25' Trojan (1967). Renewing bottom planking.
19' Chris-Craft (1937). Restoring hull and engine.
21' Delta Craft (1956). Restoring hull and engine.
23' Century Coronado (1959 & 1965 models). Restoring hulls and engines.

Yard Information
Services:
    Overland transport
    Diesel and gas engine repair
    Sailmaking
    Rigging
Storage:
    Number of boats stored per year: 20
    Percentage of wooden boats: 50
    Inside storage facilities
    Maximum size for hauling and storing:
        Length: 40'
        Draft: 12'
        Tonnage: 16
Maintenance:
    Number of boats maintained per year: 12
    Percentage of wooden boats: 100
    Owner maintenance allowed above and below rail.
Retail supplies:
    Parts and supplies for antique classic power craft. Trailers and hitches.

DON FORREST INC.—Don Forrest
303 Cedar Pt. Roadway
(shop at 713 Dutch Lane)
Sandusky, OH 44870
419-625-5547

Builder Information
Years in business: 11
Carpenters employed: 3
Shop capacity: Boats to 30'
Willing to travel for on-the-site building projects.

Recent Repair Projects
18-30' Lyman runabouts. Restoration work has included laying new teak decks, replacing frames, planks, transoms, stems, knees, and keels. Cabin and windshield renewal and installation of equipment. Approximately 75 boats repaired per year.

(continues)

OHIO

(Don Forrest Inc., continued)

Yard Information
Services:
  Overland transport
Storage:
  Number of boats stored per year: 20
  Percentage of wooden boats: 80
  Maximum size for hauling and storing:
    Length: 30'
    Tonnage: 4
Maintenance:
  Number of boats maintained per year: 75
  Percentage of wooden boats: 90
  Owner maintenance allowed.

HURON LAGOONS MARINA, INC.—Thomas Solberg
100 Laguna Dr., P.O. Box 231
Huron, OH 44839
419-433-3200

Builder Information
Years in business: 15
Carpenters employed: 2
Shop capacity: Boats to 50'

Recent New Construction
131'6" plywood canoe. Designed in-house and built in 6½ hours by
  15 people. With a rowing crew of 76, the canoe set a world's record
  in the 1985 Huron Jaycees Crazy Craft Race!

Recent Repair Projects
40' Chris-Craft (1959). Renewed planking, refinished brightwork, and repainted boat.
34' Post (1966). Modified and rebuilt boat from deck up.

Yard Information
Services:
  Marina facilities
  Launching facilities
  Overland transport
  Moorage
Storage:
  Number of boats stored per year: 250
  Percentage of wooden boats: 40
  Inside storage facilities
  Maximum size for hauling and storing:
    Length: 45'
    Draft: 5'
    Tonnage: 20
Maintenance:
  Number of boats maintained per year: 150
  Percentage of wooden boats: 30
  Owner maintenance allowed above and below rail.
Retail supplies:
  Paint, bronze fastenings, and planking stock, including mahogany, teak,
    and marine plywood.

OHIO

LYMAN MANUFACTURING CO.—Bob G. Thrash
1615 First St.
Sandusky, OH 44870
419-625-4755

Builder Information
Years in business: 108
Shop capacity: Boats to 30'

Recent New Construction
27' runabout. Plywood lapstrake construction. Lyman design. Built 1984.

Repair Projects
Rebuilding of Lyman boats. Numerous projects to date.

Yard Information
Services:
    Launching facilities
    Overland transport
    Moorage
Storage:
    Number of boats stored per year: 65
    Percentage of wooden boats: 90
    Maximum size for hauling and storing:
        Length: 39'
Maintenance:
    Number of boats maintained per year: 60
    Percentage of wooden boats: 95

OUTER LIMITS YACHTS—Duncan Schaefer
1073 Summit Ave.
Lakewood, OH 44107
216-221-3846

Builder Information
Years in business: 3
Carpenters employed: 1
Willing to travel for on-the-site building projects.

Recent New Construction
16'4" International Fireball-class sloop. Stitch-and-tape plywood composite construction. Peter Milne design. 7 built 1982-'85.

Recent Repair Projects
Repairwork has included refinishing decks and hulls, modifying racing sailboats, and replacing decks.

Yard Information
Services:
    Overland transport
    Rigging
Maintenance:
    Number of boats maintained per year: 4
    Percentage of wooden boats: 80

OHIO

SAYRE BROTHERS MARINE—Bud & Zenna Sayre
P.O. Box 65, 5171 North Bank S.E.
Buckeye Lake, OH 43008
614-928-3691

Builder Information
Years in business: 82
Carpenters employed: 2
Shop capacity: Boats to 25'

Recent Repair Projects
15-25' Chris-Craft runabouts. Restoration work has included
    replacing planks and other wooden members, engine rebuilding, and hull refinishing.

Yard Information
Services:
    Marina facilities
    Launching facilities
    Overland transport
    Moorage
    Gas engine repair
Storage:
    Number of boats stored per year: 100
    Percentage of wooden boats: 50
    Inside storage facilities
    Maximum size for hauling and storing:
        Length: 28'
Maintenance:
    Number of boats maintained per year: varies
    Percentage of wooden boats: 50
Retail supplies:
    On-the-water marine store. Paints, marine plywood, mahogany, hardware, canvas.
      Complete line of products to repair and refinish wooden boats. Full service
      for inboard and I/O boats.

RICHARD WOGISCH, JR.
300 Miles Rd.
Chagrin Falls, OH 44022
216-247-5965

Builder Information
Years in business: 10
Carpenters employed: 1

Recent Repair Projects
28' Morse Friendship sloop MORNING STAR (1904). Completely rebuilt boat. 1975-'76.
17' Thistle-class sloop. Renewed centerboard trunk. 1984.
20' sloop. Replaced laminated tiller. 1985.
22' Lyman runabout. Repaired transom delamination, renewed deck and waterways. 1985.

OREGON

APPLEGATE BOATWORKS—Laura and John McCallum
25380 Fleck Rd.
Veneta, OR 97487
503-935-2370

Builder Information
Years in business: 9
Carpenters employed: 1
Shop capacity: Boats to 23'
Willing to travel for on-the-site building projects.

Recent New Construction
Boats designed by John McCallum for taped-seam plywood construction:
- 16' sailing proa. Built 1984.
- 16' power bateau. 2 built 1984.
- 8' proa. 6 built 1984.
- 16' recreational rowing gig. Built 1985.

Recent Repair Projects
14' hot-molded Wagemaker Wolverine runabout. Replanked half of deck. Refastened keel, stringers, and transom. Built new seats, floorboard, and dashboard. Patched transom, stripped and refinished boat. 1984–'85.
20' Century Resorter (1954). Refastened hull, stripped and refinished boat. 1985.
16' M-scow class (1962). Repaired planking, recaulked hull. 1985.
16' Chestnut canoe. Renewed hull canvas, repaired stem and planking. 1984.
13' Enterprise 13 (1960s). Refastened keel, replaced 2 planks, renewed deck and caulking. 1984.
16' MacKenzie River drift boat. Rebuilt aft 2' of stern. 1983.
18' plywood faering. Replaced frames, mast partner, and yard. 1982.
19' Thistle-class sloop. Replaced gunwale. 1985.

Yard Information
Services:
- Engine repair (on sub-contract basis)
- Rigging repair (on sub-contract basis)

CLIPPER CRAFT MFG. CO.—James E. Staley
10130 N. North Portland Rd.
Portland, OR 97203
503-286-3013

Builder Information
Years in business: 30
Carpenters employed: 4
Shop capacity: Boats to 26'

Recent New Construction
17' and 20' lapstrake powerboats (Jet Sled model). Jim Staley design.
20', 23', and 26' lapstrake West Bank dory for cruising and fishing. Jim Staley design.
1,500 to 2,000 boats built to date.

OREGON

FLYNN & FLYNN CUSTOM BOAT WORKS—Rik Flynn
3005 Bay Ocean Rd.
Tillamook, OR 97141
503-842-7819

Builder Information
Years in business: 15
Carpenters employed: 2
Shop capacity: New construction to 21'
Willing to travel for on-the-site building projects.

Recent New Construction
Boats designed by Rik Flynn:
    16' dory. 5 built 1980-'85.
    16' McKenzie River drift boats. 5 built 1980-'85.

Recent Repair Projects
70' motoryacht. Renewed frames and planking. 1981.
65' halibut schooner-type motorsailer. Renewed rigging and sails. Completed mechanical and woodwork repairs. 1979-'84.
40' schooner. Renewed frames and planking. 1981.
28' power fishing boat. Renewed frames and planking. 1982.
18' kayak. Renewed frames and hull canvas. 1985.

Yard Information
Services:
    Moorage
    Rigging
Storage:
    Number of boats stored per year: 4
    Percentage of wooden boats: 50
    Inside storage facilities
    Maximum size for hauling and storing:
        Length: 21'
Maintenance:
    Number of boats maintained per year: 3
    Percentage of wooden boats: 30
    Owner maintenance allowed above rail.
Retail supplies:
    Will order supplies on request.

DON HILL RIVER BOATS—Donald L. Hill
P.O. Box CC
Springfield, OR 97477
503-747-7430 or 461-2949

Builder Information
Years in business: 25
Carpenters employed: 1 (part-time)
Shop capacity: Boats to 26'
Willing to travel for on-the-site building projects.

Recent New Construction
10', 12', 15', and 16'1" McKenzie River drift boats. Plywood construction. Don Hill design.
    Over 1,000 built to date.

Recent Repair Projects
12-16' McKenzie River drift boats. Replaced side and bottom planking and carried out other necessary repairs. 1985.

Yard Information
Services:
  Overland transport
Maintenance:
  Number of boats maintained per year: 20
  Percentage of wooden boats: 100
  Owner maintenance allowed above and below rail.
Retail supplies:
  Marine plywood, fastenings, trailers, oars and oarlocks, epoxy, lumber, and more. Also supplies plans and kits for the McKenzie River drift boat.

JORDAN WOOD BOATS—Warren L. Jordan
305 S.E. 35th St., P.O. Box 194
South Beach, OR 97366
503-867-3141

Builder Information
Years in business: 8
Carpenters employed: 1
Shop capacity: New construction to 24'
Willing to travel for on-the-site building projects.

Recent New Construction
16' lapstrake Sea Bright skiff. Plans by John Gardner. Built 1980.
11' plywood and lapstrake catboats. Atkin design. 2 built 1983.
20' plywood outboard dory. W. Jordan design. Current project.
22' plywood outboard dory. Wike design. Built 1977.
11' wood-and-canvas double-paddle peapod/canoe type. W. Jordan design. Built 1984.
8' plywood lightweight pram. W. Jordan design. Built 1985.
11' plywood garvey/duckboat. W. Jordan design. Built 1983.
14' plywood river drift boat. W. Jordan design. Current project.
9$^1/_2$' plywood V-bottomed pram. John Gardner design. Built 1984.

Recent Repair Projects
55' power yacht. Repaired deck and keel, modified interior. 1984.
30' Chris-Craft. Modified cabin interior, repaired hull and cabin. 1984.
58' halibut boat. Modified and repaired pilothouse. 1983.
20' Calkins surf dory. Completed general repairs and restoration work. 1983.

NORTHRUP BOAT WORKS—Bruce Northrup
37368 Moss Rock Dr.
Corvallis, OR 97330
503-745-5064

Builder Information
Years in business: 16
Carpenters employed: Varies, depending on work at hand
Shop capacity: Boats to 55'
Willing to travel for on-the-site building projects.
(continues)

OREGON

(Northrup Boat Works, continued)

Recent New Construction
56' pungy schooner. Bruce Northrup design. Built 1984.
22' cat schooner. R.D. Culler design. Built 1984.
17' lapstrake bateau. R.D. Culler design. Built 1985.

Recent Repair Projects
42' Alden ketch. Renewed frames, planking, floor timbers, and keelbolts. 1985.
32' Hess ketch. Replaced about half the planking. 1985.
32' cutter. Renewed rig and spars. 1985.

Yard Information
Services:
  Sailmaking
  Rigging

STEVEN RANDER
2346 N.W. Glisan #45
Portland, OR 97210
503-220-0352

Builder Information
Years in business: 30
Carpenters employed: 6
Shop capacity: Boats to any length

Recent New Construction
Boats of cold-molded construction:
    42' ocean-racing sloop. Smith design. Built 1983.
    24' Friendship sloop. Smith design. Built 1983.
    18' canoe yawl EEL. Wm. Garden design. 3 built 1979-'82.

RAY'S RIVER DORIES—C. Ray Heater
3345 N.E. 84th
Portland, OR 97220
503-254-5847

Builder Information
Years in business: 12
Carpenters employed: 1
Shop capacity: Boats to 20'

Recent New Construction
12' plywood McKenzie drift boat. C. Ray Heater design. 3 built to date.
14' plywood McKenzie drift boat. Heater design. 40 built to date.
14' plywood Rogue drift boat. Heater design. 30 built to date.
16' plywood Rogue drift boat. Heater design. 50 built to date.

Recent Repair Projects
14-16' drift boats. Have replaced bottoms, chines, caps, gunwales, sheers, and stems.

Yard Information
Storage:
  Number of boats stored per year: 2
  Percentage of wooden boats: 100
  Maximum size for hauling and storing:
    Length: 18'

Maintenance:
    Number of boats maintained per year: 2
    Percentage of wooden boats: 100
    Owner maintenance allowed above and below rail.
Retail supplies:
    Drift-boat kits. Oars and other accessories. Trailers.

RIVER SPIRIT CANOES—Robert E. Bjornstedt
40487 Snow Peak Rd.
Lebanon, OR 97355
503-451-4365

Builder Information
Years in business: 6
Carpenters employed: 1
Shop capacity: Boats to 21'

Recent New Construction
15-20' canoes. Strip-plank or cold-molded construction. Designs by D. Hazen,
    Robert Bjornstedt, and American Indians. 7 built 1979-'83.
14'6" strip-planked canoe. Design originated with Têtes de Boule Indians; lines published
    in Adney and Chapelle's *Bark Canoes and Skin Boats of North America*. Current project.

Recent Repair Projects
Canoes. Minor repairs to complete restorations.

SCHOONER CREEK BOATWORKS—Dave Huggins
515 N.E. Tomahawk Dr.
Portland, OR 97217
503-285-9786

Builder Information
Years in business: 8
Carpenters employed: Varies
Shop capacity: Boats to any size
Willing to travel for on-the-site building projects.

Recent New Construction
18' cold-molded canoe-yawl EEL. William Garden design.
    Built 1985.
10' plywood sport boat. Glen-L Marine design. Built 1985.
6'4" sailing tender. Plywood stitch-and-glue construction. In-house design.
    3 built 1985.

Recent Repair Projects
25' Prothero sloop (1938). Restored completely from garboard up.
    1983-'85.

Yard Information
Services:
    Overland transport
    Rigging
Retail supplies:
    WEST System epoxy, paint, fastenings, and wood.

OREGON

STEELE'S BOATS—Keith Steele
44976 McKenzie Highway
Leaburg, OR 97489
503-896-3279

Builder Information
Years in business: 35
Carpenters employed: 1
Shop capacity: Boats to 20'
Willing to travel for on-the-site building projects.

Recent New Construction
McKenzie River drift boats. Plywood construction. Keith Steele design.

Recent Repair Projects
McKenzie River drift boats. All types of repair.

Yard Information
Maintenance:
　Number of boats maintained per year: 50
　Percentage of wooden boats: 100

SWANSON, BAGGINS & CO.—Mark Swanson
156 Greenway Cl.
Medford, OR 97504
503-779-2850

Builder Information
Years in business: 6
Carpenters employed: 1
Shop capacity: Boats to 40'
Willing to travel for on-the-site building projects.

Recent New Construction
9½' lapstrake Norwegian Arendal pram. 12 built through 1985.

Recent Repair Projects
15' Danish Klitmoller skiff (1971). Reframed hull and replaced plank. Renewed thwarts, gunwales, rails, oars, and spars, refinished. 1985.

Yard Information
Services:
　Rigging and repair
　Overland transport
Maintenance:
　Number of boats maintained per year: 1-5
　Percentage of wooden boats: 100
　Owner maintenance allowed above and below rail.

AMBLER BOAT WORKS—John Smith
P.O. Box 1214
Lansdale, PA 19446
215-368-8474

Builder Information
Years in business: 27
Carpenters employed: 3
Shop capacity: New construction to 32′

Recent New Construction
19′ lapstrake motor launch for antique engine. John Smith design. Current project.
16′ St. Lawrence River rowing skiff. Cold-molded construction. Lines taken from original 1880 skiff. 19 built 1978 to present.

Recent Repair Projects
12′ Dyer Dink (1932). Complete reconstruction. Renewed frames, centerboard trunk, stem, seats, inwale, rubrail, and rudder. Refinished boat and spars. 1985.
23′ lapstrake rowing gig (ca. 1910). Reglued laps, replaced 2 iron fittings, and refastened all internal joinery. Refinished boat. 1985.
60′ Pocock 8-person shells (ca. 1965). Refastened all joinery and refinished hulls. 3 repaired in 1984, 2 in 1985.
23′ Lyman runabout (ca. 1940s). Renewed transom and 2 frames. 1985.
18′ Old Town wood-and-canvas canoe. Stripped and refinished boat. 1985.

Yard Information
Services:
  Overland transport
  Sailmaking
  Rigging
Maintenance:
  Number of boats maintained per year: 30-50
  Percentage of wooden boats: 40-50
Retail supplies:
  Wood, fastenings, rigging supplies. Custom new and replacement wood parts.

FRANK FLICKER & SONS, RACING SHELL REPAIRS
Frank Flicker
6381 Ditman St.
Philadelphia, PA 19135
215-332-4811

Builder Information
Years in business: 6
Carpenters employed: 1
Shop capacity: Shells to 60′
Willing to travel locally for on-the-site building projects.

Recent Repair Projects
32′ Donorotico double shell. Repaired skin and damage between wash box and bow. Renewed chine stringers. 1985.
26′ Stampfli single shell. Repaired hole in skin; renewed deck, slide tray, and tray support. Refinished boat 1985.
32′ Kaschper ZX. Completely rebuilt boat. Repaired hole in skin, renewed bow and washboards. 1985.

(continues)

PENNSYLVANIA

(Frank Flicker & Sons, Racing Shell Repairs, continued)
Yard Information
Services:
　　Launching facilities
　　Overland transport
Maintenance:
　　Number of boats maintained per year: 50 shells
　　Percentage of wooden boats: 99
Retail supplies:
　　Carry small supply of materials for shell repair.

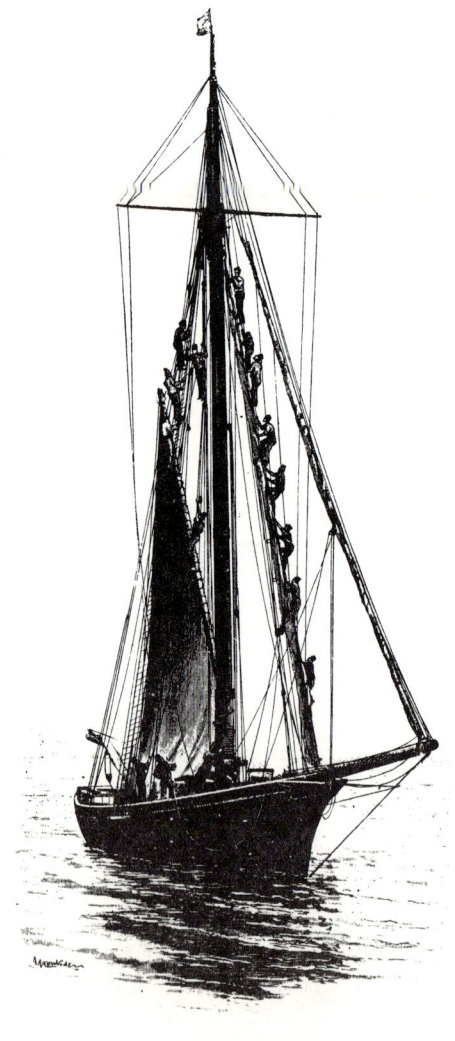

RHODE ISLAND

WALTER C. BECKMANN, LIMITED—Walter C. Beckmann
93 Harbor Island Rd.
Narragansett, RI 02882
401-783-1859

Builder Information
Years in business: 45
Carpenters employed: 3
Shop capacity: Boats to 70'
Willing to travel for on-the-site building projects.

Recent New Construction
23' cold-molded steam launch. Walter Beckmann design. 2 built 1982 and 1984.
20' cold-molded electric launch. Walter Beckmann design. Built 1983.
20' composite gas launch. Walter Beckmann design. 2 built 1983 and 1985.
23' composite steam tug. Walter Beckmann design. 2 built 1984-'1985.
8' plywood dinghy. Walter Beckmann design. 2 built 1985.

Recent Repair Projects
16' catboat. Replaced stem and some planking. 1985.
43' yawl. Reincarnation! 1983 to current.

Yard Information
Services:
    Launching facilities
    Overland transport
    Steam engine repair
    Rigging
Storage:
    Number of boats stored per year: 6
    Percentage of wooden boats: 25
    Inside storage facilities
    Maximum size for hauling and storing:
        Length: 40'
        Draft: 4'
        Tonnage: 20
Maintenance:
    Number of boats maintained per year: 12
    Percentage of wooden boats: 33
    Owner maintenance allowed above and below rail.

BEND BOAT BASIN—J. Hibbert
Rte. 114, Melville
Newport, RI 02871
401-683-4000

Builder Information
Years in business: 8
Carpenters employed: 5
Shop capacity: Boats to 70'

Recent Repair Projects
70' PT Boat #617 (1943). Rebuilding and restoring for
    display at Battleship Cove Marine Museum.
(continues)

RHODE ISLAND

(Bend Boat Basin, continued)
Yard Information
Services:
    Marine facilities
    Launching facilities
    Diesel and gas engine repair
    Rigging
Storage:
    Number of boats stored per year: 300
    Percentage of wooden boats: 15
    Inside storage facilities
    Maximum size for hauling and storing:
        Length: 70'
        Draft: 7'
        Tonnage: 70
Maintenance:
    Number of boats maintained per year: 200
    Percentage of wooden boats: 10
    Owner maintenance allowed above and below rail.
Retail supplies:
    Ship's store. Extensive inventory.

BULLOCKS POINT BOAT YARD AND MARINA, INC.—Joe Petterson
254 Riverside Dr.
Riverside, RI 02915
401-437-0477

Builder Information
Years in business: 13
Carpenters employed: 2
Shop capacity: Boats to 50'

Recent Repair Projects
39' Concordia yawl. Replaced deck canvas. 1985.
20-30' boats (3). Replaced gas engines with 2-, 3-, and 4-cylinder diesels, modified engine beds, controls, and fuel systems. 1985.
35' cruising cutter. Sheathed hull in fiberglass, using Vaitses method. 1984.
33' Weber sloop. Repaired cabintop, recaulked deck. 1985.
40' Newell sloop. Replaced maststep and refastened bottom. Recaulked deck and rebuilt hatches. 1980-'85.
50' Alden sloop. Sistered frames, replaced planks. Recaulked deck, refinished brightwork, replaced diesel engine. 1975-'84.
34' Walsted 6-meter sloop. Replaced and refastened planking on port side and transom. 1982.
38' trawler-yacht. Sheathed hull in fiberglass. 1982.
42' Warner cutter. Installed diesel generator, beds. 1984.
40' Warner sloop. Renewed horn timber, frames, and toerail. 1980.

Yard Information
Services:
    Launching facilities
    Marina facilities
    Moorage
    Engine repair
    Rigging

Storage:
    Number of boats stored per year: 85
    Percentage of wooden boats: 50
    Inside storage facilities for boats undergoing repair
    Maximum size for hauling and storing:
        Length: 50'
        Draft: 7'
        Tonnage: 20
Maintenance:
    Number of boats maintained per year: 10
    Percentage of wooden boats: 90
    Owner maintenance allowed above and below rail.
Retail supplies:
    Fastenings, paint, caulking supplies, rope, fiberglass, marine hardware, anchors, Volvo and Westerbeke engines. Extensive inventory.

CHRISTOPHER FABISZAK BOAT SHOP—Christopher Fabiszak
8 Luther St.
Jamestown, RI 02835
401-423-2563

Builder Information
Years in business: 1
Carpenters employed: 2
Shop capacity: Boats to 40'
Willing to travel for on-the-site building projects.

Recent New Construction
17' lapstrake rowing boat. Herreshoff design. Current project.

Recent Repair Projects
70' Mathis motoryacht (1912). Replaced coach roof, rebuilt tender.
32' Holiday sloop (1957). Renewed deadwood and rudder, repaired deck and cabin.
37' Egg Harbor (1967). Renewed transom, transom framing, and after hood ends of hull planking. Renewed stem and adjacent plank ends, sistered 12 frames, replaced 3 planks, refastened hull as needed. Renewed shaftlogs.
42' Rhodes 27. Installed teak toerail, caprail, transom, and taffrail. Renewed interior joinerwork.
60' Ray Hunt-designed power yacht. Installed teak interior.
18' No Man's Land boat. Refastened hull, renewed centerboard, sprits, and floorboards, repainted.
21' Indian-class sloop. Renewed stem, transom, centerboard trunk, and garboards.
34' Pacemaker. Reframed and refastened hull, renewed transom.
36' Trojan (1967). Replaced deck, bridge, and planking.

Yard Information
Retail supplies:
    Milled lumber.

RHODE ISLAND

GOETZ CUSTOM SAILBOATS—Eric Goetz
15 Broad Common Rd.
Bristol, RI 02809
401-253-2670

Builder Information
Years in business: 10
Carpenters employed: 17
Shop capacity: Boats to 80′

Recent New Construction
56′ express cruiser. Cold-molded construction. Hunt design. Built 1985.

Yard Information
Services:
   Overland transport
   Diesel engine repair

NARRAGANSETT SHIPWRIGHTS, INC.—Frank McCaffrey
61 Halsey St., Unit 25
Newport, RI 02840
401-846-3312

Builder Information
Years in business: 15
Carpenters employed: 4
Shop capacity: New construction to 45′
Willing to travel for on-the-site building projects.

Recent New Construction
32′ cold-molded sloop. Rodger Martin design. Built 1985.
16′ lapstrake peapod. Built 1984.

Recent Repair Projects
95′ Fife ketch SUMURUN. New ship's wheel and caprail forward. Cabinet work below. 1984-'85.
72′ Ticonderoga. New trailboards. 1985.
28′ Herreshoff S-boat. Complete restoration, new mast. Current.

Yard Information
Retail supplies:
   Lumber, fastenings, and other miscellaneous supplies.

RIVENDELL MARINE—Tom Wolstenholme
125 Lagoon Rd., Melville
Newport, RI 02840
401-683-1107

Builder Information
Years in business: 10
Carpenters employed: 2-5
Shop capacity: Boats to 50′
Willing to travel for on-the-site building projects.

Recent New Construction
8′ lapstrake sailing dinghy HOBBIT. Tom Wolstenholme design.
   2 built 1985.

RHODE ISLAND

Recent Repair Projects
46' Grand Banks trawler. Replaced much of plywood superstructure. 1985.
40' Owens cutter. Repaired keel and sternpost. New planks and sister frames. 1985.
32' Holiday custom sloop. New planks and laminated frames. Re-fiberglassed hull. 1985.
30' Anglemann Sea Witch ketch. Repaired strip planking, new engine, and galley equipment. 1984.
39' R-class sloop. Recanvased decks, new cabintop and canvas. Refastened hull. 1985.

Yard Information
Services:
 Marina facilities
 Launching facilities
 Engine repair
 Sailmaking
Storage:
 Number of boats stored per year: 6
 Percentage of wooden boats: 100
 Limited inside storage facilities
 Maximum size for hauling and storing:
  Length: 65'
  Draft: 6'
  Tonnage: 50
Maintenance:
 Number of boats maintained per year: 6
 Percentage of wooden boats: 100
 Some owner maintenance allowed above and below rail.
Retail supplies:
 Hardwoods, paints, fastenings. Will order supplies or equipment on request.

SOUTH CAROLINA

GRAVES BOAT WORKS—Warren M. Davies
P.O. Box 5460
Hilton Head, SC 29938
803-842-2895

Builder Information
Years in business: 15
Carpenters employed: 17
Shop capacity: Boats to 78'

Recent New Construction
Boats of cold-molded construction designed by R.L. Sherbert:
 48' sportfisherman. 2 built 1982 and 1985.
 44' sportfisherman. Built 1983-'84.
 43' sportfisherman. Built 1984-'85.

Recent Repair Projects
65' custom sportfisherman. Repowered with V12-71s and redesigned aft section for Mediterranean hardtop. Repainted boat. 1982.

Yard Information
Services (in conjunction with Palmetto Bay Marina):
 Marina facilities
 Launching facilities
 Moorage
 Diesel and gas engine repair

QUEST RACING, INC.—Kenny Adams
P.O. Box 721
St. Stephens, SC 29479
803-567-3534

Builder Information
Years in business: 15
Carpenters employed: 3
Shop capacity: Boats to 50'
Willing to travel for on-the-site building projects.

Recent New Construction
35' and 37' cold-molded racing powerboats. George Linder designs. 2 built 1984-'85.

Recent Repair Projects
Cold-molded racing powerboats. Minor repairs to complete restorations.

TENNESSEE

BEELER'S REPAIR—P.E. Beeler
Rte. 4, Povo Rd.
Madisonville, TN 37354
615-442-2753

Builder Information
Years in business: 17
Carpenters employed: 2
Shop capacity: New construction to 30'

Recent Repair Projects
22' Star-class sloop. Replaced inner keel and planking. Renewed rigging. 1985.
26' Luger sloop. Repaired topside damage. 1985.
32' Chris-Craft. Completely rebuilt boat. 1983-'84.
28' Kings Cruiser. Rebuilding boat. Renewing 20% of the hull and all of the interior. Current project.
60' barge. Replaced bottom planking. 3 boats repaired 1975-'76.

Yard Information
Services:
    Diesel and gas engine repair
    Rigging
Maintenance:
    Number of boats maintained per year: 6
    Percentage of wooden boats: 66
    Owner maintenance allowed above and below rail.
Retail supplies:
    Wood only. Crook timber, custom-sawn lumber, and $1/32$ veneers for cold molding.

TEXAS

BARLOW MARINE SERVICE—George G. Barlow
P.O. Box 34, Lake McQueeney
McQueeney, TX 78123
512-557-5000

Builder Information
Years in business: 50
Carpenters employed: 1
Shop capacity: Boats to 20'

Recent New Construction
19' V-drive runabout. Sheathed-plywood construction. Barlow design. 2 built 1971.

Recent Repair Projects
17' Chris-Craft runabout (1947). Complete restoration. Renewing deck and hull planking. 1985-'86.
18' Century Resorter (1960). Renewing bottom and transom framing. Replacing keel, stem, and hull planking. Renewing upholstery, flooring, and engine box. 1985-'86.
16' Century Resorter (1964). Replacing bungs, refinishing hull. 1985-'86.
16' Century Resorter (1957). Replacing bottom and transom. Renewing keel and stem. Refinishing hull. 1985-'86.
17' Glastron (1963). Replacing engine and engine box. Reupholstering seats. 1985-'86.

Yard Information
Services:
    Overland transport
    Gas engine repair
Maintenance:
    Number of boats maintained per year: Varies
    Percentage of wooden boats: 75
    Some owner maintenance allowed above and below rail.
Retail supplies:
    Paint, fastenings, hardware, wood. Engines and engine parts, propellers, pumps, and upholstery material.

CAMRIC BOATS—Rick Pratt
P.O. Box 2209
Port Aransas, TX 78373
512-758-3834

Builder Information
Years in business: 6
Carpenters employed: 1-4
Shop capacity: New construction to 24'
May be willing to travel for on-the-site building projects.

Recent New Construction
Boats designed by Rick Pratt:
    16' sailing skiff. Built 1984.
    14' sailing skiff. Built 1983.
    18' plywood sailing skiff. Built 1984.
    22' light-displacement inboard powerboat. Current project.
    16' bateau. Plywood and cold-molded construction. 6 built 1980-'85.
    20' bateau. Built 1984.
    16' gig. Built 1984.

Other new construction:
   16' sailing dory skiff. Phil Bolger design. Built 1982.
   20' plywood bateau. R.D. Culler design. Built 1984.

Recent Repair Projects
Herreshoff 12½-class sloop. Replaced several frames and planks. Renewed maststep and floors. 1985.
47'10" ketch. Rebuilt cabin. 1983.
38'10" Knud Reimers sloop. Replaced keel, stem, keelson, stern timbers, deck, and cabin.
37' powerboat. Replaced keel and part of stem. Refinished hull. 1984.
13' Bahamian dinghy. Totally restored boat. 1982.

Yard Information
Services:
   Overland transport
   Limited moorage
   Rigging
Maintenance:
   Number of boats maintained per year: 6-8
   Percentage of wooden boats: 75
Retail supplies:
   Fastenings, wood, paint, epoxy, fittings, oars and locks, sails. Small inventory, materials primarily by order.

FLEETWOOD BOATS—Jim Frechette
11 Bear Creek Dr.
Austin, TX 78737
512-288-5359

Builder Information
Years in business: 4
Carpenters employed: 1
Shop capacity: Boats to 30'

Recent Repair Projects
38' Wheeler sportfisherman (1954). Rebuilt flying bridge.
18' Century Resorter (1962). Repaired bottom planking, renewed brightwork.
18' Chris-Craft Riviera (1952). Total rebuild. Replaced bottom and deck planking, refinished boat.

Yard Information
Retail supplies:
   Paint, varnish, stain, fastenings, bedding and seam compounds, bungs.

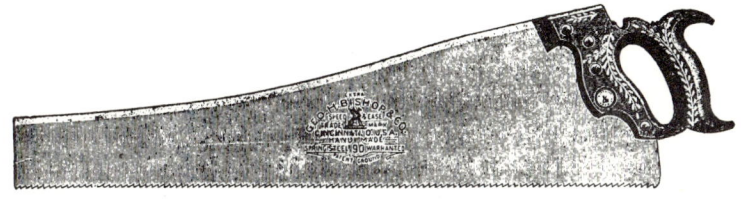

TEXAS

MICHAEL MEFFERD
2021 Sealy #1 RR
Galveston, TX 77550
409-763-1877
after 7/1/85:
11902 Knippwood
Houston, TX 77024
713-465-4413

Builder Information
Years in business: 4
Carpenters employed: 1
Shop capacity: Boats to 30'
Willing to travel for on-the-site building projects.

Recent New Construction
26' pinky schooner. Robert H. Baker design. Built 1983-'84.
16' Swampscott dory. Lapstrake construction. Built 1984.
16' lapstrake dinghy. Built 1985 for bark ELISSA.
16' peapod. Built 1983 for lighthouse service.
11' lapstrake skiff. Built 1982.

WYATT A. MOORE
P.O. Box 144
Karnack, TX 75661

Builder Information
"Dear WoodenBoat,
  "The building of my Caddo Lake bateau was featured in your January/February 1985 issue. I've just finished a 16' wooden skiff, which can be pulled with oars or propelled by a small motor.
  "I've built wooden boats as a sideline all my life, and expect I've built close to 200. I am now almost 84 years old and don't plan to build another boat—but I might build *one* more. Thanks."
—Wyatt A. Moore

THISTLE WOODWORKING—Richard G. McCloskey II
2514 Colorado
Dickinson, TX 77539
713-534-0022

Builder Information
Years in business: 10
Carpenters employed: 1
Shop capacity: Boats to 30'
Willing to travel for on-the-site building projects.

Recent New Construction
15' lapstrake canoe. Walt Simmons design. Built 1985.

Recent Repair Projects
23' double-planked sloop. Replacing frames, planking, transom, and keelbolts. Rebuilding deck and interior. Redesigning and replacing rigging. Current project.

U.S. VIRGIN ISLANDS

SPANISH MAIN BOATWORKS—Fritz Seyfarth
P.O. Box 11959
St. Thomas, U.S.V.I. 00801

Builder Information
Years in business: 20
Carpenters employed: 1 full-time, several part-time
Shop capacity: Boats to 60'
Willing to travel for on-the-site repair projects.

Recent Repair Projects
40' Alden ketch (1930). Sistered 50% of frames, refastened and cold-molded hull. Rebuilt and refastened wooden deck, then covered with fiberglass. Renewed spars and rigging.
18' double-ended sloop. Replaced part of planking and refastened hull. Renewed foredeck and spars. Refinished boat.

Yard Information
Services:
  Moorage
  Sail repair
  Rigging
Storage:
  Number of boats stored per year: 3, in water
  Percentage of wooden boats: 100
  Maximum size for storing:
    Length: 50'
Maintenance:
  Number of boats maintained per year: 6
  Percentage of wooden boats: 100
  Owner maintenance allowed above and below rail.

WEST END SLIPWAY—Morgan Sanger
Box 4376
St. Thomas, U.S.V.I. 00801

Builder Information
Years in business: 7
Carpenters employed: 3-4
Shop capacity: Boats to 100'

Recent New Construction
14' Whitehalls

Recent Repair Projects
90' ship jakt ANNE KRISTINE (1867). (Sistership to Amundson's South Pole exploration vessel). Completely rebuilt hull. Renewed frames, planking, and ceiling. Designed and installed new rig. 1983-'85.
72' Monk powerboat DESIREE. Restored hull with cold-molded overlay. 1984-'85.
37' Hood sloop IOLAIR. Gutting entire vessel. Replacing teak decks, cabinhouse, interior tanks, electrical and plumbing systems. Current project.

(continues)

U.S. VIRGIN ISLANDS

(West End Slipway, continued)
Yard Information
Services:
    Launching facilities
    Moorage
    Diesel and gas engine repair
    Rigging
Maintenance:
    Number of boats maintained per year: 50
    Percentage of wooden boats: 25-35
    Owner maintenance allowed above rail.
    Maximum size for hauling:
        Length: 120'
        Draft: 14'
        Tonnage: 200
Retail supplies:
    Paint, complete line of fastenings. 12 species of wood including pine, fir, teak, mahogany, angelique, silver bali, wana, and purpleheart. Everything a wooden boat needs!

CASTLE CREEK BOATWORKS—Paul Swanstrom
Box 33
Moab, UT 84532
801-259-8205

Builder Information
Years in business: 3
Carpenters employed: 1
Shop capacity: Boats to 20'
Willing to travel for on-the-site building projects.

Recent New Construction
14'6" and 17' whitewater dories. Plywood-and-fiberglass construction. Paul Swanstrom design. 5 built to date.

Recent Repair Projects
Whitewater dories. Minor repairs to complete restorations.

Yard Information
Maintenance:
    Number of boats maintained per year: 5
    Percentage of wooden boats: 100
    Owner maintenance allowed.
Retail supplies:
    WEST System epoxy.

VERMONT

THE ADIRONDACK GUIDEBOAT—Steve Kaulback
Box 144
Charlotte, VT 05445
802-425-3233

Builder Information
Years in business: 5
Carpenters employed: 1
Shop capacity: Boats to 16'10"

Recent New Construction
15' Adirondack guideboats. Strip-plank construction. Steve Kaulback design. 10 built 1980–'85.

CANOE IMPORTS—Robert Schumacher
RR #2, Box 2000
Shelburne, VT 05482
802-985-2992

Builder Information
Years in business: 15
Carpenters employed: 2
Shop capacity: Boats to 30'

Recent Repair Projects
12-30' canoes. Minor repairs to complete restorations. Rib, plank, and stem replacements, renewal of canvas or fiberglass hull sheathing. Stripping and refinishing of boat. 20+ canoes repaired in 1985.

Yard Information
Retail supplies:
   Materials for canoe restoration, including canvas, fiberglass, resin, filler.

DARLING'S BOATWORKS INC.
Point Bay Marina
Charlotte, VT 05445
802-425-3227

Builder Information
Years in business: 7
Carpenters employed: 2
Shop capacity: Boats to 40'

Recent New Construction
9'4" sailing skiff TETRA. Plywood lapstrake construction. Steve Redmond design. 2 built 1984.

Recent Repair Projects
18' St. Lawrence skiff. Renewed frames and split planking. Refinished boat. 1985.
20' bustle-sterned launch (1899). Completed minor hull repairs, installed new fuel tank, and refinished boat. 1985.
24' Chris-Craft cruiser (1956). Repaired double-planked bottom, replaced garboards, floors, frames, and some inner planking. 1985.
26' Dark Harbor 17½-class sloop. Recaulked bottom, stripped and repainted topsides. 1985.
30' Trojan cruiser. Replaced deck structure and aft sections of sheer planking. 1985.

VERMONT

Yard Information (provided in conjunction with nearby marina)
Services:
    Marina facilities
    Launching facilities
    Moorage
    Diesel and gas engine repair
    Rigging
Storage:
    Number of boats stored per year: 200
    Percentage of wooden boats: 10
    Maximum size for hauling and storing:
      Length: 45'
      Draft: 7'
      Tonnage: 25
Maintenance:
    Number of boats maintained per year: 15
    Percentage of wooden boats: 33
    Owner maintenance allowed above and below rail.
Retail supplies:
    Marine plywood, fastenings.

DRY HARBOR BOAT COMPANY—Tim Holloway
P.O. Box 4
Monkton, VT 05469
802-453-2884

Builder Information
Years in business: 9
Carpenters employed: 2
Shop capacity: Boats to 38'
Willing to travel for on-the-site building projects.

Recent New Construction
20' canoe yawl ELVER. Strip-plank construction. Steve Redmond
    design. Current project.
10' lapstrake yacht tender. Built 1985.

Recent Repair Projects
42' Chris-Craft. Replaced transom and transom framing. Replanked,
    refastened, and recaulked hull. 1984.
28' Controversy. Repaired lightning damage to hull, renewed cockpit. 1984.
14' Old Town canoe. Repaired planking and stems. Replaced sheerstrake and rubrails.
    Recanvased hull. 1985.
18' Lightning-class sloop. Replacing centerboard trunk. Current project.

Yard Information
Services:
    Overland transport
    Rigging
Storage:
    Number of boats stored per year: 10
    Percentage of wooden boats: 100
    Maximum size for hauling and storing:
      Length: 38'
(continues)

VERMONT

(Dry Harbor Boat Company, continued)
Maintenance:
    Number of boats maintained per year: 6-10
    Percentage of wooden boats: 100
    Owner maintenance allowed above and below rail.
Retail supplies:
    Wood, fastenings, paint. New and used hardware.

DAVE DUGDALE CEDAR STRIP CANOES—Dave Dugdale
RFD #1, Box 501
Windsor, VT 05089
802-436-2262

Builder Information
Years in business: 3
Carpenters employed: 1
Shop capacity: Boats 20-25'
Willing to travel for on-the-site building projects.

Recent New Construction
17' strip-planked Rangeley Lake boat. Ellis design. Built 1985.
16' strip-planked canoe. Built 1984.
17' strip-planked canoe. Built 1983.

Recent Repair Projects
17' strip-planked canoe. Repaired damaged fiberglass-and-epoxy sheathing. 1985.

THOMAS HILL
P.O. Box 16
Shelburne, VT 05482
802-985-3534

Builder Information
Years in business: 6
Carpenters employed: 1
Shop capacity: Boats to 25'
Willing to travel for on-the-site building projects.

Recent New Construction
Lightweight canoes and skiffs of plywood lapstrake construction. Designs
    by Ken Bausch and Steve Redmond. 65 built since 1979.

KING BOAT WORKS—Graeme King
P.O. Box 273
South Woodstock, VT 05071
802-457-1075

Builder Information
Years in business: 15
Carpenters employed: 3
Shop capacity: Shells to 60'

VERMONT

Recent New Construction
Shells designed by Graeme King for molded-plywood construction
(22 built in 1985):
23' single recreational rowing shells.
27-60' competition racing shells (23' singles, 33' doubles, 42-44' fours, and 59' eights).

Recent Repair Projects
Recreational rowing shells and competition racing shells.
Minor repairs to complete restorations.

Yard Information
Retail supplies:
Shell fittings, seats, riggers, crew shell trailers.

FUAT LATIF
RD #1, Box 1780
Moretown, VT 05660
802-496-3083

Builder Information
Years in business: 3
Carpenters employed: 1
Shop capacity: Boats to 20'

Recent New Construction
10'6" solo canoe. Lapstrake construction. J.H. Rushton design. Built 1985.
16' tandem canoe. Lapstrake construction. J.H. Rushton design. Built 1984.
12'9" solo canoe. Lapstrake construction. R.D. Culler design. Built 1983.

ONION RIVER BOATWORKS—Ken Bassett
Maple St., Box 4170
Waterbury Center, VT 05677
802-244-6495

Builder Information
Years in business: 7
Carpenters employed: 1+
Shop capacity: New construction to 24'
May be willing to travel for on-the-site building projects.

Recent New Construction
24' outboard canal cruiser. Cold-molded construction. Phil Bolger and Ken Bassett design. Built 1983.
18-24' sliding-seat touring boats. Plywood or lapstrake construction. Ken Bassett design. Over 20 built 1979-'85.
18' offshore rowing boat. Plywood construction. J. Garber and Ken Bassett design. Built 1985.
(continues)

VERMONT

(Onion River Boatworks, continued)
Recent Repair Projects
26′ McIntosh sloop. Renewed planking and centerboard trunk. Refastened bottom.
22′ Fay & Bowen launch. Renewed frames, planking, and decks. Refastened and refinished hull.
35′ Hinckley. Replaced cabintop canvas.
14′ Penn Yan outboard. Replaced transom.
16′ Lyman outboard. Modified transom.
16-18′ canoes. Complete restorations.
17′ sloop. Renewed keel, bottom planking, joinerwork, and deck and cabin framing. Refinished boat.
19′ Chris-Craft. Replaced leather upholstery.
36′ Belle Isle. Replaced transom, covering boards, and planking. Refastened hull.
30′ Chris-Craft. Replaced transom.
26′ Barnes. Renewed interior, flooring, and bulkheads.

SHELBURNE SHIPYARD
RFD 3, Box 3098, Harbor Rd.
Shelburne, VT 05482
802-985-3326

Builder Information
Years in business: 15 under current ownership
Carpenters employed: 3
Shop capacity: Boats to 60′

Recent Repair Projects
30′ workboat. Repaired engines, installed electronics, refinished hull. 1985.
Will do minor repairwork on hulls. Specialize in engine and electronic installations.

Yard Information
Services:
    Marina facilities
    Launching facilities
    Moorage
    Diesel and gas engine repair
    Rigging
Storage:
    Number of boats stored per year: 600
    Percentage of wooden boats: 5
    Inside storage facilities
    Maximum size for hauling and storing:
        Length: 58′
        Tonnage: 35
Maintenance:
    Number of boats maintained per year: 100
    Percentage of wooden boats: 20
    Owner maintenance allowed above and below rail.
Retail supplies:
    Complete inventory of parts and supplies.

JOHN W. ENGLAND III
P.O. Box 142
Wilcomico Church, VA 22579
804-580-2776

Builder Information
Years in business: 10
Carpenters employed: 1
Shop capacity: Boats to any length
Willing to travel for on-the-site building projects.

Recent New Construction
60′ replica of 16th-century sailing vessel ELIZABETH II. Lines by William Baker. Built 1983.
33′ Araminta ketch. Double-planked construction. L.F. Herreshoff design. Built 1985.
8′3″ lapstrake pram. L.F. Herreshoff design. Built 1985.

GLEBE POINT BOAT CO., INC.
TIFFANY YACHTS
Glebe Point, Box 133
Burgess, VA 22432
804-453-3464

Builder Information
Years in business: 50
Carpenters employed: 12
Shop capacity: Boats to 65′
Willing to travel for on-the-site building projects.

Recent New Construction
36′ Angler. Composite construction. Tiffany Yachts design. Built 1984.
50′ sportfisherman. Composite construction. Tiffany Yachts design. Built 1984.
62′ sportfisherman. Composite construction. Tiffany Yachts design. Built 1985.

Repair Work
Hull, engine, and electronic repairs. Restoration and redesigning.

Yard Information
Services:
    Diesel and gas engine repair
Maintenance:
    Number of boats maintained per year: 200
    Percentage of wooden boats: 75
Retail supplies:
    Mahogany, teak, paint, fastenings, pipe fittings, electronics, line. Deck and underwater hardware.

JUDSON BOATS—David Judson
P.O. Box 417
Grimstead, VA 23064
804-725-7507

Builder Information
Years in business: 14
Carpenters employed: 1
Shop capacity: New construction to 36′
(continues)

VIRGINIA

(Judson Boats, continued)
Recent New Construction
27' centerboard schooner. Dana/Judson design. Built 1983.
18' V-bottomed daysailer. Lapstrake sides. R.D. Culler design. Built 1984.
21' outboard-powered deadrise crabbing skiff. Judson design. Built 1983.

Recent Repair Projects
50' Bay-type workboat. Renewed stem and stem lining. Rebuilt foredeck. 1985.

NELSON BOATWORKS—Barry A. Nelson
5505 Ravenel Lane
Springfield, VA 22151
703-931-6181

Builder Information
Years in business: 5
Carpenters employed: 1
Shop capacity: Boats to 30'

Recent New Construction
14' strip-planked sailing peapod. John Gardner design. Built 1985.
9' double-paddle solo canoe. Strip-plank construction. Barry Nelson design. Built 1984.
6½' pram. Stitch-and-glue plywood construction. Barry Nelson design. Built 1984.

NORFOLK SCHOOL OF BOATBUILDING—Nautical Adventures, Inc.
Box 371
Norfolk, VA 23501
804-627-7266

Builder Information
Years in business: 7
Carpenters employed: 1 (plus non-paid students)
Shop capacity: Boats to 25'

Recent New Construction
20' Dark Harbor 12½ sloop. B.B. Crowninshield design. Built 1983–'85.
14' sailing skiff. Traditional design. Built 1984.
15' flat-bottomed outboard skiff. Wilson design. 2 built 1985.
16' V-bottomed outboard skiff. Plywood lapstrake construction. Wilson design. Built 1984.
16' working scow. Strip-planked topsides and plywood bottom. Wilson design. Built 1984.
11' plywood rowing skiff. Wilson design. 3 built 1983 and 1985.
13–15' flat-bottomed rowing skiffs. Traditional designs. 7 built 1983–'85.
25' Race Point surfboat. Lapstrake construction. Built 1984.
16' double-ended surfboat. Pete Culler design. 2 built 1982–'83.
10' lapstrake pram. L.F. Herreshoff design. 2 built 1983.

Recent Repair Projects
42' New York 32-class sloop. Replaced 16 planks and stem above waterline. Renewed interior. 1984–'85.
65' Primrose ketch. Replaced 45' of bulwark and caprail. 1984.
19' Chris-Craft runabout. Repaired planking and transom, laid new mahogany deck. 1985.
15' Barbour runabout. Renewed bottom and transom. 1985.
18' Hampton One Design-class sloop. Restored hull. 1982.

VIRGINIA

OCRAN BOAT SHOP, INC.—Fred Ajootian
Rte. 1, Box 783
White Stone, VA 22578
804-435-6305

Builder Information
Years in business: 45
Carpenters employed: 2-3
Shop capacity: Boats to 50′

Recent New Construction
34′6″ Presto-type ketch. Harry Bullifant design. Built 1981.
24′ utility tugboat. Scott Sprague design. Built 1983.
30′ sportfisherman. Fred Ajootian design. Built 1985.
14′ and 16′ flat-bottomed skiffs. 2 built each year.

Recent Repair Projects
53′ Elco power cruiser (1935). Replanked, refastened, and refinished hull. 1984-'85.
28′ Herreshoff H-28 ketch (1947). Completely restored. 1983-'84.
38′ yawl. Aage Nielsen design. Refastened topsides, renewed toerails, refinished hull. 1983.
26′ cat-ketch WILD DUCK. Murray Peterson design. Completely restored 1981.
43′ schooner (1927). John Alden design. Completely restored from keel up. 1984.
20′ Thompson speedboat (ca. 1948). Rebuilt, refastened, and refinished hull.
18′ Old Town canoe (ca. 1950). Replaced planks and frames, recanvased hull. 1984.

Yard Information
Services:
    Launching facilities
    Moorage
    Diesel and gas engine repair
    Rigging
Maintenance:
    Number of boats maintained per year: 150
    Percentage of wooden boats: 50
Retail Supplies:
    Paint, fasteners, wood, WEST System supplies, engine parts and supplies.
    Materials for boat maintenance.

ROCK HALL BOAT SHOP—David Scarbrough
P.O. Box 185
Burgess, VA 22432
804-453-5574

Builder Information
Years in business: 12
Carpenters employed: 1
Shop capacity: Boats to 25′

Recent New Construction
16′ sloop VIREO. Plywood lapstrake construction. D. Scarbrough design. Built 1985.
17′ flat-bottomed skiff. Lapstrake construction. D. Scarbrough design. Built 1984.
10′ sailing dory. Lapstrake construction. Chaisson design. Built 1984.
18′ houseboat RETREAT. William Atkin design. Built 1985.
(continues)

VIRGINIA

(Rock Hall Boat Shop, continued)
Recent Repair Projects
23' Staten Island oyster skiff. Renewed frames and transom.
    Replaced bottom planking, floorboards, and tonging platform. Repaired in 1984 for Staten Island Historical Society.
18' Atkin hardangersjekte. Repaired gunwales and hull as needed.
    Added mizzenmast and refinished boat. 1983-'85.

Yard Information
Maintenance:
    Number of boats maintained per year: 2
    Percentage of wooden boats: 100
    Owner maintenance allowed above and below rail.

ROLLINS BOATYARD—William M. Rollins
189 Church Rd.
Poquoson, VA 23662
804-868-6915 or 868-6710

Builder Information
Years in business: 33
Carpenters employed: 1
Shop capacity: Boats to 45'

Recent New Construction
Boats designed by Rollins Boatyard:
    26' and 38' Chesapeake Bay skipjacks. 2 built 1975 and 1983.
    26' Chesapeake log canoe. Built 1985.
    18' and 26' pleasure fishing boats. 2 built 1984-'85.
    40' crab boat. Built 1985.

Recent Repair Projects
All types of wooden boat repair.

Yard Information
Services:
    Marina facilities
    Moorage
    Engine repair
    Rigging
Maintenance:
    Number of boats maintained per year: 50-60
    Percentage of wooden boats: 95
    Maximum size for hauling:
        Length: 45'

SHERWOOD BOATBUILDING CO.—Paul S. Sherwood
Rte. 628, Box 184
Wake, VA 23176
804-776-6591

Builder Information
Years in business: 12
Carpenters employed: 2
Shop capacity: New construction to 36'
Willing to travel for on-the-site building projects.

Recent New Construction
22' cruising cutter. J. Atkin design. Built 1984.
18' lapstrake daysailer. Paul Sherwood design. Built 1985.
14'2" open fishing boat. Cold-molded. Paul Sherwood design. Built 1985.

Recent Repair Projects
36' Eldredge-McInnis sloop. Replaced deckbeams and deck, cabin, cockpit, and some planking. Refastened and refinished hull. Installed new diesel engine. 1984–'85.
42' ketch. Replaced stem, hood ends, and some planking. Renewed aft main bulkhead, cabin, deckbeams, and carlins. Recaulked bottom and refastened hull as needed. 1985.

Yard Information
Services:
  Overland transport
  Rigging
Maintenance:
  Number of boats maintained per year: 3
  Percentage of wooden boats: 100
  Owner maintenance allowed above and below rail.

VIRGINIA BOATSHOP—Carl V. Pedersen
P.O. Box 277
Seaford, VA 23690
804-898-4578

Builder Information
Years in business: 15
Carpenters employed: Up to 10
Shop capacity: Boats 100' and over
Willing to travel for on-the-site building projects.

Recent New Construction
12' plywood Pelican class. William Short design. 1984 and current projet.
40' pleasure skipjack, lines taken off old boat. Current project.
17' sloop. Pete Culler design. Built 1984.
44' 17th-century replica DISCOVERY. Fees design. Built 1982–'84.
55' 17th-century replica GODSPEED. Fees design. Built 1982–'84.
22' open deadrise boat. C.V. Pedersen design. Built 1984.
30' carvel and strip-planked net reel workboat. C.V. Pedersen design. Built 1985.
25' cypress-and-plywood 8-paddle canoe with dragon's head. Designed and built by Pedersen and crew for a raft race, which they won! Built 1983.

Recent Repair Projects
18' Hampton One-Design sloop. Replacing planks and frames. Current project.
28' 3-log canoe for Watermans Museum display, Yorktown, Virginia.
  Hull repair, rot removal, 1985.
35' Mariner ketch. New transom, bulwark repair, new caps and taffrail with stanchions. New teak cockpit and rig. Current project.
60' Crab dredger. New stem and planking. Staving for decking.
85' Scallop trawlers (numerous jobs). Frame and plank replacement. New holding tanks, cabin, and pilothouse repairs. 1979–'85.
111' 17th-century square-rigger SUSAN CONSTANT. Replaced about 95% of hull from waterline up. Work done on location and in the water at the Jamestown Festival Park, Jamestown, Virginia. 1981–'82.

(continues)

VIRGINIA

(Virginia Boatshop, continued)
Yard Information
Services:
    Overland transport
    Some diesel and gas engine repair
    Rigging
    Maintenance
Retail supplies:
    Heart pine, juniper, and white oak when sufficient quantity in to sell.

ZIMMERMAN MARINE—Steve Zimmerman
Rte. 650
Miles, VA 23114
804-725-3440

Builder Information
Years in business: 5
Carpenters employed: 3
Shop capacity: Boats to 72′

Recent New Construction
16′ cold-molded proa. Chris White design. Built 1985.
26′ cold-molded launch. Phil Bolger design. Built 1983.

Recent Repair Projects
85′ Trumpy (1931). Renewed deck with plywood and Dynel. 1983-'85.
104′ Trumpy motoryacht SEQUOIA (1928). Renewed structural beams, modified crew's quarters. 1984.
41′ ketch. Replaced stem, recaulked deck, and refinished hull. 1983-'85.
52′ motorsailer BRAVO. Refinished spars, worked on electrical system. 1982.
37′ cat yawl. Installed diesel engine, Loran, and did maintenance work. 1984.

Yard Information
Services:
    Moorage
    Diesel and gas engine repair
    Rigging
Maintenance:
    Number of boats maintained per year: 10
    Percentage of wooden boats: 50
    Owner maintenance allowed above and below rail.
    Maximum size for hauling:
        Length: 50′
        Draft: 6′6″
        Tonnage: 18
Retail supplies:
    Will order on request.

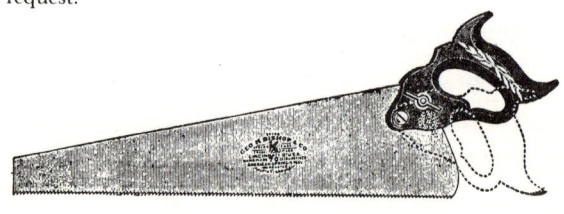

WASHINGTON

ANDREASSEN BOATWORKS—Dale Hoff
5619 Marine View Dr.
Tacoma, WA 98422
206-272-9513

Builder Information
Years in business: 4
Carpenters employed: 2
Shop capacity: Boats to 40'
Willing to travel locally for on-the-site building projects.

Recent New Construction
31' cold-molded sloop. Design by Stew Biehl. Built 1984.
11' lapstrake dinghy. Dale Hoff design. 3 built 1982-'84.
20' cold-molded, sliding-seat gig. Dale Hoff design. Built 1985.
7'5" flat-bottomed yacht tender. Plywood lapstrake construction. Dale Hoff design. 2 built 1985.
17' cold-molded canoe. Dale Hoff design. Built 1985.
12'6" lapstrake Swampscott dory. John Gardner design. 2 built 1983.

Recent Repair Projects
31' cold-molded sloop. Repaired holes and cracks in hull. 1985.
45' powerboat. Replaced cabintop. 1985.
27-33' powerboats. Repaired electrolytic rot around struts and rudderposts. 1984-'85.
17' Century runabout. Renewing planks and fastenings, refinishing. Current project.

Yard Information
Services:
  Launching facilities
  Overnight moorage for customers
  Diesel and gas engine repair
  Rigging
Maintenance:
  Number of boats maintained per year: 4
  Percentage of wooden boats: 25
  Owner maintenance allowed above and below rail.
  Maximum size for hauling:
    Length: 38'
    Draft: 7'
    Tonnage: 9
Retail supplies:
  Paint, sandpaper, epoxy, and fiberglass. Ordered on request.

L.H. BATES VOCATIONAL TECHNICAL INSTITUTE
John Possin
1101 South Yakima Ave.
Tacoma, WA 98405
206-597-7265

Builder Information
Years in business: 35
Carpenters employed: 20 students
Shop capacity: Boats to 40'

Recent New Construction
37'10" sloop. Joe Trumbly design. Built 1980.
24'7" cutter. Lyle Hess design. Current project.

WASHINGTON

BOATYARD INC.
3201 Fairview East
Seattle, WA 98102
206-323-3834

Builder Information
Years in business: 25
Carpenters employed: 10

Recent Repair Projects
Pleasure craft and commercial fishing boats. Minor repairs to complete restorations.

Yard Information
Services:
 Diesel and gas engine repair

RICHARD B. BRADEN
7781 N.E. North St.
Bainbridge Island, WA 98110
206 812 1514

Builder Information
Years in business: 8 (part-time)
Carpenters employed: 1
Shop capacity: Boats to 26'
Willing to travel for on-the-site building projects.

Recent New Construction
16' Snipe-class sloop. Wm. Crosby design. Built 1985.
14' cold-molded Port Madison pram. Wm. Garden design. Built 1985.
12' plywood skiff. Phil Bolger design. Built 1985.
8' plywood-and-fiberglass El Toro-class racing dinghy. Built 1985.

Recent Repair Projects
14' Port Madison pram. Replaced transom, forward frame, keelson, centerboard and trunk, and gunwales. Rebuilt boom and mast. 1985.
16' rowing skiff. Replaced keelson, gunwales, stem, and thwarts. 1985.
8' El Toro-class dinghy. Replaced centerboard trunk, gunwales, and boom. Repaired mast. 1985.

Yard Information
Services:
 Overland transport
 Rigging
Storage:
 Number of boats stored per year: 13
 Percentage of wooden boats: 100
 Inside storage facilities
 Maximum size for hauling and storage:
  Length: 26'
  Draft: 5'
  Tonnage: 6
Maintenance:
 Number of boats maintained per year: 6-8
 Percentage of wooden boats: 100
 Owner maintenance allowed above and below rail.

WASHINGTON

Retail supplies:
   Lumber and plywood, putty, resin, fiberglass, fastenings and fittings, paint, bedding compound, sealants.

CORUM BOATWORKS—Dennis Corum
31330 S. Highway 97
Tonasket, WA 98855
509-486-2069

Builder Information
Years in business: 8
Carpenters employed: 1
Shop capacity: Boats to 15′
May be willing to travel for on-the-site building projects.

Recent Repair Projects
14′6″ Rana sloop (ca. 1970). Replacing frames and planking. Current project.

DEVLIN DESIGNING BOATBUILDERS—Sam Devlin
2431 Gravelly Beach Loop
Olympia, WA 98502
206-866-0164

Builder Information
Years in business: 7
Carpenters employed: 4
Shop capacity: New construction to 48′
Willing to travel for on-the-site building projects.

Recent New Construction
The following were all designed by Sam Devlin for sewn-seam (stitch-and-glue) plywood construction:
31′6″ pilothouse schooner. Built 1985.
19′ Winter Wren-class sloop. Built 1985.
10′8″ to 15′6″ duckboats. 4 built 1985.
15′2″ sneakbox-type duckboats. 6 built 1985.
15′6″ Nancy's China-class sloop. 4 built 1985.
20′2″ harbor tug. Built 1985.
11′8″ Peeper-class rowboat. 8 built 1985.
15′6″ Super Peeper-class rowboat. 2 built 1985.
11′2″ lapstrake solo canoe. Built 1985.

Recent Repair Projects
26′ powerboat. Replaced transom. 1985.
82′ schooner. Repaired rot damage. 1985.

Yard Information
Services:
   Marina facilities
   Launching facilities
   Overland transport
   Rigging

(continues)

WASHINGTON

(Devlin Designing Boatbuilders, continued)
Storage:
    Number of boats stored per year: 4
    Percentage of wooden boats: 100
    Maximum size for hauling and storing:
        Length: 70'
        Draft: 8'
        Tonnage: 80
Maintenance:
    Number of boats maintained per year: 20
    Percentage of wooden boats: 100
    Owner maintenance allowed above and below rail.
Retail supplies:
    Plans for sewn-seam plywood boats (catalog available). Supplies for building are limited to stock on hand.

DOG ISLAND BOAT WORKS—David C. Hartford
368 Edens Rd.
Guemes Island, WA 98221
206-293-9361, evenings

Builder Information
Years in business: 18
Carpenters employed: 1
Shop capacity: Boats 65-75'
Willing to travel for on-the-site building projects.

Recent New Construction
51'6" schooner. Henry Scheel design. Current project.

Recent Repair Projects
55' Colin Archer Redningskoite (hull #40). Replaced deckbeams, breasthook, lodging knees, and portion of sheer clamp. Laid new planked deck, refinished hull. 1985.
42' Dave LaClerq-built Kodiak seiner. Recaulked hull and deck. 1985.
40' double-ended Alaskan troller. Replaced 15 frames and 20 planks, refastened and recaulked hull. Rebuilt fish hold and trolling cockpit, replaced some covering boards. Renewed deckbeams, deck planking and caulking, bulwarks, and railcaps. 1982-'84.
40' double-ended workboat. Replaced stem and sternpost, renewed hull planking and caulking as needed. 1984.
38' harbor tug. Worked on project involving extensive rebuilding of the boat. Replaced approximately 75% of timbers, refastened and recaulked hull and deck. 1983.
75' fish tender. Renewed and refastened 20 planks, recaulked hull. 1981.
12'6" lapstrake tender. Renewed transom, frames, and garboard planks. Replaced keel, keelson, knees, inwales, thwarts, stem, and breasthook. Current project.
42' New York 30 #17, PHRYNE. Completely restored boat. 1971-'76.

Yard Information
Services:
    Overland transport (size limitations)

WASHINGTON

FREYA BOAT WORKS—David Jackson
909 3rd
Anacortes, WA 98221
206-293-6143

Builder Information
Years in business: 30
Carpenters employed: 3
Shop capacity: Boats to 100'
Willing to travel for on-the-site building projects.

Recent New Construction
62' EAST System™ schooner. Ted Brewer design. Built 1983.
18' lapstrake Queens gig. William Garden design. Built 1984.

Recent Repair Projects
65' harbor launch. Replaced decks and bulwarks. 1985.
34' Owens cabin cruiser. Replaced keel, keelson, floors, and garboards. 1985.
22' Century Raven runabout. Completely overhauled. 1985.
65' Chris-Craft. Rebuilt transom and quarters. 1985.
40' schooner. Replaced hatches. 1985.
55' cutter. Renewed mast and rig. 1985.
34' diesel cruiser. Renewed pilothouse. 1985.

Yard Information
Services:
    Moorage
    Diesel and gas engine repair
    Rigging
Storage:
    Number of boats stored per year: 5
    Percentage of wooden boats: 100
Maintenance:
    Number of boats maintained per year: 8
    Percentage of wooden boats: 50
    Owner maintenance allowed above and below rail.

GEORGE'S LIL SHIPYARD—George Calkins
P.O. Box 222, 1441 Griffith Pt. Rd.
Nordland, WA 98358
206-385-3649

Builder Information
Years in business: 55
Carpenters employed: 1 (semi-retired)
Shop capacity: Boats to 40'

Recent New Construction
    "At age 74, I am pretty much retired and not looking for work. But I have a love for wooden boats, and as long as the Lord allows me good health, I intend to keep 'messing around in boats.'
    "I hired a couple of husky young men who spent 14 months with me, building a 37' (on deck) gaff cutter (spruce planking, wedge seam, oak frames, fir deck). Alone I am building my own takeoff of the Lincolnville wherries and recently built a 12' lapstrake double-ender after a Danish design. It's equipped with mainsail and jib, really a fun little boat.

(continues)

WASHINGTON

(George's Lil Shipyard, continued)

"I have built boats and designed them all my life. The Bartender (WoodenBoat classifieds) is my design and I have a 26-footer started. But since I also love to go boating, I don't stay home and work at it steady anymore. I sell plans for the Bartenders, but as I can't keep all my boats for pets, I have to sell them now and then. That gives me the opportunity to go on to something else. Boats are my thing!"—*George Calkins*

HADLOCK BOATYARD—Denis Dignan
Lower Hadlock Rd., P.O. Box 27
Hadlock, WA 98339
206-385-4894

Builder Information
Years in business: 8
Carpenters employed: 2
Shop capacity: Boats to 40' inside, larger outside

Recent New Construction
30' gaff sloop. William Atkin design. Built 1981.
20' sloop. George Stadel design. Built 1983.
18' powerboat. Planked sides, plywood bottom. Built 1985.
Lapstrake and plywood dinghies.

Recent Repair Projects
32' sloop (1892). Complete rebuilding is underway. To date we have renewed backbone, floors, frames, shelf, and clamp.
26' Chris-Craft (1949). Rebuilt cockpit, coamings, transom, deck, some planking, and engine. 1984-'85.

Yard Information
Services:
   Limited moorage

WALLY HARRISON, BOATBUILDER
16800 Seminole Rd.
Poulsbo, WA 98370
206-697-3830

Builder Information
Years in business: 1 full-time, 25 part-time
Carpenters employed: 1
Shop capacity: Boats to 24'

Recent New Construction
22' Liberty Bay diesel launch. Strip-plank construction. Trachi design. Built 1985.
11'8" pulling boat FAVORITE. Strip-plank construction. Plans from Mystic Seaport Museum. Built 1985.

WASHINGTON

HAUSER BOAT WORKS—Scott Hauser
607 E. 5th Ave.
Olympia, WA 98501
206-943-3076

Builder Information
Years in business: 5
Carpenters employed: 1
Shop capacity: New construction to 35'
Willing to travel for on-the-site building projects.

Recent New Construction
Boats designed by Scott Hauser for sewn-seam plywood construction:
    11'8" 2-piece nesting sailing yacht tender Roy Bean. 3 built 1982-'84.
    8' sailing pram. 10 built 1982-'85.
    15' peapod. Built 1983.
    11'8" 2-piece nesting rowing yacht tender. 3 built 1983-'84.
    8' pram. 5 built 1983-'85.
    17' racing peapod Nighthawk. Built 1984.
    23' single recreational shell. Built 1985.
    21' 5-person pilot gig. Built 1984.
Other new construction projects:
    17' cold-molded knockabout. L.F. Herreshoff design. Built 1983.
    24' Stone Horse sloop. Designed by S.S. Crocker, modified for sewn-seam plywood. Built 1983.

Recent Repair Projects
31' Mariner ketch. Rebuilt cockpit and aft cabin bulkhead. Laid new teak deck and did some interior cabinetry work. 1984-'85.
49' Sparkman & Stephens racing sloop BAY BEA. Built new aft stateroom and cabinets, replaced ceiling and forward hatch. 1984.
23' Thompson power cruiser. Installed new keel and cabintop molding. 1985.

Yard Information
Retail supplies:
    WEST System epoxy and related products. Limited stock of varnish, paint, brushes, Sikaflex, fiberglass.

HAVORN MARINE SERVICES—Lee H. Ehrheart
415 N.W. 45th St.
Seattle, WA 98107
206-789-7043

Builder Information
Years in business: 8
Carpenters employed: 2
Shop capacity: Boats to any length
Willing to travel for on-the-site building projects.

Recent Repair Projects
64' Alden ketch JESSICA (1926). Installed laminated oak stem and frames. Renewed horn timber, deadwood, and keelbolts. Replacing hull planking. 1983-'86.

Yard Information
Maintenance:
    Number of boats maintained per year: 12
    Percentage of wooden boats: 100
    Owner maintenance allowed.

WASHINGTON

HEADWATER BOATS—Tracy O'Brien
156 Bunker Creek Rd.
Chehalis, WA 98532
206-748-4089

Builder Information
Years in business: 3
Carpenters employed: 2
Shop capacity: Boats to 30'
Willing to travel for on-the-site building projects.

Recent New Construction
18', 20', and 24' plywood power Oregon dory with pilothouse. T. O'Brien design. 2 built 1983-'84, 1 in progress.
9' strip-planked pram. T. O'Brien design. 2 built 1983.
10' plywood deadrise skiff. T. O'Brien design. 2 built 1984-'85.
16' plywood pirogue. Phil Bolger design. 4 built 1982-'85.
14' plywood McKenzie drift boat. T. O'Brien design. 5 built 1982-'85.

Recent Repair Projects
16' McKenzie drift boat. Installed new horseshoe transom and bulkhead for motorwell. 1984.
16' Bolger pirogue. Replaced original bottom with ⅜" plywood, 1983.

Yard Information
Retail supplies:
   Plans available for dories, McKenzie drift boat, skiff, punt, and runabout.

ISLAND CANOE CO.—Earl Doan
3556 W. Blakely Ave. N.E.
Bainbridge Island, WA 98110
206-842-5997

Builder Information
Years in business: 5
Carpenters employed: 1, part-time
Shop capacity: Boats to 18'

Recent New Construction
17' decked sailing canoe. Lapstrake construction. E. Doan design. Built 1984.
16' lapstrake open canoe. Peterborough design modified by E. Doan. 2 built 1984-'85.

Recent Repair Projects
16' Willits canoe. Replaced stems and gunwales. Repaired hull planking and deck. 1984.
18' Old Town canoe. Renewed ribs, planking, and hull canvas. Recaned seats and added sailing rig. 1984.
16-17' canoes. Replaced stems, renewed planking and hull canvas. 1985.

Yard Information
Retail supplies:
   Paddles, life jackets, and boat carts. Sails and sail fittings, sliding-seat rowing rigs.

WASHINGTON

KARELSEN CUSTOM BOATS, INC.—Edward A. Karelsen
8516 Wallingford N.
Seattle, WA 98103
206-525-9736

Builder Information
Years in business: 33
Carpenters employed: 2
Shop capacity: Boats to 29'
Willing to travel for on-the-site building projects.

Recent New Construction
Plywood hydroplanes. Ed Karelsen design.

KNUDSON-MILLER BOATYARD CO.—John Knudson
626 W. Ewing
Seattle, WA 98119
206-285-5958

Builder Information
Years in business: 3
Carpenters employed: 5
Shop capacity: Boats to 50'
Willing to travel for on-the-site building projects.

Recent Repair Projects
50' Pacemaker. Repaired foredeck rot. 1985.
50' sloop. Repaired stem rot and electrolytic damage. Replaced plank hood ends. 1984.
38' rowing shell. Repaired skin damage, refinished boat. 1984.
30' Blanchard Senior-class sloop. Renewed frames and floors. 1984.

Yard Information
Services:
    Launching facilities
    Diesel and gas engine repair
    Rigging
Maintenance:
    Number of boats maintained per year: 200
    Percentage of wooden boats: 30
    Owner maintenance sometimes allowed above and below rail.
    Maximum size for hauling:
      Length: 45'
      Draft: 8'
      Tonnage: 10

KOLIN BOAT WORKS—Richard S. Kolin
1314 15th St.
Anacortes, WA 98221
206-293-6393

Builder Information
Years in business: 18
Carpenters employed: 1
Shop capacity: Boats to 25'
Willing to travel for on-the-site building projects.
(continues)

WASHINGTON

(Kolin Boat Works, continued)

Recent New Construction
10′ plywood flat-iron skiff Clancy. Modified stitch-and-glue construction. Designed by R.S. Kolin. 2 built 1985 as prototype kit boat.
19′ plywood bateau. Modified stitch-and-glue construction. Designed by R.S. Kolin. Built 1985 as prototype kit boat.

Recent Repair Projects
16′ Thompson outboard runabout. Replaced deck and transom, renewed interior joinerwork. 1985.

LAKE UNION DRYDOCK CO.—Jim Francis
1515 Fairview E.
Seattle, WA 98102
206-323-6400

Builder Information
Years in business: 39
Carpenters employed: 19
Shop capacity: Boats to 300′

Recent Repair Projects
165′ U.S. Navy minesweepers. Work has involved replacing engines and completing repairs to planking, sheathing, decks, and frames. 3-4 boats have been overhauled each year since 1977.
Tugs, barges, fishing boats, and historic vessels. Have routinely replaced planking and keel shoes and completed major woodworking repairs. 1946 to present.

Yard Information
Services:
    Moorage
    Diesel and gas engine repair
    Rigging
Storage:
    Number of boats stored per year: 40
    Percentage of wooden boats: 40
    Inside storage facilities
    Maximum size for hauling and storing:
      Length: 400′
      Draft: 21′
      Tonnage: 3900
Maintenance:
    Number of boats maintained per year: 400
    Percentage of wooden boats: 50
    Some owner maintenance allowed above rail.
Retail supplies:
    Materials in stock as requested.

WASHINGTON

LANGLEY BOAT & YACHT WORK—David Langley and Ivan Hope
2325 Washington St., P.O. Box 657
Port Townsend, WA 98368
206-385-4668

Builder Information
Years in business: 15
Carpenters employed: 2+
Shop capacity: Boats to 60'
Willing to travel for on-the-site building projects.

Recent New Construction
Boats designed by Langley:
- 36' commercial schooner. Current project.
- 42' scow-type houseboat. Current project.
- 28' sampan houseboat. Plywood construction. Built 1977.
- 14' skiff. Carvel and plywood construction. Built 1978.

Other new construction:
- 42' scow-schooner. Wm. Garden design. Current project.

Recent Repair Projects
24' inland cruiser ALICE LOLLIS. Completely rebuilding boat. Renewing frames, floors, sole, and interior joinerwork. Replacing decks and rails. Refastening, recaulking, and refinishing hull. 1979-'86.

37' Swedish ketch SHADOW FAX. Renewed frames, planking, horn timber, and shaftlog. Rebuilt cockpit, repaired teak deck, and refinished boat. 1983.

34' Norwegian motorsailer HAGAVIR. Rebuilt deck frame and deck. Renewed cabinhouse, rubrails, toerails, and fittings. Refinished boat. 1984.

53' Starling Burgess schooner ROSE OF SHARON. Replaced mast partners, deckbeams and deck, cabinhouse, and interior trim. Refinished boat. 1982.

Yard Information
Services:
- Marina facilities
- Overland transport
- Diesel engine repair
- Moorage
- Sail repair
- Rigging

Maintenance:
- Number of boats maintained per year: 4+
- Percentage of wooden boats: 100
- Owner maintenance allowed above and below rail.

Retail supplies:
- Materials for construction and repair of wooden boats. Fastenings, paints, fittings, etc. Will do foundry work.

LOVRIC'S SEA CRAFT—Tony Lovric
3022 Oakes Ave.
Anacortes, WA 98221
206-293-2042

Builder Information
Years in business: 25
Carpenters employed: 5
Shop capacity: Boats to 150'
(continues)

WASHINGTON

(Lovric's Sea Craft, continued)

Recent New Construction
55' strip-planked motoryacht. Monk design. Built 1981.

Recent Repair Projects
58' limit seiner. Renewed frames and starboard bottom planking. 1985.
60' seiner. Repaired damaged area on cabin. Completely rebuilt interior. 1985.
48' sailboat. Stripped and refinished hull. 1982.

Yard Information
Services:
    Marina facilities
    Launching facilities
    Moorage
    Diesel and gas engine repair
Maintenance:
    Number of boats maintained per year: 70
    Percentage of wooden boats: 70
    Owner maintenance allowed above rail.

MAGNER & SONS BOATWORKS—John F. Magner
P.O. Box 114, 214 Carlsborg Rd.
Carlsborg, WA 98324
206-683-4795

Builder Information
Years in business: 15
Carpenters employed: 2
Shop capacity: Boats to 30'

Recent New Construction
16' Great Pelican-class sloops. Plywood construction. Wm. Short design. 14 built since 1971.
16' Grand Banks sloop. Plywood construction. Garcia design. Built 1974.
12' lapstrake sailing skiff. Atkin design. Built 1979.
20' canoe yawl Elver. Strip-plank construction. Redmond design. Built 1981.
23' schooner Florence Oakland. Atkin design. Built 1983.
30' schooner Little Maid. Atkin design. Built 1983.
25' plywood Black Witch. Garcia design. Built 1985.
7' plywood skiff Precious. Atkin design. Built 1985.
21' lapstrake power skiff. Atkin design. Built 1980.

Recent Repair Projects
25' Thunder Bird. Replaced 6' of bow, rotted stem, and forefoot. 1979.

Yard Information
Services:
    Rigging
Retail supplies:
    Paint, fastenings, plywood.

WASHINGTON

CARL MEINZINGER, SHIPWRIGHT
426 S. Shore Rd.
Guemes Island, WA 98221
206-293-3634

Builder Information
Years in business: 11
Carpenters employed: 1
Shop capacity: Boats to 40'
Willing to travel for on-the-site building projects.

Recent New Construction
18' lapstrake pulling boat. Ken Bassett design. Built 1985.

Recent Repair Projects
Yachts and commercial fishing boats, 20-60'. Repair work has involved renewing planking, framing, decks, guards, and stems; caulking, making spars, fittings, and inboard joinerwork. 20-22 boats per year. 1974-'85.

Yard Information
Services:
   Rigging
Retail supplies:
   Lumber, fastenings, paint, and hardware.

NEXUS MARINE CONSTRUCTION—David Roberts
3816 Railway Ave.
Everett, WA 98201
206-252-8330

Builder Information
Years in business: 11
Carpenters employed: 3-9
Shop capacity: Boats to 45'
Willing to travel for on-the-site building projects.

Recent New Construction
18' plywood daysailer. Frank Davis design. Built 1980.
8' cold-molded pram. Frank Davis design. Built 1978.
15' plywood skiff. David Roberts design. Built 1983.
15' plywood skiff. Phil Bolger design. Built 1983.
16' plywood dory. David Roberts design. Built 1985.
20' Carolina dory. 10 built 1982-'85.
23' cabin skiff. David Roberts design. Built 1985.
26' Bartender. George Calkins design. Built 1985.
27' St. Pierre dory. David Roberts design. Built 1984.
15' rowing and sailing dory. Iain Oughtred design. Built 1983.

Recent Repair Projects
18' pocket cruiser. Replaced bottom, deck, cabin, and interior. 1985.
22' sportfisherman. Replaced chines, repaired side, hardtop, windows, bottom. 1981.
36' power yacht. Installed 24 frames, replaced canvas on cabintop. 1981.
22' sloop. Renewed frames, sheer plank, deck. 1980.
29' sloop. Recaulked deck, repaired cabintop, samson post, and cornerposts. 1979.
(continues)

WASHINGTON

(Nexus Marine Construction, continued)
Yard Information
Services:
    Launching facilities
    Moorage
    Rigging
Maintenance:
    Number of boats maintained per year: 1-3
    Percentage of wooden boats: 100
    Owner maintenance allowed.
Retail supplies:
    Will order on request. Lumber, paint, epoxy, fastenings, hardware.

NORBERG COMPANY—Norman Berg
117 Frontage Rd. N.
Pacific, WA 98047
206-833-2151

Builder Information
Years in business: 20
Carpenters employed: 2
Shop capacity: Boats to 50'
Willing to travel for on-the-site building projects.

Recent Repair Projects
21'6" Dodge (1930). Replaced bottom and deck. 1984.
36' Hacker (1950). Complete restoration of boat. 1984.
17' Fairliner (1947). Replaced bottom and a few side planks. 1984.
19' Bryant (1960). Replaced bottom and a few side planks. 1984.

NORTHERN MARINE INDUSTRIES, INC.—Ben Harry
3133 Fairview Ave. E.
Seattle, WA 98125
206-323-5945

Builder Information
Years in business: 12
Carpenters employed: 10
Shop capacity: Boats to 600'
Willing to travel for on-the-site building projects.

Recent New Construction
41' schooner COASTER III. Murray Peterson design. Launched 1985.

Recent Repair Projects
16' Chris-Craft Mod. 20 (ca. 1933). Restored foredeck and transom. 1985.
17' Chris-Craft runabout (1937). Total restoration. 1984.
52' Wheeler flush-deck cruiser. Replaced transom and transom framing. 1985.

Yard Information
Services:
    Marina facilities
    Launching facilities
    Moorage
    Rigging

Maintenance:
   Number of boats maintained per year: 100
   Percentage of wooden boats: 70

NORTH ISLAND BOAT CO.—Win Anderson and Paul Schweiss
1009 6th St.
Anacortes, WA 98221
206-293-2565

Builder Information
Years in business: 14
Carpenters employed: 4-6
Shop capacity: Boats to 60'

Recent New Construction
18' canoe yawl EEL. Carvel, wedge-seam construction. William Garden design. 4 built 1981-'85.
14' lapstrake beach boat. Traditional Danish design. 7 built 1978-'81.
10' cold-molded dinghy. Built 1979.
24' Chesapeake deadrise skiff. Herringbone lapstrake construction. Pete Culler design. Built 1985.
14' lapstrake semi-dory. John Gardner design. Built 1977.
32' lapstrake Cornish pilot gig. Built 1977.
9'6" Norse pram. Plywood lapstrake construction. Paul Schweiss design. 2 built 1984.
12' Norwegian fjord boat. Traditional design, riveted cedar over sawn-frame construction. Built 1982.
18' lapstrake gig-type pulling boat. Pete Culler design. Built 1980.
14' lapstrake Whitehall. John Gardner design. 3 built through 1984.
13' lapstrake Butternut double-paddle canoe. Pete Culler design. Built 1982.
12-22' Norwegian fjord boats. 15 built 1975-'81.

Recent Repair Projects
58' Chris-Craft. Repaired frames, renewed 12 planks. Refastened and rebuilt steering. 1985.
36' Grand Banks power cruiser. Rebuilt rotted windows and replaced decayed areas topside. 1985.
50' Kettenburg. Repaired stem and toerail, reset windows, and built pilothouse windscreen. 1984.
38' Kettenburg. Reframed, replanked, and refastened. 1985.
33' Grand Banks power cruiser. Reset windows, renewed 4 planks, refastened chine log. 1985.
42' Richardson power cruiser. Rebuilt transom and windscreen, replaced 5 planks. 1985.
33' Chris-Craft power cruiser. Replaced inner ply lining and 5 planks. 1985.
58' Chris-Craft power cruiser. Rebuilt deckhouse, replaced canvas, and built custom oval table. 1983.
56' Custom power cruiser. Totally rebuilt 2-stateroom fo'c's'le. 1983.

Yard Information
Services:
   Rigging repair
Maintenance:
   Number of boats maintained per year: 14
   Percentage of wooden boats: 4
   Owner maintenance allowed.
Retail supplies:
   Materials for repair or maintenance. Spoon-blade oars.

WASHINGTON

NORTHWEST SCHOOL OF WOODEN BOATBUILDING
Bob Prothero
251 Otto St.
Port Townsend, WA 98368
206-385-4948

Builder Information
Years in business: 5
Carpenters employed: 25 students, 2 instructors
Shop capacity: Boats to 60′

Recent New Construction
26′ sailboat. In-house design. Current project.
27′ motor launch. In-house design. Built 1985.
20′ motor launch. In-house design. Built 1985.
20′ sloop TOM COD. G. Stadel design. Built 1984.

Recent Repair Projects
22′ gillnetter. Restored aft end of hull. Renewed planking, frames, and deck. 1985.
40′ Grandy motoryacht. Renewed transom and planks. 1985.
50′ schooner. Replaced stem, planking, stanchions, and rail. Recaulked deck. 1985.

PORT TOWNSEND BOATWORKS—Mark Burn and Michael Shopenn
P.O. Box 577
Port Townsend, WA 98368
206-385-1523

Builder Information
Years in business: 8
Carpenters employed: 8-10

Recent New Construction
42′ salmon troller. Calkins design. Built 1982.

Recent Repair Projects
58′ Alaska limit seiner. Renewed 40 frames, 20 planks, and deck. 1985.
32′ Alaska troller. Replaced sternpost, horn timber, aft planks. 1985.
36′ Alaska troller. Installed new diesel engine. 1985.
40′ Alaska troller. Replaced bulwarks. 1984.
53′ motorsailer. Rewired and upgraded interior. Renewed deckhouse and refinished. 1984.

Yard Information
Services:
    Launching facilities
    Overland transport
    Moorage
    Diesel engine repair
    Rigging
Storage:
    Number of boats stored per year: 3-4
    Maximum size for hauling and storing:
        Length: 60′
        Draft: 10′
        Tonnage: 60

WASHINGTON

Retail supplies:
　　Lumber (mostly fir, oak, ironbark), galvanized and stainless steel fastenings, paint, and caulking materials. Will order marine-related equipment on request.

POULSBO BOAT WORKS—Roland Anderson
18691 Fjord Dr. N.E., P.O. Box 145
Poulsbo, WA 98370
206-779-7170

Builder Information
Years in business: 30
Carpenters employed: 1
Shop capacity: Boats to 34'

Recent New Construction
34' plywood Viking ship-type hull with modern cabin and topsides. Current project.

Recent Repair Projects
Powerboats, sailboats, and multihulls, 25-50'. Hull repairs and refinishing.

Yard Information
Maintenance:
　　Number of boats maintained per year: 60-80
　　Percentage of wooden boats: 50
　　Owner maintenance allowed.
　　Maximum size for hauling:
　　　　Length: 50'
　　　　Draft: 6'
　　　　Tonnage: 30
Retail supplies:
　　Wood, fastenings, paint.

RELIANT MARINE SERVICES—Gordon Ruby
P.O. Box 852
Bellingham, WA 98227
206-733-5583

Builder Information
Years in business: 9
Carpenters employed: 1-3
Shop capacity: Boats to 45'
Willing to travel for on-the-site building projects.

Recent New Construction
16' Gloucester Gull dory. Plywood construction. Phil Bolger design. 2 built 1983-'85.

Recent Repair Projects
87' Baltic trader SYLVIA (1897). Replaced 15 bottom planks and recaulked hull. Renewed topmast and rebuilt head. 1984-'85.
26' Nordic Folkboat WINDHORSE (1948). Renewed forefoot, planking, and deck. Repaired mast and interior joinerwork. 1981-'85.
51' longliner SWIFT II (1926). Rebuilt cabinhouse. 1984.
35' sloop CHANTY (1939). Renewed bulwarks and hatches. Recaulked deck. 1983.
41' Alden yawl VALIANT (1936). Renewed interior, hatches, and rigging. 1982-'85.
38' cold-molded sloop WANGARI. Repaired hull damage. 1981.
25' sloop LEFLEUR (1930). Renewed cabin, cockpit, and interior. 1983.

(continues)

WASHINGTON

(Reliant Marine Services, continued)
Yard Information
Services:
   Rigging
Maintenance:
   Number of boats maintained per year: 15
   Percentage of wooden boats: 100
   Owner maintenance allowed above and below rail.

RIGHTS O'MAN BOAT WORKS—Carl Brownstein
S.E. 2741 Bloomfield Rd.
Shelton, WA 98584
206-426-5276

Builder Information
Years in business: 9
Carpenters employed: 1
Shop capacity: Boats to 12 tons
Willing to travel for on-the-site building projects.

Recent New Construction
30' 10-ton cutter. Lyle Hess design. Current project.
24' dory. Heaflinger design. Current project.
21' 4-person lapstrake gig. Carl Brownstein design. 5 built to date.

Recent Repair Projects
70' schooner MERTHA. Replaced cockpit coaming. 1985.
28' Chris-Craft. Replaced bottom planks. 1985.

Yard Information
Retail supplies:
   Will order on request.

SEATTLE SHIPWRIGHTS CO-OP—Stewart McDougall
4311 Eleventh N.W.
Seattle, WA 98107
206-782-1724

Builder Information
Years in business: 5
Carpenters employed: 3
Shop capacity: Boats to 50'

Recent New Construction
17' lapstrake kayak. L. Francis Herreshoff design. 6 built 1985.

Recent Repair Projects
50' trawler. Replaced teak deck. 1985.
40' Atkin ketch INGRID. Rebuilt cockpit and bridge deck. Repaired rot. 1985.
50' ketch. Renewed cabinsides, repaired rot. 1985.
35' Richardson cruiser. Sistered 20 frames. Replaced 2 planks and part of transom. Installed new fuel tank. 1985.
20' Chris-Craft Riviera. Repaired rot in bow, renewed stem, 2 planks, and part of deck. 1985.
40' Concordia yawl. Installed hatch in cockpit floor, refurbished spars, and rebuilt masthead. Repaired rot and installed shelves. 1985.

WASHINGTON

40′ research powerboat. Sistered frames, renewed 2 planks and fuel tanks. Repaired aft deck. 1985.
40′ Reimers yawl. Rebuilt companionway hatch and installed new hatch enclosure. 1985.
45′ Atkin cutter. Repaired rot, renewed starboard bulwarks and caprail. 1985.
50′ Chris-Craft power cruiser. Renewed interior joinery, rebuilt head, and installed new cabinets. 1985.

SMITH'S BOAT SHOP—Donald Smith
764 Samish Island Rd.
Bow, WA 98232
206-766-6883

Builder Information
Years in business: 22
Carpenters employed: 1
Shop capacity: Boats to 12′

Recent New Construction
9′ plywood El Toro-class dinghy. MacGregor design. 50 built. 1985.
12′ plywood San Francisco Pelican-class dinghy. William Short design. 20 built. 1985.

Recent Repair Projects
Any repairs to El Toro and Pelican-class boats built at Smith's Boat Shop.

Yard Information
Services:
   Overland transport
   Rigging
Maintenance:
   Number of boats maintained per year: 60-70
   Percentage of wooden boats: 100
Retail supplies:
   Plywood, spruce, mahogany, paint, fiberglass, epoxy, and hardware.

RAY SPECK, BOATBUILDER
228-37th St.
Port Townsend, WA 98368
206-385-4519

Builder Information
Years in business: 16
Carpenters employed: 1
Shop capacity: Boats 100′ +
Willing to travel for on-the-site building projects.

Recent New Construction
23′ canoe yawl EEL. Lapstrake construction. Holmes and Speck design. Built 1985.
36′ Block Island schooner. Lines by H.I. Chapelle. Built 1979.
12-18′ Sid Skiff for sail and oar. Lapstrake construction. R. Speck design. 15 built 1975-'83.
22′ Banks-type power dory. Lapstrake construction. Built 1978.
26′ lapstrake lifeboats. 18th-century model, lines taken by R. Speck. 2 built 1983.
(continues)

WASHINGTON

(Ray Speck, Boatbuilder, continued)
26′ lapstrake Monomoy surfboats. U.S. Navy design.
13-18′ Whitehall pulling boats. Lapstrake construction. Gardner and Speck design. 10 built 1975-'83.
10′ lapstrake pram. H.I. Chapelle design. 5 built to date.

Recent Repair Projects
36′ Labruzzi power crusier. Replacing teak deck. Current project.
65′ limit seiner. Refitted interior for brine tank freezer. 1984.
26-90′ workboats, barges, and pleasure boats. Completed plank and frame repairs. Refitted deck and cabin, recaulked and refinished hulls. 1970-'75.

Yard Information
Services:
    Rigging
Retail supplies:
    Copper nails and roves.

STEPHENS MARINE—Barry Stephens
3016 Railway
Everett, WA 98201
206-258-9198

Builder Information
Years in business: 6
Carpenters employed: 1
Shop capacity: Boats to 40′
Willing to travel for on-the-site building projects.

Recent New Construction
12′ plywood skiff. Built 1985.

Recent Repair Projects
Northwest fishing boats. Repairwork has included replacing or sistering frames, renewing planks, and installing engines, shafts, wheels, and rudders.

Yard Information
Services:
    Sailmaking (provided on subcontract basis)

JOE TRUMBLY BOAT CO.—Joe H. Trumbly
197 Raft Island
Gig Harbor, WA 98335
206-265-3351

Builder Information
Years in business: 30
Carpenters employed: 1
Shop capacity: Boats to 72′

Recent New Construction
51′ ocean racing/cruising cutter. Cold-molded construction. Current project.

WASHINGTON

UPRIGHT BOAT WORKS—Geremy Snapp
Upright Channel
Lopez Island, WA 98261
206-468-2052

Builder Information
Years in business: 12
Carpenters employed: 2-3
Shop capacity: Boats to 36'

Recent New Construction
12'6" sailing skiff. Lapstrake construction. Thompson, Snapp, & Wehnke design. Built 1985.
32' double-ended cutter. Gillmer design. Current project.
26' Channel Pilot sloop. Mark Smaalders design. Current project.
7'6" lapstrake pram. Snapp design. Built 1981-'82.

Recent Repair Projects
14' Point Defiance lapstrake skiff. Completely rebuilt boat. Renewed keel, frames, and planking. Replaced rails, breasthook, quarter knees, and thwarts.

VALSO BOATS—Eric D. Hvalsoe
3405 Hunts Point Rd.
Bellevue, WA 98004
206-454-6533

Builder Information
Years in business: 6
Carpenters employed: 1
Shop capacity: New construction to 30'
Willing to travel for on-the-site building projects.

Recent New Construction
13' and 15'5" lapstrake sailing dinghies. Eric Hvalsoe designs. 4 built 1984-'85.
18'3" 225 cu. in.-class hydroplane. Plywood construction. John Hacker design. Current project.
10' lapstrake Norwegian Rana-type pram. 3 built 1985.
13' lapstrake dory skiff. Chamberlain design. Built 1985.

Recent Repair Projects
40' Pacemaker power cruiser. Replaced transom and portions of deck and cabinsides. Renewed planking and joinerwork. Modified flying bridge and refinished boat. 1983.
38' Pacemaker power cruiser. Extended and enclosed saloon. Modified flying bridge to accommodate 2nd steering station. 1982.
14' yacht tender. Replaced stern, frames, and garboard planks. 1984.

Yard Information
Services:
   Rigging

WASHINGTON

VIK BOAT—Gilbert Vik
275 E. Sunny Sands Rd.
Cathlamet, WA 98612
206-849-4440

Builder Information
Years in business: 10
Carpenters employed: 1
Shop capacity: Boats to 50'

Recent New Construction
Boats designed by Gilbert Vik:
    15' sprit-rigged daysailer. Built 1982.
    42' schooner. Current project.
    15' double-ended flat-bottomed tender. Batten-seam construction. Built 1984.

Recent Repair Projects
25' Columbia River gillnetter (1914). Replaced 29 frames and several planks. Renewed floor timbers, floorboards, shaftlog, bulkheads, and clamps. Replaced coaming, guardrails, and deck. Repaired cabin as needed. 1984.
34' Gillnet boat (1953). Recaulked hull, renewed decking and interior joinery. Converted to cruising boat. 1985.

Yard Information
Services:
    Sailmaking
Maintenance:
    Number of boats maintained per year: 4
    Percentage of wooden boats: 100
    Owner maintenance allowed above and below rail.
    Maximum size for hauling:
        Tonnage: 10

THE WOODPECKER SHOP—Donald E. Peters
P.O. Box 57
Nine Mile Falls, WA 99026
509-466-5306

Builder Information
Years in business: 25
Carpenters employed: 1
Shop capacity: Boats to 30'
Willing to travel for on-the-site building projects.

Recent New Construction
16' and 19' strip-planked canoes. 6 built to date.

Recent Repair Projects
28' Blanchard sailboat. Refinished. 1985.
21' Thompson inboard. Refinished. 1985.
19' Thompson outboard. Rebuilt. 1985.
20' Lyman inboard. Refinished. 1984.
21' Lyman inboard. Replaced transom. 1984.
16' Chris-Craft inboard. Rebuilt. 1984.
19' Chris-Craft inboard. Refinished. 1984.
16' Century inboard. Refinished. 1983.
30' Chris-Craft inboard. Refinished. 1983.
17' Century inboard. Rebuilt. 1983.

WASHINGTON

Yard Information
Storage:
  Number of boats stored per year: 4-5, for repair and refinishing
  Percentage of wooden boats: 100
  Inside storage facilities
  Maximum size for hauling and storing:
    Length: 30'
Maintenance:
  Number of boats maintained per year: 6-8
  Percentage of wooden boats: 100
  Owner maintenance allowed above and below rail.

WISCONSIN

BADER CUSTOM BOATS—Paul Bader
Rte. 1, Box 15
LaFarge, WI 54639
608-625-2515

Builder Information
Years in business: 6
Carpenters employed: 1
Shop capacity: Boats to 50'

Recent New Construction
19' Pomeroy 19 sloop. Cold-molded construction. J. Seward design. Built 1982.
18' lapstrake runabout. Nelson Zimmer design. Built 1984-'85.
21' lapstrake runabout. Nelson Zimmer design. Built 1983-'84.

Recent Repair Projects
17' Thistle-class sloop. Remolded bottom, renewed keelson, stem, and centerboard trunk. 1984.
19' Lightning-class sloop. Replaced stem, deck, and some frames. Refinished hull. 1985.
20' C-class racing scow. Replaced frames and bottom plank. Renewed bilge-board trunks and refinished hull. 1980.

Yard Information
Services:
    Overland transport
    Diesel and gas engine repair
    Rigging
Storage:
    Number of boats stored per year: 2-3
    Percentage of wooden boats: 100
Maintenance:
    Number of boats maintained per year: 2
    Percentage of wooden boats: 100
Retail supplies:
    Wood, fastenings, paint, and custom-made hardware.

B & H HYDROS—Sam Hemp
2405 Rockaway Lane
Brookfield, WI 53005
414-784-3265

Builder Information
Years in business: 8
Carpenters employed: 1
Shop capacity: Boats to 18'

Recent New Construction
9-12' outboard hydroplanes. Plywood construction. B & H Hydros designs. 20-30 boats built each year.
12' plywood duckboat. Built 1985.

Repair Projects
9-12' outboard racing boats. Hull repairs and improvements.
Runabouts (1950s). Limited restoration work on racing types.

WISCONSIN

Yard Information
Services (provided for B & H customers and hydroplane racers):
   Some overland transport
   Gas engine repair
   Rigging
Retail supplies:
   WEST System epoxy, plywood, custom Monel boat nails, and some custom hardware.

BEAVER BARK CANOES—Ferdy Goode
Rte. 3, Box 2
Woodruff, WI 54568
715-356-9787 or 356-3824

Builder Information
Years in business: 8
Carpenters employed: 1
Shop capacity: Boats to 20'

Recent New Construction
Birchbark canoes. Models originally built by Micmac, Ojibway, and Malecite Indians. Lines drawn by Howard I. Chapelle and published in *Bark Canoes and Skin Boats of North America*, Adney and Chapelle. Goode is building 2 canoes each summer.

MARVIN DEFOE, JR.
P.O. Box 821
Bayfield, WI 54814
715-779-5665

Builder Information
Years in business: 9
Carpenters employed: 1
Shop capacity: Boats to 40'
Willing to travel for on-the-site building projects.

Recent New Construction
Birchbark canoes. Traditional Ojibway design and construction.
   12 built 1976-85.

Recent Repair Projects
Birchbark canoes. Repairwork has included replacing bark, pitch, roots, and ribs.

JIM FRANK CANOES—Jim Frank
911 S. Sawyer St.
Oshkosh, WI 54901
414-231-7053

Builder Information
Years in business: 6
Carpenters employed: 1
Shop capacity: Boats to 18'
(continues)

WISCONSIN

(Jim Frank Canoes, continued)

Recent New Construction
15'8" canoes. Wood-and-canvas or wood-and-epoxy construction. Design by Jim Frank. 24 built in last 4 years.

Recent Repair Projects
Classic canoes and duckboats. Complete restoration and repair. 1979–'85.

FREEDOM BOAT WORKS—Anthony Bries
Rte. #1
N. Freedom, WI 53951
608-356-5861

Builder Information
Years in business: 10
Carpenters employed: 1
Shop capacity: Boats to 45'

Recent New Construction
12'8" sailing tender. N.G. Herreshoff design. Built 1984.
12' lapstrake sailing tender. Baker design. Built 1984.
18' strip-planked power launch. Dan Kidney design. Built 1983.
12'8" lapstrake canoe. J.H. Rushton design. 16 built 1985.
18' recreational pulling boat FIREFLY. Plywood construction. K. Bassett design. Built 1985.
14' lapstrake Rangeley Lake boat. 8 built 1981–'84.

Recent Repair Projects
32' Palmer Johnson sloop. Renewed cockpit, completely restored boat. 1984.
28' Chris-Craft. Renewed frames, deck, and some planking. 1985.
14–18' canoes. 12 boats restored in 1984.

GENEVA LAKE BOAT CO.—Charles Cameron
Rte. #1, Box 401
Fontana, WI 53125
414-275-6060

Builder Information
Years in business: 67
Carpenters employed: 2–3
Shop capacity: Boats to 40'
Willing to travel for on-the-site building projects.

Recent Repair Projects
Antique powerboats. Repairwork has included renewing planking and chines. Complete restoration and refinishing. 12 boats repaired in 1984.

Yard Information
Services:
    Marina facilities
    Launching facilities
    Overland transport
    Moorage
    Diesel and gas engine repair
    Rigging repair

WISCONSIN

Storage:
    Number of boats stored per year: 250
    Percentage of wooden boats: 15
    Inside storage facilities for 200 boats
    Maximum size for hauling and storing:
        Length: 45'
        Draft: 4'6"
        Tonnage: 12
Maintenance:
    Number of boats maintained per year: 45
    Percentage of wooden boats: 20
    Owner maintenance allowed above and below rail.
Retail supplies:
    Full-service marina. Good inventory of parts and supplies.

THE LOON WORKS—Tom MacKenzie
525 Orchard Dr.
Madison, WI 53711
608-231-2192

Builder Information
Years in business: 12
Carpenters employed: 1
Shop capacity: Boats to 30'
Willing to travel for on-the-site building projects.

Recent New Construction
10-16' birchbark or wood-and-canvas canoes. Designs from historic sources or by Tom MacKenzie or David Yost.

Repair Projects
Most types of repairs have been made to canoes of wood-and-canvas or birchbark construction.

MURPHY BOAT WORKS LTD.—F.J. Murphy
220 North Front St.
La Crosse, WI 54601
608-782-7650

Builder Information
Years in business: 30
Carpenters employed: 10
Shop capacity: Boats to 35'
Willing to travel for on-the-site building projects.

Recent New Construction
18-35' powerboats. Cold-molded, lapstrake, carvel, or strip-plank construction. Nelson Zimmer designs. 18-24 boats built per year.

Recent Repair Projects
Repairwork limited to boats built by Murphy Boat Works.
(continues)

(Murphy Boat Works Ltd., continued)
Yard Information
Services:
    Marina facilities
    Launching facilities
    Moorage
    Gas engine repair
Storage:
    Number of boats stored per year: 35
    Percentage of wooden boats: 100
    Inside storage facilities
    Maximum size for hauling and storing:
        Length: 50'
Maintenance:
    Number of boats maintained per year: 25
    Percentage of wooden boats: 100
Retail supplies:
    Wood, fastenings, paint, hardware.

F M NIMPHIUS
Rte. 2, Box 155
Neshkoro, WI 54960
414-293-4465

Builder Information
Years in business: 60
Carpenters employed: 8
Shop capacity: Boats to 30'
Willing to travel occasionally for on-the-site building projects for Nimphius-built boats and other projects of interest.

Recent New Construction
47' schooner. F.M. Nimphius design. Built 1984.
20' sloop. Nimphius design. Built 1985.
20' ketch. Nimphius design. Current project.
36' ketch. John G. Hanna design. Current project.
39' strip-planked boat (hull only). Eldredge-McInnis design. Built 1985.
25' strip-planked sloop. Nimphius design. Current project.
17' pulling boat SKÅL. Paul Erickson design. 1985.
19' hardangersjekte VALGERDA. Lapstrake plywood construction. John Atkin design. Current project.

Recent Repair Projects
19' Chris-Crafts. Transom, frame, and planking repairs. Did engine and other structural work. 3 models repaired. 1985.
19' Century. Transom, frames, and planking repairs. Did engine work. 1985.
34' custom Gentleman's Runabout. Complete overhaul. New teak-maple inlaid floor. 1984-'85.
26', 39', and 43' auxiliary sailboats. Structural repairs, rigging work. 1981-'85.

Yard Information
Services:
    Overland transport
    Diesel and gas engine repair
    Sail repair
    Rigging

Storage:
    Provided for Nimphius-built boats only
    Percentage of wooden boats: 100
    Inside storage facilities
    Maximum size for hauling and storing:
        Length: 60'
        Draft: 6'7"
        Tonnage: 40
Maintenance:
    Provided for Nimphius-built boats only.
    Percentage of wooden boats: 99
    Owner maintenance allowed above and below rail.
Retail supplies:
    Just about everything, but limited to over-the-counter sales.

NORTON BOAT WORKS—Joe Norton
Box 464, 16103 Depot Rd.
Green Lake, WI 54941
414-294-6813

Builder Information
Years in business: 16
Carpenters employed: 2 to 6
Shop capacity: Boats to 60'
Willing to travel for on-the-site building projects.

Recent New Construction
12' DN iceboats. Cold-molded construction. Joe Norton design. 300 built since 1970.
30' MORC sloop. Cold-molded construction. Built 1979.
44' cold-molded cat-ketch. David Hubbard design. Built 1981.
43' sportfishing lobsterboat. Strip-plank construction. Spencer Lincoln design. Current project.

Recent Repair Projects
Totally restored following boats in 1984-'85
    (bottoms sheathed in WEST System):
    26' Chris-Craft Sportsman (1937).
    17' Neenah Boat Works rowing skiff (1920).
    22' Chris-Craft Cadet (1931).
    24' Chris-Craft Cadet (1929).
    18' 225 Three Point racer (1948).
    22' Chris-Craft Sportsman (1947).
    26' Chris-Craft Continental (1957).

Yard Information
Services:
    Marina facilities
    Launching facilities
    Overland transport
    Moorage
    Diesel and gas engine repair
    Rigging
(continues)

WISCONSIN

(Norton Boat Works, continued)
Storage:
    Number of boats stored per year: varies
    Percentage of wooden boats: 100
    Inside storage facilities
    Maximum size for hauling and storing:
        Length: 30'
Maintenance:
    Number of boats maintained per year: 13
    Percentage of wooden boats: 100
    Owner maintenance allowed above and below rail.
Retail supplies:
    Materials for repair and construction of wooden boats.

POVERTY ISLAND BOATWORKS—Tony Hodges
P.O. Box 195, 7154 Green Bay Rd.
Sturgeon Bay, WI 54235
414-743-5092

Builder Information
Years in business: 6
Carpenters employed: 1
Shop capacity: Boats to 190'

Recent New Construction
16' Banks dory. Strip-plank construction. 2 built 1982-'83.
16' plywood Banks dory. Built 1982.
9' strip-planked skiff. Wm. Atkin design. 2 built 1983.
12' skiff. Wm. Atkin design. 16 on order for 1986.

Yard Information
Services:
    Overland transport
    Diesel and gas engine repair
Storage:
    Number of boats stored per year: Varies
    Maximum size for hauling and storing:
        Length: 30'
        Draft: 6'
        Tonnage: 5
Maintenance:
    Owner maintenance allowed above and below rail.

SHEA MARINE BUILDERS, INC.—Dan Shea
4237 Cottage Row Rd.
Fish Creek, WI 54212
414-868-3772

Builder Information
Years in business: 12
Carpenters employed: 4
Shop capacity: Boats to 50'
Willing to travel for on-the-site building projects.

WISCONSIN

Recent New Construction
Boats of cold-molded construction:
    30' IOR one-half-tonner. Sparkman & Stephens design. Built 1982.
    40' PHRF race boat. T. Wylie design. Built 1982.
    42' IOR 2-tonner. Sparkman & Stephens design. Built 1983.
    24' runabout. Phil Bolger design. Built 1984.
Other new construction:
    32' strip-planked schooner. Traditional design. Built 1981.
    24' lapstrake dory. Traditional design. Built 1984.
    Great Lakes schooner CLIPPER CITY. Built 'midship section for Manitowoc Maritime Museum exhibit.

Recent Repair Projects
65' schooner MALABAR X. Renewed frames, stem, floors, bottom planking. Refastened ballast keel.
60' HMS Hood's Admirals Gig. Repaired hull with glass sheathing.
25' Dodge Water Car. Restored and refinished.

Yard Information
Storage:
    Provided for boats undergoing repair.
    Maximum size for hauling and storing:
        Length: 50'
Maintenance:
    Number of boats maintained per year: 4
    Percentage of wooden boats: 100
    Owner maintenance allowed.
Retail supplies:
    By special order.

TROUT RIVER BOAT WORKS—Jeffrey F. Trapp
Rte. 2, Box 304
Manitowish Waters, WI 54545
715-543-2577

Builder Information
Years in business: 6
Carpenters employed: 1
Shop capacity: Boats to 30'
Willing to travel for on-the-site building projects.

Recent New Construction
Boats of lapstrake construction:
    16' Swampscott dory for oar and sail. J. Gardner design. Built 1985.
    10'6" sailing tender. W. Simmons design. Built 1983.
    17' Rangeley Lake guideboat. Traditional design. Built 1984.
    13' double-paddle canoe. Design by W. Simmons. Built 1983-'84.
    13'6" Adirondack guideboat. Traditional design. Built 1985.
    14' double-ended pulling boat. J.H. Rushton design. Built 1985.
Other new construction:
    15' dory canoe. Plywood sewn-seam construction. Roger Long design. Built 1983.
(continues)

WISCONSIN

(Trout River Boat Works, continued)
Recent Repair Projects
17′ Century inboard (1966). Renewed 7 planks, transom and transom framing, forward frames, and floor. Refinished hull. 1985.
13′ Racine Mfg. Co. double-paddle canoe. Renewed frames and planking. Refinished hull. 1984.
20′ Sunflower Boat Works launch. Replaced deck, 3 frames, and shaftlog. Recaulked and refinished hull. 1984.
17′ Chris-Craft Deluxe runabout. Replaced transom, frames, and two planks. Refinished hull. 1985.
15-18′ wood-and-canvas canoes. Various repairs including frame, gunwale, and canvas renewal. 8 boats repaired 1984-'85.

Yard Information
Services:
    Overland transport
    Rigging
Storage:
    Number of boats stored per year: 2-5
    Percentage of wooden boats: 100
    Inside storage facilities
    Maximum size for hauling and storing:
      Length: 20′
Maintenance:
    Number of boats maintained per year: 6-8
    Percentage of wooden boats: 100
    Owner maintenance allowed above and below rail.
Retail supplies:
    Wood, fastenings, paints, hardware, and plans.

VINTAGE ANTIQUE & CLASSIC BOAT RESTORATION—Brian Wilburn
RR Box 207
Port Washington, WI 53074
414-285-3163 or 612-339-4708

Builder Information
Years in business: 10
Carpenters employed: 1

Recent Repair Projects
22′ runabout (1935). Replaced deck, transom, and several topside planks.
20′ runabout (1942). Renewed frames and some of hull planking.
24′ runabout (1950). Replaced deck and bottom planking.
20′ rowing boat (1920). Renewed frames and chines.

Yard Information
Services:
    Launching facilities
    Overland transport
    Gas engine repair

Storage:
    Number of boats stored per year: 25
    Percentage of wooden boats: 100
    Inside storage facilities
    Maximum size for hauling and storing:
        Length: 40'
        Draft: 6'
        Tonnage: 15
Maintenance:
    Number of boats maintained per year: 10
    Percentage of wooden boats: 100
    Owner maintenance allowed above and below rail.

JEAN WOOD BOATS—Jean Wood Anderson
1304 Nishishin Trail
Madison, WI 53716
608-222-6790

Builder Information
Years in business: 3
Carpenters employed: 1
Shop capacity: Boats to 30'
May be willing to travel for on-the-site building projects.

Recent New Construction
16' plywood skiff WHISP. Steve Redmond design. Built 1985.
18' sliding-seat rowing boat TORPEDO. Plywood construction. Robert Barker design. Built 1986.

Recent Repair Projects
16' cold-molded canoe. Repaired dry rot. Renewed gunwales and epoxy/fiberglass sheathing. Revarnished hull. 1985.

Yard Information
Services:
    Launching facilities for company-built boats
    Overland transport
    Rigging
    Maximum size for hauling:
        Length: 25'
        Draft: 2'
        Tonnage: 2

CAN

BRITISH COLUMBIA

GRAND BANKS DORY WORKS—Peter B. Legere
Box 1583
Squamish, BC Canada V0N 3G0
604-892-3713 or 892-5555

Builder Information
Years in business: 15
Carpenters employed: 1-3
Shop capacity: Boats to 45'
May be willing to travel for on-the-site building projects.

Recent New Construction
6'11" ultralight pram dinghy WILLOW LEAF. Plywood lapstrake construction. Bill Peterson design. 18 built 1981-'85.

Recent Repair Projects
30' Atkin schooner AMERICA JUNIOR. Completely rebuilt hull. Redesigned and renewed house and deck. 1984.

Yard Information
Services:
  Rigging
Maintenance:
  Number of boats maintained per year: 3-4
  Owner maintenance allowed.
Retail supplies:
  Wood, fastenings, milled boat lumber.

HEAD OF THE LAKE BOATS—Jur Bekker
General Delivery
Argenta, BC Canada V0G 1B0
604-366-4484

Builder Information
Years in business: 1
Carpenters employed: 1
Shop capacity: Boats to 16'
Willing to travel for on-the-site building projects.

Recent New Construction
15'6" sharpie skiff. Plywood lapstrake construction. Redmond design. Built 1985.
16' strip-planked canoe. *Popular Mechanics* design. Built 1971.

Recent Repair Projects
12' lapstrake peapod. Replaced frames, planking, gunwales, breasthook, knees, and thwarts. 1985.

ADA

BRITISH COLUMBIA

Yard Information
Storage:
  Number of boats stored per year: 8
  Percentage of wooden boats: 100
Inside storage facilities
  Maximum size for hauling and storing:
    Length: 20'

BENT JESPERSEN BOATBUILDERS, LTD.—Bent Jespersen
10001 5th St.
Sidney, BC Canada V8L 2X8
604-656-5096

Builder Information
Years in business: 11
Carpenters employed: 4
Shop capacity: Boats to 60'

Recent New Construction
Boats of cold-molded construction:
  52' sloop. R. Perry design. Built 1983.
  25' Vertue-class sloop. Laurent Giles design. Built 1984.
  34' 6-meter sloop. Bruce Kirby design. Built 1985.
  44' 8-meter sloop. Bruce Kirby design. Built 1984.
  41' cutter. Francis Kinney design. Built 1985.

Recent Repair Projects
25' sloop BOUNTY. Renewed deck, cabin, and interior. 1984.
50' sloop COURAGEOUS. Replaced sheer plank and mahogany covering board. 1985.
40' Owens cutter FALCON. Cold-molded hull, built new cabin. 1984.

Yard Information
Services:
  Rigging

PETER LONDON SHIPWRIGHT LTD.—Peter Henry London
2220 Harbour Rd.
Sidney, BC Canada V8L 2S1
604-656-8011 or 656-9281

Builder Information
Years in business: 30
Carpenters employed: 2
Shop capacity: Boats to 60' +
May be willing to travel for on-the-site building projects.
(continues)

(Peter London Shipwright Ltd., continued)
Recent New Construction
57' motor schooner. William Garden design. Built 1980-'81.
18' sloop. Pete Culler design. Built 1983.
18' power workboat. William Garden design. Built 1981.
18' power workboat. Paul Gartside design. Current project.

Recent Repair Projects
36' gaff cutter. Completely rebuilt from keel up. Converted from fish boat to cutter. 1975.
36' and 42' fishing boats. Major repairs to hull and fish hold. Renewed frames and planking. 1983.
42' Nicholson powerboat. Completely rebuilding boat. Current project.

Yard Information
Services:
    Marina facilities
    Moorage
    Diesel and gas engine repair
    Sailmaking
    Rigging
Maintenance:
    Number of boats maintained per year: 12
    Percentage of wooden boats: 100
    Owner maintenance allowed above and below rail.
    Maximum size for hauling:
      Length: 60'
      Draft: 6'6"
      Tonnage: 40

MILLER MARINE SERVICES LTD.—Paul Miller
Box 1499
Port Hardy, BC Canada V0N 2P0
604-949-7806

Builder Information
Years in business: 15, present owner
Carpenters employed: 4
Shop capacity: Boats to 110'

Recent New Construction
36' cutter, Cape Scott 36 Pilot. Cold-molded construction. Jay Benford design. Built 1985.
36' cutter, Cape Scott 36. Cold-molded construction. Jay Benford design. Built 1985.
20' plywood-and-epoxy passenger ferry. 2 built 1985.
19'6" gunkholer/catboat. Plywood construction. 2 built 1981 and 1983.

Recent Repair Projects
42' Stephens power cruiser. Replaced 52 frames, renewed interior. 1982.
38' fishing boat. Renewed stern and wheelhouse. 1980.

BRITISH COLUMBIA

SKIFF WORKS—Davyd McMinn
1068 Primrose Rd.
Victoria, BC Canada V8Z 4S5
604-479-6197

Builder Information
Years in business: 3
Carpenters employed: 1
Shop capacity: New construction to 16'
Willing to travel for on-the-site building projects.

Recent New Construction
10' sharpie-type rowing boat. 4 built 1985.

Recent Repair Projects
26' double-ended Navy whaleboat. Renewed canvas decks and self-bailing cockpit. Replaced rigging and spars and refitted boat. 1984.
25' Danish Folkboat-class sloop. Renewed frames, companionway and hatch, and rudder. Sheathed deck in Dynel and epoxy. Rebuilt cockpit and refinished boat. 1985.
16' Canadian Navy motor launch. Renewed transom and 25% of planking. Rebuilt interior and replaced engine. 1984.

Yard Information
Maintenance:
    Number of boats maintained per year: 2-3
    Percentage of wooden boats: 100
    Some owner maintenance allowed above rail.

ALEC SPILLER, MASTER SHIPWRIGHT
Box 766
Chemainus, BC Canada V0R 1K0
604-246-3216

Builder Information
Years in business: 15
Carpenters employed: Up to 10
Shop capacity: Boats to 150'
Willing to travel for on-the-site building projects.

Recent New Construction
65' brigantine SPIRIT OF CHEMAINUS. 1900 East Coast design. Built 1985.
50' West Coast fishing trollers. Wahl Bros. design. 4 built 1981-'85.
30' fishing sailboats. Wahl Bros. design. 2 built 1980.
37' motorsailer. Brandlmayr design. Built 1979.
26' high-speed power cruiser. Batten-seam construction. Alec Spiller design. 2 built 1983.

Recent Repair Projects
30-50' West Coast trollers and gillnetters. Total restorations, including stern and wheelhouse replacements. 1970-'85.
Chris-Crafts and other classic power cruisers. Total restorations, including stern replacements. 1970-'85.

Yard Information
Services:
    Marina facilities
    Launching facilities
    Overland transport
    Diesel engine repair
(continues)

BRITISH COLUMBIA

(Alec Spiller, Master Shipwright, continued)
Maintenance:
    Number of boats maintained per year: 100
    Percentage of wooden boats: 75
    Owner maintenance allowed.
    Maximum size for hauling:
        Length: 70'
Retail supplies:
    Extensive inventory of marine supplies.

TUULOS CUSTOM YACHTS LTD.—Tim Tuulos
16655 - 25A Ave.
Surrey, BC Canada V4B 5E7
604-531-8023

Builder Information
Years in business: 15
Carpenters employed: 1-3
Shop capacity: Boats to any size
Willing to travel for on-the-site building projects.

Recent New Construction
40' Panda 40 cutter. Strip-plank and cold-molded construction. R. Perry design. Built 1985.
22'4" 680 sloop. Cold-molded construction. T. Tuulos design. 2 built 1985.
32'10" 10-meter sloop. Cold-molded construction. T. Tuulos design. 4 built 1980-'85.

Recent Repair Projects
33'10" Slingshot 34 racing sloop. Repaired hull damage after boat ran aground.

Yard Information
Services:
    Rigging
Maintenance:
    Number of boats maintained per year: 2
    Percentage of wooden boats: 100
    Owner maintenance allowed above and below rail.

WAHL BOATS—Gordon Wahl
9317 River Rd.
North Delta, BC Canada V4G 1B4
604-584-0322

Builder Information
Years in business: 62
Carpenters employed: 3
Shop capacity: Boats to 80'
Willing to travel for on-the-site building projects.

Recent New Construction
Boats designed by Wahl:
    44' and 52' full-displacement powerboat. Built 1982 and 1985.
    38', 40', and 42' hard-chined powerboats. Built 1983 and 1985.
    25' cold-molded utility powerboats. Current project.
Other new construction:
    20' plywood oyster skiff. J. Gardner design. Built 1985.

Recent Repair Projects
32' power cruiser (1928). Replaced transom and engine beds and ⅔ of hull planking. 1984.
34' Chein Wa trawler (1975). Replaced forward cabin sole, fore and aft cabins, and main cabin sides. 1984.
35' hard-chined power cruiser (1955). Refastened hull and built new flying bridge. Applied epoxy finish to trunk cabin and wheelhouse. 1985.
31' Fairliner cruiser (1965). Lengthening hull by 3' and building enclosed wheelhouse and flying bridge. Replacing deck and cockpit. Current project.

WHALER BAY BOAT YARD—Greg Foster
Box 43
Galiano Island, BC Canada V0N 1P0
604-539-5822

Builder Information
Years in business: 15
Carpenters employed: 1-13
Shop capacity: Boats to 50'
Willing to travel for on-the-site building projects.

Recent New Construction
80' topsail schooner. Replica of 1778 SWIFT. Current project.
45' lapstrake Finnish scoote. 18th-century design. 2 built 1982-'84.
18'6" sailing Shetland sixern. Lapstrake construction. 2 built 1985.
16'6" shallop for oar and sail. 2 built 1984.

Yard Information
Services:
    Sailmaking
    Rigging
Maintenance:
    Number of boats maintained per year: 6
    Percentage of wooden boats: 100
Retail supplies:
    Stockholm pine tar and pine-tar-based compounds.

WINARD WOOD INC.—Hugh W. Campbell
10563 McDonald Park Rd.
Sidney, BC Canada V8L 3J3
604-656-5466

Builder Information
Years in business: 5
Carpenters employed: 1-6
Shop capacity: Boats to 50'
Willing to travel for on-the-site building projects.

Recent New Construction
17' sailing Whitehall. Lapstrake construction, J. Gardner design. Built 1985.

Recent Repair Projects
47' powerboat. Lowered and rebuilt aft deck. Added canopy. 1985.
32' powerboat. Repaired holes in plywood bottom. 1985.
(continues)

BRITISH COLUMBIA

(Winard Wood Inc., continued)
Yard Information
Services
    Marina facilities
    Launching facilities
    Rigging
Maintenance:
    Number of boats maintained per year: 12
    Percentage of wooden boats: 100
    Owner maintenance allowed above and below rail.
    Maximum size for hauling:
        Length: 45'
        Draft: 14'
        Tonnage: 13
Retail supplies:
    Copper rivets and clench nails. Paints, varnishes, and hardware.

MANITOBA

WATSON MARINE, LTD.—Tom Watson
Box 34, Group 31, RR #1B
871 Grassmere Rd.
Winnipeg, MB Canada R3C 4A3
204-334-5161

Builder Information
Years in business: 34
Carpenters employed: 2
Willing to travel for on-the-site building projects.

Recent Repair Projects
19′ Chris-Craft Capri runabout (1958). Replaced portion of planking, refinished boat inside and out.
53′ Chris-Craft Cruiser (1965). Renewed bottom planking, replaced trim and flying bridge windshield.
19′ Shepherd runabout (1960s). Replaced cockpit floor, repaired seats and rotted section of starboard gunwale.
20′ Chris-Craft custom runabout (1947). Repaired leaking transom, recaulked bottom, and refinished hull.

Yard Information
Services:
    Diesel and gas engine repair
    Rigging
Maintenance:
    Number of boats maintained per year: 75-100
    Percentage of wooden boats: 25-50
    Owner maintenance allowed above and below rail.
Retail supplies:
    Wood, paints, fasteners, hardware. Caulking materials, glues, and fiberglass.

NEW BRUNSWICK

MILLER CANOES—William V. Miller III
RR #1, Plaster Rock
Nictau, NB Canada E0J 1W0
506-356-2409

Builder Information
Years in business: 60
Carpenters employed: 1
Shop capacity: Boats to 26'
Willing to travel for on-the-site building projects.

Recent New Construction
Boats of wood-and-canvas or wood-and-fiberglass construction:
    11' duckboat. B.S. Moore design.
    16' and 17' canoes. W.V. Miller III design.
    18', 19', and 20' guide and fishing canoes. W.V. Miller designs.
    20-26' V-sterned guide and fishing canoes. B.S. Moore designs.

Recent Repair Projects
Canoes. All types repair and restoration.

CAPE BRETON BOATYARD LTD.—Henry W. Fuller
Box 247
Baddeck, NS Canada B0E 1B0

Builder Information
Years in business: 10
Carpenters employed: 2
Shop capacity: Boats to 40'

Recent New Construction
38' lobsterboat. Royal Lowell design. Built 1983.

Recent Repair Projects
Have repaired numerous boats. Work has included renewing transoms, decks, and planking. Currently replacing a teak deck on a 46' sloop.

Yard Information
Services:
    Launching facilities
    Moorage
    Diesel and gas engine repair
    Rigging repair
Storage:
    Number of boats stored per year: 25
    Percentage of wooden boats: Varies
    Maximum size for hauling and storing:
        Length: 60'
        Draft: 7'
        Tonnage: 30
Maintenance:
    Number of boats maintained per year: 25
    Percentage of wooden boats: 20
    Owner maintenance allowed above rail.
Retail supplies:
    Marine store. Good inventory of supplies.

COOMBS SHIPWRIGHT SERVICES—R.T. Coombs
216 Main St.
Dartmouth, NS Canada B2X 1S6
902-435-0751

Builder Information
Years in business: 2
Carpenters employed: 1
Shop capacity: Boats to 30'
Willing to travel for on-the-site building projects.

Recent New Construction
12' DN iceboat. Built 1985.
15'6" skiff WHISP. Steve Redmond design. Planned for 1986.
16' strip-planked canoe. Chestnut Prospector design. Planned for 1986.

Recent Repair Projects
16' Mahone Bay plywood runabout. Repaired hull planking and sheathed in fiberglass. 1985.
26' Bush Island double-ender. Converted from fishing boat to yawl. Added 12" to keel and built cabin with accommodations for 3. Sheathed hull in fiberglass. 1984–present.
16' Wayfarer class. Sheathed hull in fiberglass. Epoxied interior and deck. 1985.

NOVA SCOTIA

COVEY ISLAND BOATWORKS—John Steele
Bush Island Post Office
Lunenburg County, NS Canada B0R 1B0
902-688-2843

Builder Information
Years in business: 6
Carpenters employed: 10
Shop capacity: Boats to 50′
Willing to travel for on-the-site building projects.

Recent New Construction
33′ strip-planked sloop. Concordia design modified by Joel White. Built 1984.
38′ strip-planked Covey Island ketch. S. Lincoln design. 2 built 1981 and 1985.
36′ cold-molded cutter. Roberts design. Built 1984–'85.
32′ strip-planked Covey Island 32. S. Lincoln design. 2 built 1984–'85.
38′ strip-planked Covey Island 38. S. Lincoln design. 3 built 1985.
27′ plywood Covey Island boat. J. Steele design. Built 1984.
22′ strip-planked whaleboat. S. Lincoln design. Built 1983.

Recent Repair Projects
47′ schooner ATLANTICA. Renewed frames, garboards, decks, house, and cockpit. 1985.
41′ schooner HAKADA. Replaced decks. 1984.
34′ schooner SYBARITE. Completely refitted. Renewed starboard side of hull, rebuilt decks, house, and interior. 1983.

Yard Information
Services:
　Launching facilities
　Moorage
　Diesel and gas engine repair
　Rigging
Retail supplies:
　Materials for construction and finish work. Wiring and plumbing supplies, WEST System epoxy.

DANNY'S BOAT BUILDING—Daniel Stevens
P.O. Box 14
Chester, NS Canada B0J 1J0
902-275-4502

Builder Information
Years in business: 35
Carpenters employed: 2
Shop capacity: Boats to 30′
Willing to travel for on-the-site building projects.

Recent New Construction
18′ Connecticut drag boat. Lapstrake construction. Bill Stamper design. Built 1984.
30′ Cape Island lobsterboat. Built 1984.
22′ Mini Cape pleasure boat for inboard or outboard. Built 1984.
10′ dinghies. Lapstrake or plywood construction. 10 built 1985.

Recent Repair Projects
25' lobsterboat. Replaced frames, part of keel, floor, and house. Installed new engine. 1984.
30' Cape Island pleasure boat. Replaced frames, floor, and house. Installed new engine. 1985.
30' English sloop. Replaced keel, stern knee, gripe. Renewed bottom and topside planking, deck, and gunwales. 1983-'84.

Yard Information
Services:
    Moorage
    Gas engine repair
Storage:
    Number of boats stored per year: 5
    Percentage of wooden boats: 95
    Inside storage facilities
    Maximum size for hauling and storing:
        Length: 28'
        Draft: 5'
        Tonnage: 2
Maintenance:
    Number of boats maintained per year: 10
    Percentage of wooden boats: 95
    Owner maintenance allowed.

CAMILLE D'EON BOATBUILDERS, LTD.—Camille D'Eon
Middle West Pubnico
Yarmouth Co., NS Canada B0W 2M0
902-762-2326

Builder Information
Years in business: 30
Carpenters employed: 7
Shop capacity: Boats to 50'
Willing to travel for on-the-site building projects.

Recent New Construction
45' fishing boat. MacGuire & Associates design. Built 1985.
42' fisheries patrol boat. D'Eon design. Built 1984.

Recent Repair Projects
38' lobsterboat. General repairs to hull and fish hold. 1985.
45' fish dragger. General repairs to hull and fish hold. 1985.

Yard Information
Services:
    Launching facilities
    Rigging
Storage:
    Number of boats stored per year: 4
    Maximum size for hauling and storing:
        Length: 40'
        Draft: 5'
        Tonnage: 12
Maintenance:
    Owner maintenance above and below rail.

NOVA SCOTIA

ROY M. DOUCETTE BOATBUILDERS LTD.—Paul Doucette
Comp. 8, Site 3, RR #1, Yarmouth
Cape St. Mary, NS Canada B5A 4A5
902-645-3445

Builder Information
Years in business: 60
Carpenters employed: 4
Shop capacity: Boats to 55'
Willing to travel for on-the-site building projects.

Recent New Construction
42' lobsterboat and dragger. In-house design. Built 1985.

Yard Information
Services:
    Diesel and gas engine repair

GILLIES CANOES—John Gillies
General Delivery
Margaretville, NS Canada B0S 1N0
902-825-3725

Builder Information
Years in business: 7
Carpenters employed: 1
Shop capacity: Boats to 25'

Recent New Construction
Boats designed by J. Gillies for cedar-strip construction:
    16' canoes. 15 built since 1977.
    17' canoes. 20 built since 1977.
    18' canoes. 12 built since 1977.

Recent Repair Projects
16' Hornet-class daysailer. Replaced planking and fiberglass sheathing. 1985.
16' Peterborough lapstrake canoe (ca. 1915). Renewed planking, gunwales, decks, and keel. Sealed hull in epoxy. 1985.
17' Peterborough canoe (ca. 1920). Renewed planking, gunwales, and seats. Sheathed in fiberglass. 1985.

Yard Information
Services:
    Sailmaking and rigging for canoes
Retail supplies:
    Materials for fiberglassing, epoxies, and fastenings.

LANGILLE BOAT BUILDING—Ernest J. Langille
Oakland, RR #2
Mahone Bay, NS, Canada B0J 2E0
902-624-8462

Builder Information
Years in business: 40
Carpenters employed: 1
Shop capacity: Boats to 40'

Recent New Construction
Cape Island-style powerboats. Ernest J. Langille design. 2 built 1984-'85.

Recent Repair Projects
26' schooner. Rebuilt 80% of boat. 1983-'84.

Yard Information
Services:
   Launching facilities
   Diesel and gas engine repair
   Rigging

ROY LEVY & SONS—Randy D. Levy
RR #2, Sheet Harbour
Halifax, NS Canada B0J 3B0
902-885-2930 or 885-2611

Builder Information
Years in business: 50
Carpenters employed: 2
Shop capacity: Boats to 40'
Willing to travel for on-the-site building projects.

Recent New Construction
Boats designed by R.D. Levy:
   26', 28', and 30' Cape Island-style lobsterboat. 3 built 1985.
   18' Cape-style pleasure boat. Built 1985.
   17' Nova Scotia dory. Lapstrake construction. 6 built 1985.

Yard Information
Services:
   Overland transport
Storage:
   Number of boats stored per year: 2
   Maximum size for hauling and storing:
      Length: 40'
      Draft: 5'

LUNENBURG REGIONAL VOCATIONAL SCHOOL
75 High St.
Bridgewater, NS Canada B4V 1V8
902-543-4608

Builder Information
Years in operation: 16
Carpenters employed: 8-12 students per year
Shop capacity: Boats to 30'

Recent New Construction
25' Pemaquid-type Friendship sloop. 1 built 1982, 1 under construction.
18' strip-planked sloop PICAROON. Sam Rabl design. Current project.
19'4" general-purpose power launch. W. Atkin design. Built 1984.
11' flat-bottomed skiff. Plywood construction. N. Cutler design. Built 1985.
16' strip-planked canoe. Gilpatrick design. 2 built 1983, 8 in progress.
15' plywood dory skiff. Chamberlain design, modified by J. Gardner and N. Cutler. Built 1985.
(continues)

NOVA SCOTIA

(Lunenburg Regional Vocational School, continued)
Yard Information
Maintenance:
　　Number of boats maintained per year: 2-3
　　Percentage of wooden boats: 50-60

THE MOUNTAIN BOAT SHOP LTD.—Jeff Mitton
RR #1
Scotsburn, NS Canada B0K 1R0
902-351-2613

Builder Information
Years in business: 5
Carpenters employed: 2
Willing to travel within Atlantic Canada for on-the-site building projects.

Recent New Construction
20′ cold-molded class C Friendship sloop. Bolger design. Built 1983-'85.
11′ plywood lapstrake tender. Lawley design. 4 built 1984-'85.
14′ strip-planked peapod. Built 1984-'85.

NEW DUBLIN WATERCRAFT—Wayne D. Mosher
Dublin Shore
Lunenburg County, NS Canada B0R 1C0

Builder Information
Years in business: 3
Carpenters employed: 2
Shop capacity: Boats to 30′

Recent New Construction
13′6″ Banks dory. Plywood construction. In-house design. 4 built 1985.
16′6″ wood-and-canvas canoes. Chestnut design. 4 built 1985.

Recent Repair Projects
12-16′ skiffs and dories. Repairwork has included replacing frames, centerboard trunks, and other timbers. Renewal of fiberglass sheathing.
16′ canoes. Repairwork has included renewing keels, ribs, gunwales, and hull canvas.

ROSBOROUGH BOATS LTD.—J. Douglas Rosborough
55 Purcells Cove Rd.
Halifax, NS Canada B3L 4J9
902-477-1415

Builder Information
Years in business: 30
Carpenters employed: 4
Shop capacity: Boats to 65′

Recent New Construction
Boats designed by J.D. Rosborough:
   40' ketch. 2 built 1984.
   45' privateer. Current project.
   30' lobsterboat. Built 1982.
   20' lapstrake longboat. Built 1984.

Yard Information
Services:
   Marina facilities
   Moorage
   Rigging

SLAUNWHITE'S BOAT & JOINERY SHOP—Stephen H. Slaunwhite
RR #1
Mahone Bay, NS Canada B0J 2E0
902-624-8861

Builder Information
Years in business: 9
Carpenters employed: 1
Shop capacity: Boats to 40'

Recent New Construction
Boats designed by Stephen Slaunwhite:
   29' sloop. 2 built 1978 and 1981.
   36' ketch. Built 1981-'82.
   30' and 32' lobsterboats. 2 built 1984-'85.
   17' lapstrake outboard runabout. Built 1983.
   12' lapstrake peapod. Built 1983.
   18' plywood dory. Current project.
Other new construction:
   30'3" Wagonbox sloop. L.F. Herreshoff design. Current project.
   39' pinky schooner. Chapelle design. Built 1979-'80.
   27' power cruiser. D. Mason design. Built 1983.

Recent Repair Projects
30' flying-bridge cruiser. Built interior. 1983.
26' cruiser. Renewed hull planking. 1983.

SNYDER'S SHIPYARD LTD.—Philip Snyder
Dayspring RR #3, Bridgewater
Lunenburg County, NS Canada B4V 2W2
902-543-8323

Builder Information
Years in business: 45
Carpenters employed: 30
Shop capacity: Boats to 110'

Recent New Construction
52'6" longliner. P. Snyder design. Built 1983.
45' powerboat for hunting and fishing. J.B. McGuire Associates design. Built 1984.
65' stern dragger. P. Snyder design. Built 1985.
(continues)

NOVA SCOTIA

(Snyder's Shipyard Ltd., continued)
Recent Repair Projects
92' dragger. Renewed topsides, rails, deck, and deckhouse. 1984.
105' dragger. Renewed topsides, rails, deck. Installed new engine. 1985.
58' dragger. Raised aft deck and installed new beams and deck. 1985.
90' D.O.T. ferry. Refinished and refitted boat. 1985.
D.O.T. scow. Replaced damaged wood, repainted boat. 1985.

STEVENS BOATWORKS—Steven Swinamer
Western Shore, Box 2
Lunenburg, NS Canada B0J 3M0
902-627-2951

Builder Information
Years in business: 10, current owner
Carpenters employed: 2
Shop capacity: Boats to 50'

Recent New Construction
23' Bluenose-class sloop. W.J. Roue design. Built 1984.
28–30' lobsterboats. Steven Swinamer design. 4 built 1981–'85.
7'6"–18' skiffs and dinghies. Lapstrake, plywood, or carvel construction.
    Atkin, Stevens, and Swinamer designs. 25 built 1980–'85.
28'2" sharpie EGRET. R.M. Munroe design. Current project.
26' power cruiser. Current project.
32' lobsterboat. Current project.

Recent Repair Projects
28–48' powerboats, schooners, and other craft. Repairs to planking,
    transoms, decks, stems, gunwales, horn beam, and interiors. 1978–'85.

Yard Information
Services:
    Launching facilities
    Rigging
Storage:
    Number of boats stored per year: 6
    Percentage of wooden boats: 100
    Maximum size for hauling and storing:
      Length: 40'
      Draft: 5'
    Owner maintenance above and below rail.

A.F. THERIAULT & SON, LTD.
Meteghan River
Digby County, NS Canada B0W 2L0
902-645-2327

Builder Information
Years in business: 46
Carpenters employed: 62
Shop capacity: Boats to 152'

Recent New Construction
64–102' scallop draggers. In-house design. 5 built 1984.

NOVA SCOTIA

Recent Repair Projects
64-102' scallop draggers and fish draggers. General overhauls.

Yard Information
Services:
    Marina facilities
    Launching facilities
    Moorage
    Diesel and gas engine repair
    Rigging
    Storage
Maintenance:
    Number of boats maintained per year: 150
    Owner maintenance allowed.
    Maximum size for hauling:
        Length: 110'
        Draft: 8'

ONTARIO

BAYCREST MARINA
Big Island
Demorestville, ON Canada K0K 1W0
613-476-5357

Builder Information
Years in business: 30
Carpenters employed: 2
Shop capacity: Boats to 40'
Willing to travel for on-the-site building projects.

Recent New Construction
Daysailers. Holt design. 3 built 1980–'82.

Recent Repair Projects
22' Grew runabout Jolly Giant (1948). Replaced several frames and bottom planking. Refinished boat. 1985.

Yard Information
Services:
    Marina facilities
    Launching facilities
    Overland transport
    Moorage
    Engine repair
Storage:
    Number of boats stored per year: 150
    Percentage of wooden boats: 30
    Inside storage facilities
    Maximum size for hauling and storing:
      Length: 46'
      Draft: 5'
      Tonnage: 20
Maintenance:
    Number of boats maintained per year: 300
    Percentage of wooden boats: 30
    Owner maintenance allowed above and below rail.

THE BEAR MOUNTAIN BOAT SHOP—Ted Moores
Box 1041
Bancroft, ON Canada K0L 1C0
613-332-4456

Builder Information
Years in business: 13
Carpenters employed: 2
Shop capacity: Boats to 30'

Recent New Construction
Boats of strip-plank construction:
    30' C15 (15-person) sprint racing canoe. Ted Moores design. 2 built 1984–'85.
    20' C4 (4-person) sprint racing canoe. Ted Moores design. 6 built 1984–'85.
    13-18' recreational canoes. Designs by Rushton, Culler, W. Dean, Peterborough, and Moores. 8 built 1984–'85.

ONTARIO

Recent Repair Projects
Dispro (1952). Restoration work.
24' Greavette Streamliner runabout (1954). Replaced transom and frame. Renewed hull framing, planking, interior, and engine. Rechromed hardware and refinished hull. (1985 winner of "People's Choice," Tahoe Club, Concours d'Elegance.)
17'6" Ditchburn runabout (1937). Renewed frames, keel, stem, bottom, transom, and planking.
20' St. Lawrence canoe launch (1910). Renewed frames, planking, and sponsons. Replaced keel, skeg, and false stems. Recanvased hull. (1985 winner of "Best Motorized Launch," Manotick ACBS, Clayton.)
16' Sunny Side cruiser's canoe (1910). Renewed frames, planking, and deck. Refinished hull. 2 repaired.
17' Chris-Craft Sportsman. Restoration work.
24' Shepherd runabout. Restoration work.

GILL BIBBY, BOATBUILDER
230-7 Hempstead Dr.
Hamilton, ON Canada L8K 5K2
416-388-0761

Builder Information
Years in business: 30
Carpenters employed: 2
Shop capacity: Boats to 50'
Willing to travel for on-the-site building projects.

Recent New Construction
18' catboat. Composite construction. Vandersleen design. 7 built 1979-'81.
16' St. Lawrence skiff. Lapstrake construction. 2 built 1983.
14'6" Delaware ducker. Lapstrake construction. Built 1984.
16' strip-planked canoe. 3 built 1984-'85.

Recent Repair Projects
26' Chris-Craft. Renewed hull, deck, and interior. Repaired engine and repainted hull. 1983-'84.
18' sloop. Completely rebuilt. 1985.
16' outboard boat. Replaced transom. 1985.
26' Shepherd. Rechromed hardware, renewed brightwork. 1985.
45' Egg Harbor. Renewed hull, built flying bridge. 1984.
37'6" Ditchburn. Rebuilt and refinished hull. 1983-'84.

Yard Information
Services:
    Diesel and gas engine repair
    Rigging
Storage:
    Number of boats stored per year: 10
    Percentage of wooden boats: 60
Maintenance:
    Number of boats maintained per year: 30
    Percentage of wooden boats: 75
Retail supplies:
    Complete line of supplies.

ONTARIO

CARRYING PLACE CANOE WORKS—Joseph Ziemba
RR #1
Kleinburg, ON Canada L0J 1C0
416-893-1350

Builder Information
Years in business: 5
Carpenters employed: 1
Shop capacity: Boats to 16'
Willing to travel for on-the-site building projects.

New Construction
12-16' wood-and-canvas canoes. Designs by Joseph Ziemba.

Repair Projects
12-19' canoes. Restoration and structural repairs, including rib, stem, and gunwale replacement. Recanvasing and refinishing hulls.

Yard Information
Retail supplies:
  Wood, fastenings, seats, stem bands, canvas, paint, and lead-based filler.

CEDARGLAS LTD.—David Good
11 Allaura Blvd. #11
Aurora, ON Canada L4G 3N2
416-727-4484

Builder Information
Years in business: 10
Carpenters employed: 2
Shop capacity: Boats to 19'

Recent New Construction
Boats designed by Cedarglas Ltd. for strip-plank construction:
  14' and 16' canoes.
  8' and 10' yacht tenders
  17' rowing shells
Other new construction:
  15' sailing Whitehall

Recent Repair Projects
16' Century Resorter runabout. Renewed frames and planking. Refinished boat.
17' Chris-Craft. Refinished boat.
17' Muskoka skiffs, wood-and-canvas canoes. Minor repairs to complete restorations.

Yard Information
Retail supplies:
  Good selection of materials.

CLARION BOAT CO.—Dwight Boyd
246 Front St. N., P.O. Box 389
Campbellford, ON Canada K0L 1L0
705-653-3820

Builder Information
Years in business: 8
Carpenters employed: 2
Shop capacity: Boats to 45′

Recent Repair Projects
24′ Borneman launch (1924). Major restoration. Renewed stem, keel, transom, and cockpit furnishings. Replaced all frames and bottom planks. 1984.
21′ Ditchburn launch (1924). Replaced frames and hull planking. Renewed stem, keel, transom, and cockpit furnishings. 1984.
27′ Shepherd commuter (1960). Replaced several planks and refastened hull. Renewed cockpit furnishings and refinished boat. 1985.
16′ Lakefield runabout (ca. 1960). General refurbishment. 1985.
24′ Crusader sloop (ca. 1940). Major restoration. Renewed frames, floors, deckbeams, deck, and cabin. Replaced some deadwood, repaired spar, and refinished boat. 1985.

Yard Information
Services:
    Launching facilities
    Overland transport
    Inside storage facilities for boats undergoing repair
    Maximum size for hauling and storing:
        Length: 35′
        Tonnage: 20

CLASSIX—Robert C. Elliott
Box 2536
Bracebridge, ON Canada P0B 1C0
705-645-6336

Builder Information
Years in business: 7
Carpenters employed: 1
Shop capacity: Boats to 30′

Recent Repair Projects
22′ Century runabout. Renewed stem, transom, and splash rails. Replaced 8 planks. Refinished boat.
22′ Grew runabout. Replaced 12 frames and several planks. Reinforced engine-bearing beams and refinished boat.

Yard Information
Services:
    Overland transport
    Engine repair
Storage:
    Number of boats stored per year: 5-6
    Percentage of wooden boats: 100
    Maximum size for hauling and storing:
        Length: 32′

(continues)

(Classix, continued)
Maintenance:
  Number of boats maintained per year: 6-8
  Percentage of wooden boats: 100
  Owner maintenance allowed.

COWAN CANOES—Ted Cowan
RR #5,
Brussels, ON Canada N0G 1H0
519-887-6116 or 887-9342

Builder Information
Years in business: 8
Carpenters employed: 1
Shop capacity: Boats to 40'
Willing to travel for on-the-site building projects.

Recent New Construction
Boats designed by Cowan Canoes:
  36' power "wooden pointer." Strip-plank construction. 2 built 1982-'83.
  24' ice canoe. Built 1984.

Recent Repair Projects
18' Dispro. Renewed frames and planking. Refinished boat. 1981.
17' Port Carling runabout. Renewed planking. 1984.

Yard Information
Services:
  Overland transport
Maintenance:
  Number of boats maintained per year: Varies
  Percentage of wooden boats: 10

DISAPPEARING PROPELLER BOAT COMPANY LIMITED
Paul Dodington
Port Carling Post Office
Muskoka, ON Canada P0B 1J0
705-765-5037

Builder Information
Years in business: 1
Carpenters employed: 1
Shop capacity: Boats to 20'

Recent Repair Projects
16'3" Dispro (1923). Restored woodwork, engine, and mechanical
  systems. Renewed planking, stem, frames, seats, and floorboards.
18'6" Dispro (1952). Restored engine and mechanical systems. Replaced 3
  planks and refinished boat.
18'6" Dispro (1952). Restored engine and mechanical systems.
18'6" Dispro (1922). Restored engine and mechanical systems.
16'3" Dispro (1927). Restored engine and mechanical systems.
18'6" Dispro (1946). Restored woodwork, engine, and mechanical systems.
  Refinished boat.

Yard Information
Services:
    Overland transport
    Gas engine repair
Maintenance (for Dispros only):
    Number of boats maintained per year: 25-40
    Percentage of wooden boats: 100
    Owner maintenance allowed above and below rail.
Retail supplies:
    New and used materials for the restoration of vintage Dispros.
    Custom-made hardware and spare parts for Dispros.

DOVE INDUSTRIES INC.—Ian Ross
RR #1, Manitoulin Island
Tehkummah, ON Canada P0P 2C0
705-859-3973

Builder Information
Years in business: 4
Carpenters employed: 8
Shop capacity: Boats to 50'

Recent New Construction
39' skipjack. Composite ply construction. Atkin design. Built 1985.
18' strip-planked St. Lawrence skiff. Ian Ross design. 25 built 1985.
13' strip-planked canoe. Ian Ross design. 2 built 1985.
16' plywood Halcyon punt. Wayne design. 8 built 1984-'85.

Recent Repair Projects
16' Peterborough skiff. Replaced seats and gunwales. Stripped and varnished hull. 1985.
16' Berry outboard. Replaced transom. 1985.
16' Peterborough outboard. Replaced transom. 1985.
16-17' canoes. Hull repairs and recanvasing.

Yard Information
Services:
    Launching facilities
    Overland transport
    Diesel and gas engine repair
    Sailmaking
    Rigging
Storage:
    Number of boats stored per year: 6
    Percentage of wooden boats: 50
    Inside storage facilities
    Maximum size for hauling and storing:
        Length: 30'
        Draft: 3'
        Tonnage: 15
Maintenance:
    Number of boats maintained per year: 20
    Percentage of wooden boats: 50
    Owner maintenance allowed above and below rail.
Retail supplies:
    WEST System products. Wood, paint, fastenings, glue, and fiberglass.

ONTARIO

ESPECIALLY WOOD—Juerg Schattin
36 Stanton Dr.
Orillia, ON Canada L3V 2K1
705-326-6194

Builder Information
Years in business: 4
Carpenters employed: 1
Shop capacity: Boats to 60'
Willing to travel for on-the-site building projects.

Recent Repair Projects
42' Chris-Craft (1948). Replaced chines and double-planked hull bottom.
50' Chris-Craft (1950). Repaired dry rot in cabintop, replaced chines.
18' Shepherd runabout (1956). Refastened bottom planking. Replaced sheerstrake, aft deck, and hatch. Refinished boat.
16' Ski-Bee (1961). Refastened bottom planking, replaced quarter rails, and refinished boat.

Yard Information
Services:
    Overland transport for runabouts
Maintenance:
    Number of boats maintained per year: 5
    Percentage of wooden boats: 100

ROB HAGGAR WOODEN BOATS LTD.—Rob Haggar
Medora St., P.O. Box 102
Port Carling, ON Canada P0B 1J0
705-765-6036

Builder Information
Years in business: 8
Carpenters employed: 2
Shop capacity: Boats to 32'

Recent Repair Projects
31' Ditchburn Commodore (1926). Replaced bottom plank and installed new ceiling in main cockpit. Stripped and refinished hull, renewed upholstery, and rechromed hardware. 1983-'84.
16'6" Dispro (1923). Completely restored. Replaced all frames and 20 planks. Renewed engine bed, floorboards, stem, keel, and rudder. Refinished boat. 1985.
18'6" Dispro (1923). Replaced 7 frames and 3 planks. Renewed engine bed, floorboards, stem, sternpost, and ½ of keel. Replaced knees, gunwales, splashboards, rudder, dashboard, seats, and seat backs. Refinished boat. 1985.

Yard Information:
Maintenance:
    Number of boats maintained per year: 25
    Percentage of wooden boats: 100

ONTARIO

ED HUCK MARINE LTD.—Morris Huck
Thousand Islands
Rockport, ON, Canada K0E 1V0
613-659-3408

Builder Information
Years in business: 75
Carpenters employed: 1

Recent Repair Projects
28' Gar Wood. Renewed planking, refinished boat. 1985.
19' Chris-Craft. Renewed planking and refinished boat. 1985.

Yard Information
Services:
    Marina facilities
    Launching facilities
    Moorage
    Gas engine repair
Storage:
    Number of boats stored per year: 200
    Percentage of wooden boats: 10
    Inside storage facilities
    Maximum size for hauling and storing:
        Length: 50'
        Draft: 6'
        Tonnage: 30
Maintenance:
    Number of boats maintained per year: 350
    Percentage of wooden boats: 10
    Owner maintenance allowed above rail.
Retail supplies:
    Mahogany, brass screws, and paint.

HURLEY CANOE WORKS—Jack Hurley
Box 42
Dwight, ON Canada P0A 1H0
705-635-1565

Builder Information
Years in business: 10
Carpenters employed: 1
Shop capacity: Boats to 16'

Recent New Construction
9' wood-and-canvas Trapper canoe. C. Bouges design.
16' wood-and-canvas Cruiser canoe. Peterborough design.
15' wood-and-canvas solo cruiser canoe. Peterborough design.
Square-sterned outboard wood-and-canvas canoe. Jim Kay design. Built 1985.
Square-sterned outboard wood-and-canvas canoe. C. Bouges design.

Repair Projects
All kinds of canoe repairs. 100–150 boats since 1978.
(continues)

ONTARIO

(Hurley Canoe Works, continued)
Yard Information
Storage:
  Number of boats stored per year: 20
  Percentage of wooden boats: 100
  Inside storage facilities
  Maximum size for hauling and storing: 150 lbs
Maintenance:
  Number of boats maintained per year: 15
  Percentage of wooden boats: 100
Retail supplies:
  Materials for canoe construction and repair.

LUDLOW BOAT WORKS—Philip Ludlow
RR #4
Kemptville, ON Canada K0G 1J0
613-258-4270

Builder Information
Years in business: 7
Carpenters employed: 2
Shop capacity: Boats to 60'

Recent New Construction
Boats designed by P. Ludlow:
  17' cold-molded sloop. Built 1983.
  7'1" cold-molded tender. 9 built since 1980.
  7' plywood tender. 5 built since 1980.
  6'6" plywood pram. 3 built since 1980.
  20' Thames River punt. Plywood and planked construction. 16 built 1984.
Other new construction:
  40' plywood catamaran. Wharram design. Built 1985.
  19' cutter. Garcia design. Built 1977.
  27' strip-planked pilot launch. Built 1983.
  22' runabout. Chris-Craft replica. Built 1985.

Recent Repair Projects
33' Century cruiser. Renewed deck and above deck structures. 1985.
30' Revel-Craft. Replaced transom, laid new teak deck. 1985.
33' cutter (1902). Cold-molded hull. 1985.
30' Dragon class. Renewed frames and floors. 1985.
18' Mason runabout. Replaced deck, transom, and bottom planking. 1985.
23' sloop. Replaced mast, boom, and rigging. 1985.
16' Cliff-Craft. Renewed aft section of bottom. 1985.

Yard Information
Services:
  Limited moorage
Storage:
  Number of boats stored per year: 5-10
  Percentage of wooden boats: 99
  Maximum size for hauling and storing:
    Length: 60'
    Draft: 5'6"

ONTARIO

Maintenance:
    Number of boats maintained per year: 6
    Percentage of wooden boats: 99
    Owner maintenance allowed above and below rail.
Retail supplies:
    Lumber, plywood, epoxy, bronze fastenings, and sealants. Caulking materials, paint, rope, and sanding supplies.

McCLELLAND BOATWORKS—Jim McClelland
Longbow Lake Post Office
Kenora, ON Canada P0X 1H0
807-548-4768

Builder Information
Years in business: 20
Carpenters employed: 1
Shop capacity: Boats to 50'

Recent New Construction
41' cold-molded ketch. Bruce King design. Built 1980.
34' cold-molded sloop. Gary Mull design. Built 1982.
34' cutter. Bruce King design. Built 1984.
26' sloop. Gary Mull design. Built 1985.

MILLAR-POTTER BOAT RESTORATION
James Potter and John Millar
P.O. Box 56
Manotick, ON Canada K0A 2N0
613-692-3455

Builder Information
Years in business: 4
Carpenters employed: 4
Shop capacity: Boats to 30'

Recent New Construction
16' wood-and-canvas canoe.

Recent Repair Projects
To date, have restored 6-8 Shepherds, 2 Ditchburns, several Jeffries runabouts, and several canoes and cedar-strip runabouts.

Yard Information
Services:
    Overland transport
    Gas engine repair
Storage for work in progress:
    Percentage of wooden boats: 100
    Maximum size for hauling and storing:
        Length: 30'
Maintenance:
    Number of boats maintained per year: 15
    Percentage of wooden boats: 100
(continues)

ONTARIO

(Millar-Potter Boat Restoration, continued)
Retail supplies:
    Wood, fastenings, and paint. Hard-to-find antique marine engine parts and accessories.

NORTH BAY CANOE CO.—William P. Schorse
166 Campbell Ave.
North Bay, ON Canada P1A 1W3
705-472-7204 or 752-1770

Builder Information
Years in business: 8
Carpenters employed: 1
Shop capacity: Boats to 17'

Recent New Construction
17' wood-and-canvas canoes. William Schorse designs. 14 built 1980-'85.
15' wood-and-canvas canoes. William Schorse designs. 8 built 1980-'85.
16' wood-and-canvas canoes. William Schorse designs. 8 built 1980-'85.

Recent Repair Projects
12-20' wood-and-canvas canoes. Work ranges from minor repairs to complete restoration, and has included replacing ribs, planking, decks, gunwales, thwarts, and canvas, as well as hull refinishing. 35 canoes repaired last year.

Yard Information
Storage:
    Number of boats stored per year: 7 canoes
    Percentage of wooden boats: 100
    Inside storage facilities
    Maximum size for hauling and storing:
        Length: 25'
Retail supplies:
    Wood, canvas, filler, paint, and fastenings. Trim materials, epoxy and polyester resins, fiberglass cloth.

PEEL MARINE LIMITED
96 Clementi St.
Lakefield, ON Canada K0L 2H0

Builder Information
Years in business: 39
Carpenters employed: 1
Shop capacity: Boats to 30'

Recent New Construction
Boats of strip-plank construction:
    9' sailing dinghy
    14'6" and 16'6" runabouts/fishing boats
    16' double-ended rowing skiff
    14' and 16' canoes
Other new construction:
    14' and 16' wood-and-canvas canoes
    30' war canoe
    20' C-4 sprint-racing canoe

ONTARIO

PHOENIX WOODWORK—J. Stanton
RR #1
Janetville, ON Canada L0B 1K0

Builder Information
Years in business: 23
Carpenters employed: 3
Shop capacity: Boats to 40'
Willing to travel for on-the-site building projects.

Recent New Construction
Bilge-keeled boats of plywood-and-epoxy construction (built 1979
    to present).
24' Eventide sloop. Maurice Griffiths design.
30' Waterwitch sloop-ketch. Maurice Griffiths design.
37' cutter-rigged motorsailer Nova. Lawrence Jump and J. Stanton design.

RAINBOW CANOES—Leslie Jackson
RR #1
Apsley, ON Canada K0L 1A0
705-656-4759

Builder Information
Years in business: 6
Carpenters employed: 1
Shop capacity: Boats to 20'

Recent New Construction
Boats designed by Leslie Jackson and constructed between 1978 and 1985:
    15' canoe. 5 built to date.
    16' canoe. 6 built to date.
    16' rowing skiff. 1 built to date.
    14' canoe. 3 built to date.

Recent Repair Projects
12-17' canvas canoes, wood canoes, runabouts, and rowing skiffs (Peterboroughs, Chestnuts,
    Tremblays, and other boats built by Canadian companies). Repairwork has included
    renewing ribs, planking, decks, gunwales, stems, keels, and seats. Recanvasing
    and refinishing of hulls. 1978-'85.

Yard Information
Retail supplies:
    Seats, ribs, planking blanks, stem bands and other wooden parts for canoe construction and
        repair. Brass and copper nails, tacks, and screws.

CLIFF RICHARDSON BOATS LTD.—Alan Richardson
103 Bayfield St., Box 819
Meaford, ON Canada N0H 1Y0
519-538-1940

Builder Information
Years in business: 51
Carpenters employed: 2
Shop capacity: Boats to 60'
(continues)

ONTARIO

(Cliff Richardson Boats Ltd., continued)
Recent Repair Projects
32' 5.5-meter sloop. Replaced frames. Splined hull seams. 1985.
31' Trojan cruiser. Renewed planking, chines, decks, cabin, and wiring. 1985.
40' Huckins. Renewed flying bridge, installed new engines and generator.
　　Refinished boat. 1984–'85.

Yard Information
Services:
　　Marina facilities
　　Launching facilities
　　Moorage
　　Diesel and gas engine repair
　　Rigging
Storage:
　　Number of boats stored per year: 105
Maintenance:
　　Number of boats maintained per year: 120
　　Percentage of wooden boats: 15
　　Some owner maintenance allowed above and below rail.
Retail supplies:
　　Mahogany, white oak, bronze and stainless steel fastenings, paint.

SUNDANCE CANOE—Mike Shumaker
Box 1769, Sagamo Dr.
Gravenhurst, ON Canada P0C 1G0
705-687-2554

Builder Information
Years in business: 10
Carpenters employed: 2
Shop capacity: Boats to 18'6"

Recent New Construction
Boats of strip-plank construction:
　　13'8" solo canoe. D. Yost design. Built 1985.
　　15'6" solo canoe. D. Yost design. 6 built 1984–'85.
　　17' canoe. In-house design. 100 built 1978–'85.
　　16' canoe. Chestnut design. 3 built 1985.
　　17' skiff. Peterborough design. 20 built 1976–'85.
　　17'10" kayak. In-house design. 2 built 1985.
Other new construction:
　　16'6" wood-and-canvas canoe. In-house design. 21 built 1981–'85.

Recent Repair Projects
12–18' canoes. Repairs to ribs, gunwales, keels, rails, stem, keelsons, and
　　planking. Recanvasing and refinishing. Approximately 250 canoes repaired since 1976.

Yard Information
Services:
　　Storage
Retail supplies:
　　Complete line of materials for canoe construction and repair.

SUPERIOR SAILBOATS LTD.—Victor A. Carpenter
Port McNicoll, ON Canada L0K 1R0
705-534-7741

Builder Information
Years in business: 38
Carpenters employed: 6
Shop capacity: Boats to 100'

Recent New Construction
Boats designed by V.A. Carpenter:
    45' triple-planked custom sloop.
    45' single-planked custom sloop.
    64' single-planked custom sloop.
    33' custom power cruiser.
Other new construction:
    35' launch. Minett replica.
    18' Minett replica.
    33' Purdy replica.

Recent Repair Projects
Complete restorations, including:
    35' Minett (1931).
    18' Minett (1934). 3 boats restored.
    33' Minett (1927).
    38' Minett (1928).
    54' Hacker (1934).
    70' steam launch (1903).

Yard Information
Services:
    Launching facilities
    Overland transport
    Diesel and gas engine repair
    Sailmaking
    Rigging
Maintenance:
    Number of boats maintained per year: 25
    Percentage of wooden boats: 100
Retail supplies:
    Wood, paint, glue, fastenings. Custom hardware fabrication.

THE TENDER CRAFT BOATSHOP—Barbara Williams
67 Mowat Ave. #031
Toronto, ON Canada M6K 3E3
416-531-2941

Builder Information
Years in business: 6 in Toronto, 60 in North Bay
Carpenters employed: 2 in Toronto, 12 in North Bay
Shop capacity: Boats to 18'
(continues)

ONTARIO

(The Tender Craft Boatshop, continued)

Recent New Construction
Strip-planked boats of Peterborough and Lakefield styles:
  16′ sailing skiff.
  11′ sailing tender.
  14-18′ runabouts.
  16′ rowing skiff.
  11′ rowing tender.
  16′ canoe.
Other new construction:
  14′6″ wood-and-canvas kayak.

Recent Repair Projects
8-18′ tenders, rowboats, canoes, and runabouts. Work has included repairing ribs, planks, canvas, stems, decks, and gunwales.

Yard Information
Retail supplies:
  Wood, fastenings, paint, epoxy, glue, bronze and brass fittings, oars, paddles, seats, spars, kit boats.

UHH ENTERPRISES—Ulf H. Hansen
82 Willow Ave., Apt. 46
Toronto, ON Canada M4E 3K2
416-699-7774

Builder Information
Years in business: 19
Carpenters employed: 3-7
Shop capacity: Boats to 45′
Willing to travel for on-the-site building projects.

Recent New Construction
9′ cold-molded sailing dinghies. Ulf Hansen design. 3 built 1984-'85.

Recent Repair Projects
Restoration of following boats:
  24′ Shepherd (1954).
  27′ Hunter (1937).
  26′ Chris-Craft (1956).

Yard Information
Maintenance:
  Number of boats maintained per year: 10
  Percentage of wooden boats: 100
  Owner maintenance allowed above and below rail.

WALKER BOAT BUILDING LTD.—Willie Walker
Box 272
Kingston, ON Canada K7L 4V8
613-542-0841

Builder Information
Years in business: 9
Carpenters employed: 4-8
Shop capacity: Boats to 50′

ONTARIO

Recent New Construction
23′ sloop-rigged motorsailer. Strip-plank construction. William Garden design. Built 1985.
20′ cold-molded Tornado-class catamaran. 2 built 1984-'85.
51′ 6-man fixed-seat rowing shell. Strip-plank construction. Built 1985.

Recent Repair Projects
20′ Tornado-class catamarans. Repaired molded hull, replaced centerboard gasket, refinished hull. 7 boats repaired 1984-'85.
20′ Lyman Islander launch. Completely rebuilt. Renewed frames, planking, and deck. Refinished hull. 1984-'85.
24′ Warrington Smyth 6-tonner. Renewed planking, cockpit, and teak decks. Installed engine and refinished boat. 1984-'85.
63′ 8-man shells. Reglued inner structures and refinished hulls. 2 boats repaired 1984-'85.
26′ Chris-Craft Sea Skiff. Repaired bottom, replaced props, rudders, and shafts. Repaired engine. 1985.
22′ Cliff-Craft outboard runabout. Replaced transom, decks, and some planking. Refinished hull. 1985.
16-18′ canoes. Repaired rails, recanvased and refinished hulls. 4 boats repaired 1984-'85.
17-26′ antique launches. Renewed planking, transoms, keels, stems. Refinished hulls. 4 repaired 1984-'85.

Yard Information
Services:
  Launching facilities
  Diesel and gas engine repair
  Rigging
Storage:
  Number of boats stored per year: 15
  Percentage of wooden boats: 100
  Maximum size for hauling and storing:
    Length: 50′
Maintenance:
  Number of boats maintained per year: 4
  Percentage of wooden boats: 100
Retail supplies:
  Marine plywood, mahogany, teak, Sitka. Epoxy, nonferrous fastenings, specialty hardware, and other items.

WEBB WOOD WORK—Mervyn Webb
General Delivery
Gilford, ON Canada L0L 1R0
416-775-6801

Builder Information
Years in business: 7
Carpenters employed: 1
Shop capacity: Boats to 26′
Willing to travel for on-the-site building projects.
(continues)

ONTARIO

(Webb Wood Work, continued)
Recent Repair Projects
26' Gilbert launch (1910). Renewed bottom frames and planking. Replaced keel and keelson.
16' Chris-Craft Riviera runabout (1950). Stripped and refinished boat.
18' Chris-Craft Riviera runabout (1951). Repaired dry rot and restored boat.
15'6" Shepherd outboard runabout. Completely refinished boat.
19' Delcraft utility runabout (1950). Repaired rot and restored boat.

Yard Information
Services:
   Marina facilities
   Launching facilities
   Moorage
Maintenance:
   Number of boats maintained per year: 10
   Percentage of wooden boats: 80

ZAPPENUFF GENERATORS—Peter O. Andersen
RR #2
Wahnapitae, ON Canada P0M 3C0
705-694-5581

Builder Information
Years in business: 3
Carpenters employed: 1
Shop capacity: Boats to 30'
Willing to travel for on-the-site building projects.

Recent New Construction
16' canoe. Composite construction. Peter Andersen design. Built 1985.
16' strip-planked canoe. Current project.

Recent Repair Projects
14' canoe. Refinished hull. 1983.

Yard Information
Services:
   Gas engine repair
   Sailmaking
   Rigging
Maintenance:
   Number of boats maintained per year: 2
   Percentage of wooden boats: 50
Retail supplies:
   Miscellaneous parts, glues, cloth. By order only.

CAMP NOMININGUE INC.—Peter Van Wagner
119 Cragmore Rd.
Pointe Claire, PQ Canada H9R 3K7
514-694-4020

Builder Information
Years in business: 27
Carpenters employed: 1-2
Shop capacity: Boats to 18'

New Construction
16' wood-and-canvas canoes. P. Van Wagner and Lucien Desroches design. 360 built since 1968.

Repair Projects
Wood-and-canvas canoes. Complete rebuilding and recanvasing.

THE DINGHY SHOP—Timothy M. Cox
169 St. Francis Blvd.
Chateauguay, PQ Canada J6J 1Y9
514-691-8688

Builder Information
Years in business: 1
Carpenters employed: 1
Shop capacity: Boats to 14'

Recent New Construction
Boats designed by Cox for strip-plank construction:
    7' sailing pram. 4 built 1984.
    8' sailing dinghy. 2 built 1984.
    9' and 10'6" Rushton-type double-paddle canoes. 2 built 1985.

DAVID GIDMARK
Box 26
Maniwaki, PQ Canada J9E 3B3

Builder Information
Years in business: 7
Carpenters employed: 1
Shop capacity: Boats to 26'
Willing to travel for on-the-site building projects.

Recent New Construction
12' and 14' birchbark canoes. 3 built 1985.
David has acted as paid consultant on birchbark canoes for the National
    Museum of Man, Canadian Broadcasting Corp., and Astral-Bellevue-Pathe.
    He has lectured on the subject in Canada, the United States, and
    Sweden, and has written books and articles on birchbark canoe construction.
    Several of his canoes are in the collection of the National Museum of Man, Ontario.

QUEBEC

NAVIGATEURS JEL LTEE.
572 St. Germain Est.
Rimouski Est, PQ Canada G5L 1G4
418-722-5011

Builder Information
Years in business: 9
Carpenters employed: 1
Shop capacity: Boats to 60'

Recent New Construction
Boats of plywood construction:
    28' sloop. P. Harlé design. Built 1983.
    20' sloop. P. Harlé design. 12 built to date.
    16' sloop. Herbulot design. 7 built to date.
    32' trawler. Glen-L Marine design. Built 1983.
    30' power catamaran. In-house design. 3 built to date.
Other new construction:
    33' cold-molded Barbara 33 sloop. Architectes Navals Associés design.

Yard Information
Services:
    Overland transport
    Diesel and gas engine repair
    Rigging
Storage:
    Number of boats stored per year: 10
    Percentage of wooden boats: 50
    Maximum size for hauling and storing:
      Length: 40'
      Tonnage: 15
Maintenance:
    Number of boats maintained per year: 25-30
    Percentage of wooden boats: 25
    Owner maintenance allowed above rail.
Retail supplies:
    Extensive inventory. Fastenings, wood, electrical and mechanical supplies. Electronic gear.

INDEX

Abel, William H., 51
Acadia Canoe Shop, 56
Adams, Albert E. (Bud), 34
Adams, Kenny, 204
Adams, Kim, 34
Adams Boatbuilding Co., 34
Adams Custom Boats Inc., 34
The Adirondack Guide Boat, 212
The Adirondack Guideboat Shop, 164
Ajootian, Fred, 219
Alder Creek Boat Works, 164
Alexander, Eugene, 56
Allen, Taylor, 97
Alred Marina, 2
Ambler Boat Works, 197
Andersen, Peter O., 290
Anderson, David, 117
Anderson, Jean Wood, 255
Anderson, Roland, 239
Anderson, Win, 237
Andreassen Boatworks, 223
Androscoggin Boat Co., 56
Applegate Boatworks, 191
The Apprenticeshop of Maine Maritime Museum, 57
Aquatec Boat Co., 21
Ariel Boatworks, 58
Arundel Shipyard, 58
Atkins, Frederick J., 118
Avery, Dexter C., 22
B & H Hydros, 246
Back River Boat Shop, 59
Bader, Paul, 246
Bader Custom Boats, 246
Baggins, Abe, 69
Baker, Anne W., 113
R.H. Baker Boat & Launch Works, 113
Ballentine, Stephen, 113
Ballentine's Boat Shop, Inc., 113
Don Baman, Boatbuilder, 60
Barber, Mark W., 128
Barker, Robert, 129
Barlow, George G., 206
Barlow Marine Service, 206
Barnegat Bay Boatworks, 158
Barnegat Bay Sneakboxes, 158
Baron, Walter, 129
Barrow, David, 2
Bassett, Ken, 215
L.H. Bates Vocational Technical Institute, 223
Bauser, Ken, 21
Bausman, Lawrence, 35
Baycrest Marina, 274
Beal, Osmund M., 91
The Bear Mountain Boat Shop, 274
Beavan, Leslie, 114
Beaver Bark Canoes, 247
Walter C. Beckmann, Ltd., 199
Bedell, Chester S., 165
Bedell Marine Carpentry, 165
Beebe, Douglas, 94
Beeler, P.E., 205
Beeler's Repair, 205
Bekker, Jur, 256

Beltman, John, 143
J.W. Beltman Woodworking, 143
Bend Boat Basin, 199
Benjamin, Donald A., 155
Benjamin, Nat, 120
Berg, John, 122
Berg, Norman, 236
Betula Canoe, 115
Gill Bibby, Boatbuilder, 275
Bielinski, Jon, 15
Bigelow, Myron C., 115
R. Bigelow and Co., Inc., 115
Bigfork Canoe Trails, 54, 143
Billings, Harlan, 60
Billings Diesel & Marine Services, Inc., 60
Bingham, Joseph, Jr., 132
Bingham Boat Works, 132
Biscayne Bay Boat Works, 182
Bitterroot Boat Works, 35
Bjornstedt, Robert E., 195
Black Bottom Runabouts, Inc., 165
Blair, Ronald, 18
Blake, Bryan, 182
Blake Boatworks, 182
Blevins, Thomas, 61
Blevins Company, 61
Block, Gus, 12
Boatyard Inc., 224
Bock, James W., 100
Boessel, Ray, Jr., 144
Boone, Jim, 5
Borland, Gerald, 168
Boyd, Dwight, 277
Braden, Richard B., 224
Brass Tacks Canoe Shop, 62
Brechtel, Dan, 20
Brendze, Arthur, 58
Bries, Anthony, 248
Briggs, Daniel C., 126
Brigham, Walter L., 165
Bright Craft Boatworks, 6
Brochetti, Louie, 7
Bronstien, James E., 43
Brooklin Boat Yard, 62
Brown, Foy W., 63
Brown, J.W., 142
J.O. Brown & Son, Inc., 63
Brownstein, Carl, 240
Bruno, Peter and Steven, 36
Bruno's Marine Service, 36
Bryant, Paul, 95
Buffalo Bateaus, 5
Bullock's Point Boat Yard and Marina, Inc., 200
Bulman, Larry, 42
Burgess, John T., 80
Geoffrey Burke, Boatbuilder, 151
Burke, John, 57
Burn, Mark, 238
Caddis Canoe, 64
C and B Marine, 7
California Custom Yachts and
    Marine Hardware, Inc., 6
Calkins, George, 227

INDEX

Camber Craft, 7
Cameron, Charles, 248
Campbell, Hugh W., 261
Camp Nominingue, Inc., 291
Camric Boats, 206
Cannell, Bill, 64
Wm. Cannell Boatbuilding Co., Inc., 64
Canoe Imports, 212
Canoesport, 132
The Canoe Works, 65
Cape Breton Boatyard Ltd., 265
Cape Fear Technical Institute, 183
Capozza, Jon, 56
Carl's Canvas Canoe Care Co., 21
Carney, Patrick, 165
Carpenter, Victor A., 287
The Carpenter's Boatshop, 65
Carroll, Gregory C., 98
Carrying Place Canoe Works, 276
Carter Boat Building Co., 166
Cassell, Charles, 187
Cassell, Jerry, 133
Cassell Marine, 187
Castle Creek Boatworks, 211
Cedar Bay Works, 188
Cedarglas Ltd., 276
Chalk, Duane J., 167
H. Chalk & Son, Inc., 167
Chamberlain, Richard, 50
Chamberlain Marine, 50
Charles, Ted, 177
Chebeague Marine, Inc., 66
The Chicagoland Canoe Base, Inc., 50
Clarion Boat Co., 277
Clark, Bill, 8
Clark Custom Boats, 8
Clarke, Dick, 16
Classix, 277
William Clements, Boatbuilder, 116
Clipper Craft Mfg. Co., 191
Coecles Harbor Marina & Boatyard, Inc., 167
Collins, Thomas J., Jr., 37
R.S. Colson Boatworks, 67
Comb, Alex, 146
Concordia Co., Inc., 116
Condino, David, 119
Conner, P., 106
Coombs, R.T., 265
Coombs Shipwright Services, 265
Corum, Dennis, 225
Corum Boatworks, 225
Covey Island Boatworks, 266
Cowan, Ted, 278
Cowan Canoes, 278
Cox, Timothy M., 291
Cranberry Island Boatyard, 68
Crockett Bros. Boatyard, 106
Chester A. Crosby and Sons, 117
Crown Point Marine, 183
Custom Boats, 151
Custom Building, 68
Custom Canoes, 168
Custom Wood Services, 169

Cutts, Edmund A., 106
Cutts & Case, Inc., 106
Cyr, Guy A., 65
Dahmen, Emerson, 131
Dana Creek Boatworks, 69
Danny's Boat Building, 266
Dark Harbor Boatyard Corp., 69
Darling's Boatworks Inc., 212
Davies, Warren M., 204
Davis, Gary, 186
Davis, Tony, 118
Davis Custom Boats, 118
Dawe, Ernie, 8
Dawe Craft Boats, 8
Defoe, Marvin, Jr., 247
Camille D'Eon Boatbuilders, Ltd., 267
Derecktor-Gunnell, Inc., 36
Derwinski, Stevan, 8
Desco Marine, Inc., 37
De Silva Boats, 46
Devlin, Sam, 225
Devlin Designing Boatbuilders, 225
Dexter Boats, 22
Dibble, Keith, 70
Dibble & Thomas, 70
Dignan, Denis, 228
The Dinghy Shop, 291
Dion, Elmer L.J., 70
Fred J. Dion Yacht Yard, 118
Dion's Yacht Yard, Inc., 70
Disappearing Propeller Boat Company Ltd., 278
Doan, Earl, 230
Dodington, Paul, 278
Dog Island Boat Works, 226
The Dory Shop, 71
Doucette, Paul, 268
Roy M. Doucette Boatbuilders Ltd., 268
Dove Industries Inc., 279
Downeast Peapods, 71
Dragseth, Jim, 45
Driscoll, Gerald, 9
Driscoll Custom Boats, Inc., 9
The Drydock, 150
Dry Harbor Boat Company, 213
Duck Trap Woodworking, 72
Dave Dugdale Cedar Strip Canoe, 214
Dullum, Ted, 145
East Bay Boat Works, 184
East/West Custom Boats, 72
Ehrheart, Lee H., 229
Elliott, Robert C., 277
England, John W., III, 217
Era-Past Boat Co., 37
Graham Ero Wooden Boat Shop, 22
Especially Wood, 280
Essex Bay Boat Co., Inc., 119
Essex Boat Works, 23
The Everett Boat Works, 169
Christopher Fabiszak Boat Shop, 201
Faering Design, 133
Farley, Edward, 107
Farnham, Stuart, 103
Farrin, Bruce A., 73

294

INDEX

Farrin's Boatshop, 73
Feather Canoes, Inc., 38
Fesenmeyer, W. Jack, 41
Fewtrell, Richard A., 24
Fiske, John, 131
Fitzgerald & Hollins, 38
Flaherty Marine, Inc., 39
Fleetwood Boats, 207
Frank Flicker & Sons, Racing Shell Repairs, 197
Flyer's Boat Shop, 120
Flynn, Rik, 192
Flynn & Flynn Custom Boat Works, 192
Jeffrey R. Fogman Yacht Builder, Inc., 151
Forden, Harvard, 156
Don Forrest Inc., 187
Foss, John, 88
Foster, Barry K., 169
Foster, Greg, 261
Douglas Fowler Sailmaker, 170
Francis, Jim, 232
Francis, Sam, 59
Jim Frank Canoes, 247
Franklin Cedar Canoes, 73
Frechette, Jim, 207
Frechette, Joe, 149
Freedom Boat Works, 248
Frenette, Robert W., 179
Frese, Ralph C., 50
Freya Boat Works, 227
Fuller, Henry W., 265
Gagnon, George, 91
Gallant, Peter, 152
Gallant Custom Yachts, 152
Gannon & Benjamin, Inc. Marine Railway, 120
The Gar Wood Boat Co., 170
Geneva Lake Boat Co., 248
George's Lil Shipyard, 227
Gidmark, David, 291
Giles, Bill, 121
Gillies, John, 268
Gillies Canoes, 268
Gillikin, Vance, 184
Glebe Point Boat Co., Inc., 217
Goetz, Eric, 202
Goetz Custom Sailboats, 202
Good, David, 276
Goode, Ferdy, 247
Grand Banks Dory Works, 256
Grand Craft, 134
Graves Boat Works, 204
Gray, Edward, 68
Great Canadian Canoe, 122
Great Heron Works, 73
The Great River Small Boat Co., 51
Grosjean, Charles, 73
Gunnell, Skip, 36
Hadlock Boatyard, 228
H & H Boatworks, 74
Hafeman Boat Works, 144
Rob Haggar Wooden Boats Ltd., 280
Hale, Thomas, 124
Hall, Mary D., 171
Hall's Boat Corporation, 171

Halls Boat House, 46
Hamilton, Daniel W., 122
Hamilton Canoe & Boat Shop, 122
Charles Hankins Boatbuilders, 159
Hanna, James P., 75
Hanna, Jeff, 89
Hanna, Michael R., 164
Hansen, Ulf H., 288
Harper, Jerry W., Sr., 152
Harper's Boat Restoration, 152
Wally Harrison, Boatbuilder, 228
Harry, Ben, 236
Hartford, David C., 226
Hathaway, Carl, 171
Hathaway Boat Shop, 171
Hauser, Scott, 229
Hauser Boat Works, 229
Havorn Marine Services, 229
Head of the Lake Boats, 256
Headwater Boats, 230
Heater, C. Ray, 194
Hebert, Roy, 5
Heitman, Herrick, 49
Heitman Boats, 49
Hemp, Sam, 246
Peter Henkle Inc., 139
Heritage Boatbuilders, Inc., 74
Hetrick, Jim, 14
Hibbert, J., 199
Hill, Thomas, 214
Don Hill River Boats, 192
Hingham Boat Works, Inc., 123
Art Hoban, Boatbuilder, 9
Hodgdon, Timothy, 75
Hodgdon Yachts, Inc., 75
Hodges, Tony, 252
Hoff, Dale, 223
Hogan, Robert, 48
Hogan Boat Works, 48
William Holland, Master Boatbuilder, 147
Hollins, Kim, 38
Holloway, Tim, 213
Hope, Ivan, 233
Huck, Morris, 281
Ed Huck Marine Ltd., 281
Huckins Yacht Corp., 40
Huggins, Dave, 195
Hughes, Cymbrid, 74
Hurley, Jack, 281
Hurley Canoe Works, 281
Huron Lagoons Marina, Inc., 188
Hvalsoe, Eric D., 243
Iris Boat Works, 75
Irwin, Jack, 153
Irwin Marine, 153
Island Canoe Co., 230
Island Falls Canoe, 76
Island Woodworking, 76
Ives, Robert E., 65
Jackson, David, 227
Jackson, Leslie, 285
Jason, Terence T., 77
T. Jason Boats, 77

INDEX

Jenkins, Roy, 87
Jenkins, Spencer, 166
Bent Jespersen Boatbuilders, Ltd., 257
John's Bay Boat Co., 78
Johnson, Elmer L., 134
Johnson, Janine Dion, 70
Johnson, Ralph F., Jr., 123
J. Ervin Jones, Boatbuilder, 79
Jordan, Warren L., 193
Jordan Wood Boats, 193
Judson, David, 217
Judson Boats, 217
Karelsen, Edward A., 231
Karelsen Custom Boats, Inc., 231
Kass, Peter H., 78
Kaulbach, Steve, 212
Kealiher, Cliff, 79
Keegstra, Brian, 64
Kelly, William (Bill), 158
Kendall, Philip A., 153
Kindervater, Eric, 159
King, Graeme, 214
King, Howard A., 53
King, Mary, 137
King Boat Works, 214
King Marine, 53
Klondike Wood Works, 134
Knudson, John, 231
Knudson-Miller Boatyard Co., 231
Kolin, Richard S., 231
Kolin Boat Works, 231
Konitzky, Gustav A., 80
Konitzky Boat Works, 80
Kortchmar, Michael, 172
Kortchmar & Willner, Inc., 172
William Krase, Boatwright, 10
Krautkremer, Steve, 90
Kretzer Boat Works, Inc., 172
Kruger, Evan, 87
Kuhn, Chester, 173
Kuhn's Marine Service, 173
Kurz, Walter and Karl, 83
Labelle, Lee K., 56
Lake Union Drydock Co., 232
The Landing School of Boatbuilding and Design, 80
Langille, Ernest J., 268
Langille Boat Building, 268
Langley, David, 233
Langley Boat & Yacht Work, 233
Mortimer Lapointe Wooden Boat Restoration
 & Repair, 25
Latif, Fuat, 215
Laurentian Boatworks, 144
Leavitt, James A., 81
Leavitt Quality Canoe, 81
Lee, Doug and Linda, 88
Lee, Lance, 97
Leelanau Boat Repair, 135
Legere, Peter B., 256
Leight, Dennis M., 81
D.M. Leight & Co., 81
Lenowitz, David, 82
Levy, Randy D., 269

Roy Levy & Sons, 269
Liebow, M. Chas., 76
Lincoln, Bob, 96
Link, Ron, 10
Little, John D., 86
Peter London Shipwright Ltd., 257
Longfield Dory Co., 83
The Loon Works, 249
Lovric, Tony, 233
Lovric's Sea Craft, 233
Lowell, William, 74
Pert Lowell Co., Inc., 123
Lowell's Boat Shop, Inc., 124
Lowery, Maynard W., 108
Lowery Boat Yard, 108
Ludlow, Philip, 282
Ludlow Boat Works, 282
Lunenburg Regional Vocational School, 269
George Luzier Boatbuilder, Inc., 40
Lyman Manufacturing Co., 189
Macey, Don L., 10
Machiasport Marine Railway Co., 83
MacKenzie, Bruce, 183
MacKenzie, Tom, 249
Mackie, Alan, 145
Mackie's Boat Repair, 135
MacMurray, Peter, 84
Magner, John F., 234
Magner & Sons Boatworks, 234
Malone, Bruce, 84
Malone Boatbuilding Co., 84
The Marine Exchange, 11
Marine Exhibits Restoration Co., 25
Marks, Stephen, 108
Marks Boat Yard, 108
Marshall, Thomas F., 136
Marshall Marine & Woodworking, 136
Martha's Vineyard Shipyard, 124
Martin, Kevin, 154
Martin's, 145
Mason, Mark, 154
Matheson, Michael, 182
Mayea, Larry, 137
Mayea Boat Works, 137
McCaffrey, Frank, 202
McCallum, Laura and John, 191
McCarthy, Henry, 38
Lucy McCarthy Boatshop, 85
McClelland, Jim, 283
McClelland Boatworks, 283
McCloskey, Richard G., II, 208
McDougall, Stewart, 240
David McFadden, Boatbuilder, 3
McGreivey, John, 173
McGreivey's Canoe Shop, 173
McIntosh, Edward D. (Ned), 151
McKee, Philip W., 111
Damian McLaughlin Jr. Corporation, 125
McMinn, Davyd, 259
McMullen, Stephen, 104
Meads, Charles E., 126
Meads Boatbuilding Co., 126
Mefferd, Michael, 208

296

INDEX

Carl Meinzinger, Shipwright, 235
Mele, Andre, 178
Mentha Wooden Boat Co., 137
Midcoast Marine Service, Inc., 85
Mile Creek Boat Shop, 86
Milford Boat Works, 25
Millar, John, 283
Millar-Potter Boat Restoration, 283
Mill Cove Small Boat Works, 87
Miller, Paul, 258
Miller, William V., III, 264
Miller Canoes, 264
Miller Marine Services Ltd., 258
Mills, Jeff, 174
Mills Boatbuilding, 174
Minehart, Jack, 54, 143
Minnis, Gary, 19
Mittleman, Howard, 175
Mitton, Jeff, 270
Mocksfield, Wayne A., 163
Molly's Cove Boat Works Inc., 126
Montgomery Boat Yard, 127
Montgomery, David, 127
Moore, Gregory, 58
Moore, Wyatt A., 208
Moores, James, 67
Moores, Ted, 274
Morley, Greg, 149
Morley Cedar Canoes, 149
Morrow, Ralph, 174
Morrows Boat Shop, 174
Mosher, Wayne D., 270
The Mountain Boat Shop Ltd., 270
Arthur F. Mulvey Fine Woodworking, 12
Mundschenk, Manual, 150
Murdock, James L., 73
Murphy, F.J., 249
Murphy Boat Works Ltd., 249
Murray, Robert E., 123
Mystic Seaport Small Boat Shop, 26
Nagelbach, Fred, 51
Nantucket Shipyard, 128
Narragansett Shipwrights, Inc., 202
National Maritime Museum at San Francisco, 12
Nau, Warren, 160
Nau's Boat Works, 160
Nautical Adventures, Inc., 218
Navigateurs Jel Ltee., 292
Needham, Peter, 167
Nelson, Barry A., 218
Jerry Nelson, Woodworker, 109
Nelson, Robert, 105
Nelson Boatworks, 218
New Dublin Watercraft, 270
New England Boat & Motor, Inc., 154
New Harbor Yachts, Inc., 87
Nexus Marine Construction, 235
Niangua Boat and Canoe Co., 148
Nimphius, F.M., 250
Noah Boatworks/Planecat Catamarans, 138
Norberg Company, 236
Norfolk School of Boatbuilding, 218
North Bay Canoe Co., 284

North End Shipyard, 88
Northern Marine Industries, Inc., 236
North Island Boat Co., 237
North River Boatworks, 175
Northrup, Bruce, 193
Northrup Boat Works, 193
Northwest School of Wooden Boatbuilding, 238
Northwoods Canoe Shop, 88
Norton, Joe, 251
Norton Boat Works, 251
David Nutt, Boatbuilder, 89
Oat Canoe Co., 89
O'Brien, Tracy, 230
O'Connor, Mike, 172
Ocran Boat Shop, Inc., 219
Odell, Jim, 124
Okoboji Boats, 54
Old Time Boat Co., 41
Old Town Canoe, 90
Old Wharf Dory Co., 129
Old Wooden Boatworks, 41
Olsen, John, 160
Olsen's Boat Works, 160
Onion River Boatworks, 215
Opus Yachts, 129
O'Riley, Gene, 17
Osborne, Mark, 90
Osmond's Boat Shop, 91
Outer Limits Yachts, 189
Parker, Reuel B., 175
Parker Marine Enterprises, 175
Parsons, Jay B., 115
Patrick, Bruce W., 139
Patrick's Landing, 139
Payson, Harold H., 91
Peale, Barry, 25
Pedersen, Carl V., 221
Pedersen, Wade, 161
Hans Pedersen & Sons, Inc., 161
Peel Marine Limited, 284
Pelasara, R.J., 110
Pembroke Boat Company, 91
Perkins, Robert, 6
Perlowski, Walter, 162
Perlowski Bros. Boatworks, 162
Perry, Ted, 72
Persson, Jon, 27
Seth Persson Boatbuilders, 27
Peters, Donald E., 244
Pettegrow, Richard S. and Nettie J., 92
Pettegrow Boat Yard, 92
Petterson, Joe, 200
Chuck Petty Custom Boats, 13
Phelps, Ivan, 156
Phoenix Woodwork, 285
Pierce, Bill, 148
Pierce, Bob, 135
Robert Pieri, Inc., 93
Pilots Point Marine, 28
Plettner, Bill, 130
Pt. La Jolla Custom Boats, 13
Port Townsend Boatworks, 238
Porter, Michael, 66

INDEX

Possin, John, 223
Potter, James, 283
Potts, Rives, 28
Poulsbo Boat Works, 239
Poverty Island Boatworks, 252
Pratt, Rick, 206
Proctor, E. Tyler, 68
Prothero, Bob, 238
Pulsifer, Richard S., 94
R.S. Pulsifer Co., 94
Quest Racing, Inc., 204
Rainbow Canoes, 285
Rander, Steven, 194
Ray's River Dories, 194
Reliant Marine Services, 239
Renaissance Yacht Co., 94
Reverence for Wood Boat Shop, 5
Richardson, Alan, 285
Cliff Richardson Boats Ltd., 285
James H. Rich Boat Yard, 94
Ridgway, J., 23
Rights O' Man Boat Works, 240
Curtis Rindlaub, Amateur Boatbuilder, 28
Ritter, Jim, 176
Rivendell Marine, 202
Riverside Boat Company, 95
River Spirit Canoes, 195
RKL Boatworks, 96
Roberts, David, 235
Rock Hall Boat Shop, 219
The Rockport Apprenticeshop, 97
Rockport Marine Inc., 97
Rogala, Richard, 138
Rogers, John, 176
Rogers, Paul, 98
Rogers Marine, Inc., 98
Rollins Boatyard, 220
Rollins, William M., 220
Ronning, Larry J., 144
Rosborough, J. Douglas, 270
Rosborough Boats Ltd., 270
Ross, Ian, 279
Ruby, Gordon, 239
Rumery's Boat Yard Inc., 98
Russell, Jake, 13
Rutherford, Jeffrey, 13
Rutherford's Boat Shop, 13
Ryder, Richard G., 29
Ryder & Son Woodworking, 29
Sag Harbor Yacht Yard, 176
Sagman's, 177
St. Clair Flats Marina & Scripps Marine Engine, 139
St. Claire, Jerry, 87
Saint, Col. Hugh M., USAF (Ret.), 42
Saint Marine Replicraft, 42
Salt Creek Boat Works and Trading Company, 14
Salt River Boat Works, 140
Sanford, Alfred, 14
Sanford Boat Co., 14
Sanger, Morgan, 209
Santos, Francis, 120
Saroukos, George, 42
Saroukos Boat Building, 42

Sausalito Shipwright's Co-op, 15
Sauvage, Gretchen, 135
Sayre, Bud and Zenna, 190
Sayre Brothers Marine, 190
Scalzo, Eugene, 102
Scarbrough, David, 219
Schaefer, Duncan, 189
Schattin, Juerg, 280
Schneider, Ralph R., 54
Schooner Creek Boatworks, 195
Schorse, William P., 284
Schroeder, Glenn, 158
Schumacher, Robert, 212
Schweiss, Paul, 237
Scott, Michael, 185
Scott Boatyard, 185
Scully, John, 52
Seal Cove Boatyard Inc., 99
Seattle Shipwrights Co-op, 240
Seaway Boat Repairs, 42
Seyfarth, Fritz, 209
Sharples, Ned, 132
Shea, Dan, 252
Shea Marine Builders, Inc., 252
Shelburne Shipyard, 216
Sherwood, Paul S., 220
Sherwood Boatbuilding Co., 220
Shew & Burnham, 100
Shipskills, Inc., 178
Shopenn, Michael, 238
Shumaker, Mike, 286
Shuman, Bill, 103
Sierra Boat Company, 16
Sill, Stewart, Jr., 178
Sill's Marina, Inc., 178
Silva, Nelson L., 185
N.L. Silva & Co., 185
Simmons, Walter J., 72
Skiff Works, 259
Skoriak, John D., 11
Slaunwhite, Stephen H., 271
Slaunwhite's Boat & Joinery Shop, 271
Sleepy Creek Boat Works, 186
Sligh, Dick, 134
Slingerland, Jack, 179
Slingerland Classic Boats, 179
Smith, Arnie, 71
Smith, Donald, 241
Smith, F. Everett, 169
Smith, John, 197
Smith, Melbourne, 109
Smith's Boat Shop, 241
Skip Snaith Canoes & Kayaks, 30
Snapp, Geremy, 243
Snyder, Philip, 271
Snyder's Shipyard Ltd., 271
Solberg, Thomas, 188
Sorensen, Darrell, 17
Sorensen Woodcraft, 17
South Cove Boat Shop, 129
Spanish Main Boatworks, 209
Ray Speck, Boatbuilder, 241
Spectrum Woodwork, 110

INDEX

Spencer Boat Co., 43
Alec Spiller, Master Shipwright, 259
Spring, John B., 164
Spruce Knee Boatbuilding, 179
Staley, James E., 191
Stanton, J., 285
Stauter Boats, 2
Steele, James, 71
Steele, John, 266
Steele, Keith, 196
Steele's Boats, 196
Stelmok, Jerry, 76
Stephens, Barry, 242
Stephens Marine, 242
Newton S. Sterling Products, 162
Stevens, Daniel, 266
Stevens Boatworks, 272
Stewart River Boatworks, 146
Stimson, David, 87
Story, D. Bradford, 130
Story Shipyard, 130
Stubing, Paul T., 25
Stulen, Chip, 133
Sundance Canoe, 286
Sun Junction Boatworks, 130
Sunrise Designs—Boatbuilding & Repair, 149
Superior Sailboats Ltd., 287
Swans Island Boatshop, 100
Swanson, Baggins & Co., 196
Swanson, Mark, 196
Swanstrom, Paul, 211
Sweet, David, 101
Swift, Gordon, 155
Swift Custom Boats, 155
Swinamer, Steven, 272
Sylvia, Robert T., 85
Tassell, Dale, 37
Tassier, Marvin and Gary, 141
Tassier Boatworks, 141
The Tender Craft Boat Shop, 287
Teutsch, Arthur E., 140
Thayer, Edwin A., 101
Thayer's Y-Knot Boatyard, 101
A.F. Theriault & Son, Ltd., 272
Thistle Woodworking, 208
Thomsen, Bob, 7
Thomson, Schuyler, 30
Thomson Canoe Works, 30
Thrash, Bob G., 189
Thunder Bay Canoes, 142
Thurlow, Rollin, 88
Tiffany Yachts, 217
Tobias, Archie, 144
Tolman, Renn, 3
Tolman Skiffs, 3
Traditional Ship Caulking, 102
Traditional Wooden Craft, 180
Trapp, Jeffrey F., 253
Trout River Boat Works, 253
Trull, Alden, 116
Joe Trumbly Boat Co., 242
Turcotte, Thomas R., 170
Tuulos, Tim, 260

Tuulos Custom Yachts Ltd., 260
UHH Enterprises, 288
Ungarean, Gary L., 129
Upright Boat Works, 243
Valso Boats, 243
Van Bibber, V.H., 44
Van Dam, Stephen, 142
Van Dam Wood Craft, 142
Van Dell, Kenneth, 52
Van Dell Canoes, 52
Van Mar Boat Co., 44
Van Syckel, Steven, 62
Van Wagner, Peter, 291
Vaughan, Robert, 99
Vik, Gilbert, 244
Vik Boat, 244
Vintage Antique & Classic Boat Restoration, 254
Virginia Boatshop, 221
Voyager Marine, 17
Wahl, Gordon, 260
Wahl Boats, 260
Wahlman, Erik, 6
Walker, Willie, 288
Walker Boat Building Ltd., 288
Washington County Vocational Technical Institute, 102
Rick Waters, Boatbuilder, 30
Watson, Tom, 263
Watson Marine, Ltd., 263
Wayfarer Marine Corp., 103
Wayne's Marine Inc., 163
Webb, Mervyn, 289
Webb Wood Work, 289
Gary Weisenburger, Boatbuilder, 31
Wells Boat Shop, 103
Wenzel, Jack, 110
Wenzel Boat Co., 110
John Wermescher, Boatbuilder, 47
West Cove Boat Yard, 104
West End Slipway, 209
Whaler Bay Boat Yard, 261
White, Jean T., 46
White, Joel, 62
White, Paul R., 180
Whiticar Boat Works Inc., 45
Wikander, Stuart, 111
Wikander Yacht Yard, 111
Wilburn, Brian, 254
Willard, Emerson, 183
Williams, Barbara, 287
Williams, C., 180
Williams, Carl H., 21
Williams Wood Boat Shop, 180
Willis, Melvin, 104
Willis Enterprises, Inc., 104
Willmann, Olga Lange, 64
Willner, Andrew, 172
R.K. Wilmes, Boatbuilder, 32
Winard Wood Inc., 261
Winnipesaukee Canoe Co., 131
Wisner, J.D., 32
Wisner Bros., 32
Wogisch, Richard, Jr., 190

299

INDEX

Wolfeboro Restoration Center, 155
Wolstenholme, Tom, 202
Wooden Boat Center, 18
The Wooden Boat Shop, 156
Wooden Ship Boatworks, 19
The Gar Wood Boat Co., 170
Jean Wood Boats, 255
The Woodpecker Shop, 244
The Woodsmith, 105
Woodwinds, 19
Yachtcraft, 131
Yacht Maintenance Co., Inc., 111
Yacht Standard, 52
Young, Gary, 19
Zappenuff Generators, 290
Z-Craft Custom Race Boats, 4
Zebcraft, 156
Ziemba, Joseph, 276
Zimmerman, Steve, 222
Zimmerman Marine, 222
Zorkan, Frank, 4

rattling windows and doors. The streets had not been cleaned in years, and we left a wake of leaves, papers, trash, and angry cyclists. It was like a caricature by Dubout. A difference also in taxis, with the square and commodious London type succeeded by small cars unable comfortably to accommodate either people or luggage, and driven by apache types.

It was a day or two before the charm of Paris began to work, so different is it from London's magic to which we had become accustomed. Composed of smells, sights, and sounds, the charm of Paris is irresistible, though one is repelled at first by an initial impression of brutality and a price for everything. This is why Henry Miller's *Tropic of Cancer* is a great book, banned though it be in the English-speaking countries, so perfectly does it embody the ambiance of Paris unbuttoned.

We lodged in a doll-size hotel on the Quai Saint-Michel, overlooking the bookstalls, the Seine, the Palaces of Commerce and Justice, and Notre Dame, gloriously floodlit at night. Traffic on the street below had only two tempos around the clock: standstill for red light, full speed for green. Parisians once drove with their horns; now throttles do it. Half a block away the Place Saint Michel boiled with student life. A walk up the boulevard to the Sorbonne was like running the rapids of the Colorado in reverse. No color line. The blacker the man's skin, the blonder the girl. A sense of youth's vitality. Be-bops the modern *fauves*. Immemorial atmosphere of freedom within the restraints of custom.

Uphill we took sanctuary in the Pantheon and saw the

pastel murals of Puvis de Chavannes, delicate as the music of Debussy. We reached the Luxembourg Garden at closing time, and watched people of all ages shuffling out through rainbow leaves, herded by a gendarme with lock and key and thirst for an *apéritif*. Big-leafed chestnuts were towers of gold. Little-leafed trees launched their relics like yellow butterflies. The ground was carpeted. No one raked, no one burned.

Choice of eating places in Paris is nearly limitless among the four thousand restaurants in the city. Whatever the choice, there was always *soupe du jour* of potato, leek, carrot, turnip, or spinach, a meal in itself, served family style. *Choucroute garnie* at Brasserie Lipp. *Omelette aux champignons* at Calvet next door. *Filet de boeuf charolais* at the Relais de St. Germain, tender and succulent, garnished with watercress, hemmed with wild rice and chopped mushrooms. A steak to end steaks at the Rôtisserie Périgourdine on the night of the general strike, when only those restaurants with charcoal were able to serve. *Poisson dorade,* a kind of Mediterranean goldfish, Chez Joséphine, followed by coffee at the Closerie des Lilas, in an atmosphere of deep peace, polished brass, mahogany walls, marble-top tables, and leather seats, with the habitués—man with poodle, a couple reading Camus together, chess players, poet in the throes of creation, there in the café on the edge of Montparnasse, once a country inn, the Lilac Farm, on the road to Orléans.

Paris in the fall, dirty, bittersweet, fatal, all things to all people regardless of age, sex, or purse, city of light and lust. Along the Quai des Orfèvres grow tall elms, and one looks up at blue sky through a filigree of golden leaves, while down below he sees barges on the river, bearing master, wife, children, dogs, and the family washing on a deck line. And sees the eternal fishermen who catch naught. The bookstalls fascinated my wife—not their trite contents, but rather the men and women who ran them and the people who browsed and sometimes bought. Day's end was the best time for sales, she observed.

One cloudy day, sans electricity, gas, transportation, and (most critical of all) morning coffee, we trudged upriver to the Jardin des Plantes, and found its denizens indifferent to the strike of workers, as well as to us. This was the zoo where Rilke walked alone, half a century before, conceiving poems to its flamingos and panthers.

> His sight from ever gazing through the bars
> has grown so blunt that it sees nothing more.
> It seems to him that thousands of bars are
> before him, and behind them nothing merely.

Toward noon we found ourselves on the Cité across from our quai, in the Brasserie des Deux Palais opposite the Sainte Chapelle. There by some culinary miracle we were served eggs on ham, crusty sweet-buttered bread, and coffee *almost* hot. Thus heartened we continued our walk, through the Louvre and the Tuileries Gardens, seeing the bust of Lenôtre (1613-1700), designer of the Tuileries and all of France's classic parks, on to the Place de la Concorde and up the Rue Royale to the Madeleine and the flower stands along its flank. Here in 1849 Chopin had been given a great funeral. "Play Mozart," he said on his deathbed, "and I will hear you." They sang the Requiem, K. 626.

IV

On a day of flying clouds we went by train to Chartres. This time, as my wife raised her eyes to the windows, I cast mine to the floor, observing its worn softness, warm to the eye, cold to the hand, laid to outlast all the feet in the world. I wanted to take her to the restaurant where years before I had seen the Great God Pan, disguised as a cheese-peddling shepherd, but feared that potent deity had long since departed. In our hunger was memory of that meal at the Relais St. Germain, and we rushed back to Paris and fell on a two thirty lunch of soup, fish, salad, and fruit, a meal which lasted till four o'clock. Lovely day!

Another trip was to Dijon one morning from the Gare de Lyon, on a *rapide* made up of through cars to Bern, Geneva, Lyon, Marseilles, Nice, and Italy, the split-up to occur at Dijon. We took red plush seats in an Italian coach destined for Milan, and observed the stream of travelers, anxiously seeking the cars of their destinations. The members of a symphony orchestra on tour arrived late, protecting an assortment of instruments from the rain. At eight ten the train soundlessly followed the electric engine out of the station on the three-hour nonstop run to Dijon, two hundred miles southeast. Rain followed us, and we looked through its curtain on brown fields and yellow woods, on shining red-roofed villages, and finally on the hills of Burgundy, with a glimpse at Alésia of the heroic statue of Vercingetorix, last of the Gallic chieftains to capitulate to Caesar, in the year 52 B.C.

A rainy Dijon underlined Victor Hugo's description of the Burgundian capital: *délicieuse ville, mélancolique et douce*. My last sight of her golden towers had been on a May afternoon. Now the limestone was drab, as I sought the scenes of my student days, a quarter century before. Huddled under a single umbrella we trudged the cobbled streets, past the home shop of Grey-Poupon mustard, the Patisserie Michelin which baked the flakiest of goodies, the Restaurant Racouchot, *Aux Trois Faisans*, statues of the Grape Treader, of Rameau, Bossuet, and Rude. In the four-storied building of the Faculté des Lettres where, twenty-five years ago to the month, I had faced the jury in defense of my thesis and been awarded the Doctorate of the University of Dijon, students were jammed and the foyer stank of wet wool. Down the narrow Rue du Petit-Potet we splashed to the pension at Number 14 where I had lived, neighbor to the Mayor of Dijon and the Bishop of Burgundy, though with medieval plumbing. The limestone was lifeless, the cobbles rough, the rain cold; the only color was of the multihued tile roofs.

We took shelter in the museum, quartered in a wing of the Hôtel de Ville, the former ducal palace, and found it refurbished by a new director, the inner sanctum occupied, as of yore, by the tombs of the Dukes and their wives, the masterpiece of the Flemish sculptor, a bronze statue of whom by Rude stood in the courtyard, austere, aproned, chisel and hammer in hand, indifferent to the incessant rain. *Claus Sluter, Imagier aux Ducs de Bourgogne,* read the inscription on the base.

In the Place Darcy at the opposite end of the Rue de la Liberté from the museum, we again sheltered, in the Café de la Concorde where on the banquette, under gilt-framed mirrors, we took *thé anglais,* served by a flat-footed *garçon* whom I recognized from student years. In answer to my question as to how long he had served there, he replied, *Thirty-seven years.* Next to us bridge-playing Dijonnais drank beer and conversed in the hoarse patois of Burgundy. A table of matrons sipped hot chocolate. A lone man wrote a letter on café stationery. Another read *Le Bien Public.* Nothing had changed. Only I.

Back up the hill past the Hôtel de la Cloche we walked through sodden leaves to our hosts' home overlooking Dijon. We were staying with Docteur Georges Connes, wife and daughter, the man under whom I had studied, the learned and tolerant Professor of English Language and Literature, Dean of the Faculty of Letters, Resistance hero, Mayor of Dijon, now in retirement, dividing his time between Dijon and his ancestral farm far south in the mountainous Rouergue. In his attic study under the rain-pattered shingles, he showed me the work he was doing on the local history of the Rouergue, based on family papers of several centuries, and the major work that had occupied his free time during the Occupation—the first French translation of Browning's *Ring and the Book.*

Snapshots he showed me portrayed incidents of the Liberation when, in spite of Mayor Connes' efforts, the populace had dealt direct justice by hanging from a lamppost in the Place d'Armes the Commissioner of Police who had collaborated with the Nazis, and patriots had seized, stripped, and shaved the heads of several women of *mauvaise vie*.

The next morning was clear, and we drove around town in Connes' tiny open-topped Citroën. We saw the new Faculty of Sciences building on the outskirts of town and enormous new apartment houses. The monument to patriots executed by the Nazis was impressive: simply the rifle range, with the heroes' names carved on the wall before which they had fallen. One hundred thirty-four of them.

Down the Côte d'Or toward Beaune we drove, seeing the vineyards after the vintage, golden with an occasional red clump, now open to gleaners. Growing on the eastern slopes of the limestone hills and extending a short way onto the plain, the vineyards of the red Burgundies unrolled like the wine list in a restaurant: Clos Vougeot, Corton, Romanée, Chambertin. In the village of Gevrey-Chambertin we saw the graveyard where Gaston Roupnel is buried, the old hawk-faced professor of Burgundian folklore whose lectures I had followed, a novelist whose *Nono, or the Life of the Soil* was translated into English.

We returned to Paris on the four thirty *rapide* from Marseilles, St. Etienne, and Lyon, boarding a section which came in from Besançon to be coupled to the main train. Another nonstop run, through fields and woods, along rivers and canals, seeing an occasional hunter with gun and dog, as darkness fell and crows came to roost, through a countryside unchanged in a thousand years.

Seven thirty arrival at Gare de Lyon allowed sight of the Simplon-Orient Express drawn up on the next track for eight o'clock departure to Trieste, Belgrade, Bucharest, Athens, and Istanbul, via Dijon, Geneva, and the Simplon Tunnel through the Alps. On another track stood the Blue Train on which we had once ridden to Nice. We took the Metro to the Place St. Michel and our hotel. It was like coming home. We had grown accustomed to the noise and to the street light which the drawn curtain failed to dim. Dinner was antigastronomical: fruit in our room.

V

The next day we made a rainy flight to Amsterdam on a KLM Convair. Across the aisle a Dutch burgher returned from holiday with a bird cage and a bottle of cognac. We lodged in a friend's eighteenth-century bookshop-apartment on the Keizersgracht Canal, with a view onto a secluded garden. The rain it raineth every day in Amsterdam, and we were content to spend hours in talk. The coffee shops serve rich pastries, thick cream, and coffee. Barrel organs drown out the noise of traffic. We came upon a hidden square of seventeenth-century pensioners' houses, overlooking a greensward and a statue of the gentle Jesus. Restaurants in town and country contributed to our sense of well-fed-being. We saw one windmill. Books bought included a collection of printing by Bodoni of Parma and a 1672 Dutch translation of Donne's poetry.

Wonderful was a visit to the Ryksmuseum and sight of the Rembrandts, alive with lights and shadows. The self-portraits at thirty and sixty are heartbreaking testimonials to what he acknowledged life had done to him, almost too painful to contemplate. To sit before them was to sit to Rembrandt himself, the three centuries since his passing telescoped into an eternal present.

Leaving the museum rain began to fall and we ran the short distance to our abode on the Keizersgracht, and that night at dinner with twenty booksellers and the University Librarian I wished for a Rembrandt to immortalize a meeting of deep understanding and good will.

An eleven o'clock departure found us dining earlier with our hosts, looking out on the rainy concourse where the Flying Dutchmen of KLM were coming and going to and from the ends of the earth. We boarded our DC-7 in the rain and were airborne nonstop for New York. Over England weather cleared and we saw the lights of Manchester, and later those of Dublin, like a golden hive in swarm. Then all through the night nothing but moonlit ocean and broken clouds, landfall at Newfoundland, thence down coast to an easy landing at Idlewild.

Our car had arrived on the freighter *American Scout* the day before. My wife flew on home, leaving me to drive across country alone, an experience I had relished in 1951. "First catch your Jaguar." It took me several days of misplaced papers, broken choke, and other human and mechanical delays to get the car unloaded, through customs, off dock, and over to Long Island for servicing. When I finally got behind the wheel of the sleek gray car and slipped into evening traffic, gained the Queens Midtown Tunnel, crossed Manhattan, took the Lincoln Tunnel under the Hudson, and headed south on the New Jersey Turnpike toward Los Angeles and way points, my exultation was boundless. The car ran like a watch. The radio was alive with all kinds of music. At the first Howard Johnson's I savored a plate of scallops, then drove on to the Pennsylvania Turnpike and west to Willow Grove, north of Philadelphia, where I bedded for the night.

The next day we ate up 375 miles of autumn-colored Appalachians, reached the Ohio Turnpike, then angled southwest to sleep in Columbus. Along the roads baskets of apples were for sale, but when I ordered applesauce for breakfast, it came from a can. Stops at Earlham College and at the University of Illinois slowed me a bit, but then I reached U.S. 54, on its great diagonal traject from Chicago to El Paso, crossed the Mississippi at the river town of Louisiana, the Missouri at Jefferson City, through the sered Ozarks and dropped onto the stubble fields of Kansas, leaving behind a swirl of dead leaves. In towns and villages old people were raking and burning. The car gathered the sweet smell of the smoke as I rolled southwestward. Once beside a field of dead corn, the dry rustle was music never heard in my homeland.

Weather worsened as I quit Kansas for Oklahoma, Texas, and New Mexico—rain turning to snow. Still the car ran smoothly, its heater keeping me warm, the radio never on the same station for long. I heard a faculty wives' orchestra play Mozart beautifully. Recipes for cooking broccoli. An illustrated lecture on César Franck's mastery of the canon form. All about job opportunities in Wichita. I kept rolling. Cows in the dead corn, golden ears safely cribbed. It was late in the year for autumn colors, but an occasional maple with the sun shining through was a breath-catching *luminario*. Sputnik II kept lapping the Jaguar, in spite of my haste. At Tucumcari I left 54 for 66, crossed the Sandias in a snowstorm, and descended to Albuquerque in a burst of sundown light.

The rest of the way, a mere 800 miles, was home country, nothing foreign in the color and configuration of the landscape, all mountains mapped and known—Taylor, Graham, Mingus, and finally, across desert and river and desert again, Cuyamaca, Old Saddleback, and the Santa Monicas of Southern California. Here was autumn too, the year fallen, apparent only to those with loving eyes. East, West, Home's best.

THROUGH THE BURNING GLASS

Suppose we go not through the Looking Glass, as Alice did, but through the Burning Glass. Then what? I can only report what happened to me, when I had such an experience, both symbolical and actual.

First a definition of Burning Glass: *a convex lens for focusing the sun's rays so as to produce heat or set fire to something.*

Now it should be clear what I am up to. Some books are burning glasses, whose focus on a reader can figuratively set him on fire. Four years ago a book did this to me. Not an obvious book of inspiration, it was a bibliography by a Texan which set me burning and changed my life. J. Frank Dobie's *Guide to Life and Literature of the Southwest* was the book.

First published in Lousiana Library Association Bulletin, *Spring 1957.*

THROUGH THE BURNING GLASS

I had been invited to speak to a convention of Arizona librarians, and as usual with me, I had a title, "This Dry and Wrinkled Land," before I had a talk. Almost at the last minute I reached for Dobie in desperation, and that life-giving man did not fail me. From the exciting annotations in his *Guide* I was led to choose three very different Southwest books, and to speak of the way in which they evoked for me the evergreen spirit of the semiarid Sonoran zones of Arizona and New Mexico.

The books were Will Levington Comfort's *Apache*, Willa Cather's *Death Comes for the Archbishop*, and Haniel Long's *Interlinear to Cabeza de Vaca*. Dobie's book was the burning glass which fired them for me, and they in turn proved burning glasses on the whole Southwest, which has ever since been blazing in my imagination. Through these books I entered a new-found world, living henceforth on a higher plane of places and people. From each of them I derived new relationships, proving again the power of books to change one's life. That is why librarianship can be such a powerful profession, concerned as it is, when properly practiced, with transforming the common elements of experience into the precious elements of heightened, widened, and deepened human consciousness, changing people and thereby changing the world.

Two of the authors, Will Comfort and Willa Cather, were dead and gone beyond my ken, but I did come to know Comfort's daughter Jane, also a writer. I sought to learn what had led her father to forsake magazine serials and write this novel about the rimrock Apache, the Chieftain Mangas Coloradas—Red Sleeves—which Dobie calls "the most moving and incisive of all writing known to me about the Indians of the Southwest."

She did not know. No one knew. The answer was apparently lost forever with Comfort's death in 1932, soon after the publication of *Apache*. All she remembered was that her father had been so obsessed by the subject that, in delirium before he died, he imagined that he himself was the Apache chieftain.

A few months passed, and then I heard again from Jane Comfort. She had dug into some cartons long stored in a closet of her late mother's house, and in one of them she had found the things that had been on her father's worktable the day he died—a jumble of writer's paraphernalia swept up by the widow and stored out of sight, and forgotten after her death. Included was the last thing he had been working on, a fantastically illegible sheaf of manuscript pages—which appeared to be an unfinished essay on what led him to write *Apache*. James Mink of my staff deciphered the notes and published an article based on them, called "The Making of a Southwestern Novel," in which he analyzed the complex causes which motivated Comfort, running back to his childhood reading of Westerns, army service in the Philippines with an Arizona regiment, reading in the files of the *Tombstone Epitaph,* and finally a mysterious compulsion which led inevitably to the choice of theme.*

I was led by a rereading of Willa Cather to make my first pilgrimage to Santa Fe to see the statue of Father Lamy, in front of the Cathedral, sight of which was the burning

* *Manuscripts,* Summer 1957.

glass which caught Miss Cather on fire and led to the writing of this bareboned and beautiful book called *Death Comes for the Archbishop*.

I came to Santa Fe, upriver from Albuquerque, on a summer day of thundercaps over the Sangres, dove-colored and sinister, and the wind risen, bearing the smell of piñon smoke long before I reached the City of the Holy Faith, the ancient spiritual center of the Southwest. As I crossed the Plaza toward the cathedral, a troop of Boy Scouts went by in tow of their master, headed also for the church, and I overheard one laggard say to another.

"Come on, I'll buy you a Coke at the drugstore."

"Yeah," his buddy agreed, "the church won't be much; just a lot of veils and saints."

Whereupon the two peeled off from their pious fellows and took to their heels.

This modern cathedral of Santa Fe is not beautiful, either without or within, but it serves as a place of worship and meditation for people in need of peace and quiet; and in the annals of American literature also it is a sacred place, the place where Miss Cather caught fire and in the crucible of her imagination created the book which is her immortality.

I went on to climb the rock-fast pueblo of Acoma, which figures memorably in *Death Comes for the Archbishop*, and there in the ancient church of St. Stephen I sat in solitude, seeing the naive frescoes, hearing the murmur of men on the roof rolling new logs into place, my heart filled with the riches that came from reading a book.

Who says that reading is a substitute for living? When

one goes through the Burning Glass, he finds that living and reading are as inseparable as two flames which have come together and made one.

My journey to Acoma recalled Willa Cather's description of the same approach:

> After early Mass the next morning Father Latour and his guide rode off across the low plain that lies between Laguna and Acoma. In all his travels the Bishop had seen no country like this. From the flat red sea of sand rose great rock mesas, generally Gothic in outline, resembling vast cathedrals. They were not crowded together in disorder, but placed in wide spaces, long vistas between. This plain might once have been an enormous city, all the smaller quarters destroyed by time, only the public buildings left,—piles of architecture that were like mountains. The sandy soil of the plain had a light sprinkling of junipers, and was splotched with masses of blooming rabbit brush,—that olive-coloured plant that grows in high waves like a tossing sea, at this season covered with a thatch of bloom, yellow as gorse, or orange like marigolds.
>
> This mesa plain had an appearance of great antiquity, and of incompleteness; as if, with all the materials for world-making assembled, the Creator had desisted, gone away and left everything on the point of being brought together, on the eve of being arranged into mountain, plain, plateau. The country was still waiting to be made into a landscape.
>
> Ever afterward the Bishop remembered his first ride to Acoma as his introduction to the mesa country. One thing which struck him at once was that every mesa was duplicated by a cloud mesa, like a reflection, which lay motion-

less above it or moved slowly up from behind it. These cloud formations seemed to be always there, however hot and blue the sky. Sometimes they were flat terraces, ledges of vapour; sometimes they were dome-shaped, or fantastic, like the tops of silvery pagodas, rising one above another, as if an oriental city lay directly behind the rock. The great tables of granite set down in an empty plain were inconceivable without their attendant clouds, which were a part of them, as the smoke is part of the censer, or the foam of the wave.

The widening circles carried me deep into Texas where I visited Frank Dobie, that good human being who stands for all that is decent in the American tradition. Austin is tree-green in summertime, and its streets, named for the rivers of Texas, are a prose poem: Brazos, Nueces, Pecos, and Guadalupe, Colorado, Neches, and Rio Grande. Later I dedicated to him my book, *Heart of the Southwest,* which his book had inspired. I wish that he could be sent around the world to speak to people everywhere. Not even speak; just grin. Dobie's grin has more humor in it than a network of comics. People of the world would trust Americans more if they could know ambassadors like Dobie.

All men in one way or another feel the need of the mystery which is much the same under the names of corroboration, self-justification, benediction, and which means the courage to be oneself. Down into this life of ours, this succession of daily emergencies each filled with the need of reality, certain men can thrust their roots deeper and deeper. Others can not. When one examines the careers of men, something of the greatness of those who are truly great may dawn on one like a white-crested mountain, K2 or Everest, so far away that it seems to be a white sheep lying down in a pasture.

This was written by Haniel Long, at the beginning of his book about Walt Whitman, a beautiful book in content and format, published at Santa Fe in 1938 by Writers' Editions, the co-operative publishing house founded by Long and others to foster the growth of American literature by regional publishing.

All through the 1940's I was discovering the books of Haniel Long—this one on Whitman, the *Interlinear to Cabeza de Vaca,* still another on Cortés's companion, the Indian girl Malinche, *Piñon Country* in the American Folkways series, and others, all without knowing anything about their author, other than that he had been born in 1888 of missionary parents in Rangoon, had gone to Exeter and Harvard, taught English for twenty years at Carnegie Tech before "retiring" to Santa Fe in 1929, where he became spokesman for the Southwestern literary tradition.

These books, mostly published in Santa Fe, seemed precious as examples of independence from New York. I never wrote to him of my pleasure in his books, since I had first learned from his former fellow Pittsburgher, Robinson Jeffers, that writers are better employed in writing more books than in answering fan mail.

And so the forties passed and the fifties began. Then in that fateful month of April 1953, when I caught fire from Dobie's book and chose Haniel Long's work on Cabeza de Vaca as the final one of my Southwestern trio, I reread the *Interlinear* and found it better than ever, truly an American classic; and finally, when "This Dry and Wrinkled Land" appeared in the *Arizona Librarian*, I sent a copy to Long.

His reply led to correspondence and friendship, and to a mutual affection that increased during the three years of life that remained to him. He was sixty-five when I met him, tall, gray, partly blind, gentle and kind, and he might have said of himself the words he gave his Conquistador:

> In youth the human body drew me and was the object of my secret and natural dreams. But body after body has taken away from me that sensual phosphorescence which my youth delighted in. Within me is no disturbing interplay now, but only the steady currents of adaptation and of sympathy.

In 1953, '54, '55, and '56 I went to Santa Fe to see Haniel Long, each time more certain of his stature, in the way he ascribed greatness to Whitman, as being possessed of the courage to be himself and to thrust down roots deeper than others dare.

Each time, I took one of his books to be autographed. The last time it was the one called *Notes for a New Mythology,* and on its flyleaf he wrote, "Dear Clark"—he always called me by my middle name, for his middle name also was Clark—"Dear Clark, this book is full of youthful dreams, and gratitude to those who caused them—and now getting along in years, I have a lot of gratitude to you for a youthful dream come true—and another memorable visit."

Haniel Long and his wife Alice, herself a poet and rare person, lived near the heart of Santa Fe in one of the old adobe houses, walled with adobe, and filled with old New England furniture and family portraits. There was a garden too, of flowers and vegetables and peach trees. Once I took them a Japanese wind-bell, and each spring Long reported that he had hung it out again from a branch of the fruit tree when the blossoms first burst forth.

Tea was our drink. Alice Long knew how to brew Darjeeling so that it had strength without bitterness. While she sat and knitted and nodded, Long and I talked and read aloud, or listened to Mozart. Once I read to them from his nearly finished first novel, and his intense pleasure in hearing spoken the words he had labored so long to put in order, was good to see.

Another time he and the city and state librarians sponsored a lecture by me in the Santa Fe museum. Long sat in the front row, his eyes closed most of the time, his face relaxed and peaceful; and now and then he would open his eyes and smile at me, nod approval, and close his eyes again.

This man was father, brother, friend to me, asking no questions, making no demands, accepting me as I was, giving me the courage one needs to be his deepest self. He began to transfer his manuscripts to my custody, and when he died he willed his journals to the Library in my care. His books are being widely translated and his influence will widen. He is in the great tradition of Thoreau, Emerson, Melville, and Whitman.

One of the dearest of lovers' wishes is that they die

together, and not leave one in a living death after the other has gone. Alice and Haniel Long were granted this wish, dying last fall three days apart.

I have used the Burning Glass to symbolize the power of some books to fire the imagination, and also to burn away the dross of experience, leaving the bones of lasting literature. In this way fire is a friend. Fire can also be an enemy. It is ranked by William Blades as one of the chief enemies of books. Last winter I had an experience, not symbolical but actual, with fire itself, which was one of the most frightening and at the same time most purifying experiences of my life. I mean the Malibu fire which in three days after Christmas burned over twenty-five miles of coastal mountains in Southern California and destroyed a hundred homes.

We live on the Malibu coast and were in the fiery heart of this furnace, three miles from where it started to burn at three o'clock in the morning and, fanned by a fifty-mile wind, ran like tigers on the loose.

We were awakened by the glare and the roar of the approaching flames, and barely had time to round up our cats and dog, load them in the station wagon, and drive it to the narrow beach below our cliffside house.

The heat and the smoke and the ashes kept my wife and me there on the sand at water's edge, looking up at our house, surrounded by potential torches of cypress, pine, and eucalyptus trees. Somehow we were reconciled to losing it and all it contained, knowing a sudden serenity and freedom from concern.

Other people were on the beach and the things they had chosen to save were curious: a stamp collection; a drawerful of cleaning rags mistaken for the one holding the lady's silk underwear; a pair of shoes, both lefts, one brown, one black; a bottle of cognac and a bottle of water; one horse and one burro, given to me to tether.

Then my wife remembered her handbag, and up the cliff I went, wet towel around my face, and entered the house somehow not yet on fire. I went through the smoke-filled rooms looking for her handbag, and in the search, I found my brief case, containing the notes for this essay.

As I went from room to room, I said goodbye to clothes, rugs, pictures, phonograph records (all of Mozart's piano sonatas), our Steinway; and finally to my books, the ones I keep at home in the room that serves as study and guest room. Long and Cather, Comfort and Dobie, Wright's *Islandia,* and a thousand more, each volume rich with many-layered meaning, each volume as dear to me as our own grown sons. In the smoky room, with fire at the window and sparks raining on the tile roof, which books did I save? None. I didn't take even a single book. It was all or none. "Let them burn!" I said, and ran for it, handbag in one hand, brief case in the other, down to the water's edge.

They didn't burn. Everything was saved. At the last minute the wind changed and drove the fire away from the house, long enough for a neighbor and us to beat it out of our burning fences and trees with shovels and wet sacks, as the water failed. It approached the miraculous. Or perhaps our readiness to give them up, led the Lord to let us keep our house and things.

Twenty-four hours and several quarts of cold milk later, the wind fell, and the burning fields and fence posts and tree trunks were quenched. Then my wife lay down and slept, all the animals gathered round her—a most beautiful still life seen by candlelight. I blew the flame out, unable to bear sight of fire, and tiptoed away, lay down in my dirty clothes and slept for two hours, secure in the selfish knowledge that there was nothing left to burn for miles around.

I had been through the Burning Glass in every sense, and since then I have felt free and easy as never before. "I had been down Old Age River in the log, with sheet-lightning and rainbows and soft rain, and the gods on either side to guide me." Books mean both less and more to me, for the essence of life is in the spirit, not in things.

ABOUT THE AUTHOR

LAWRENCE CLARK POWELL was born in Washington, D.C., in 1906 of Quaker parents, and soon moved to South Pasadena, California, where he attended public schools. He is a graduate of Occidental College in Los Angeles, and received his Doctorate in Letters from the University of Dijon, having written his dissertation on Robinson Jeffers. His professional training for librarianship was at the University of California at Berkeley. Dr. Powell's experience in the booktrade, before entering librarianship, is reflected in several of his writings, including *Recollections of an Ex-Bookseller* and *Vroman's of Pasadena*. He has been University Librarian on the Los Angeles campus of the University of California and Director of the William Andrews Clark Memorial Library since 1944. He is also a Lecturer in English at UCLA, and has been a visiting professor at the Columbia University School of Library Service. Dr. Powell was a Guggenheim Fellow in Great Britain in 1950-51. He has been president of the Bibliographical Society of America, the California Library Association, and the Zamorano Club of Los Angeles, and is also a member of the Roxburghe

Club of San Francisco, the Caxton Club of Chicago, and the Grolier Club of New York. He gave the Randolph G. Adams Memorial Lecture at the University of Michigan in 1953, the Annual Library Association Lecture in Great Britain in 1957, and has been a tireless traveler and speaker on behalf of books and reading. Under Dr. Powell's directorship the libraries at UCLA have tripled in size, now numbering a million and a quarter volumes. He has become internationally known as a do-it-himself book collector for his university, having gone into the field to bag such noted collections as Michael Sadleir's Victorian Fiction and the 80,000-volume library of C. K. Ogden, originator of Basic English.

Dr. Powell's writing embraces a dozen books, scores of pamphlets, and hundreds of articles and reviews. His books classify roughly into two categories, about books, book-collecting, and reading, and about Southwestern literature, and include *Islands of Books, The Alchemy of Books, The Manuscripts of D. H. Lawrence, Robinson Jeffers, the Man and His Work, Philosopher Pickett, Land of Fiction, Heart of the Southwest, A Southwestern Century,* and *The Malibu* (with W. W. Robinson). His concern for the education and training of bookish and humane librarians has resulted in a number of his staff going out to major library positions throughout the country, and is expected to culminate in the establishment of a library school at UCLA. When their two sons had grown up, he and his wife moved to the Malibu coast, thirty miles from Los Angeles, where their hobbies are gardening and beachcombing, their companions three land-loving cats and one sea-going poodle.

This book was set in Baskerville and Bulmer types, printed, and bound by The Haddon Craftsmen. The paper is Perkins and Squier's RRR Smooth Antique made by P. H. Glatfelter Company. Designed by Abe Lerner and Lawrence S. Kamp.